Torchbearers

by Carolyn Wilde

Cover painting by Larry Davis

Solid Rock Books, Inc.
Woodburn, Oregon

First Printing, September, 1994

Published by

Solid Rock Books, Inc.
979 Young Street, Suite E
Woodburn, Oregon 97071
(503) 981-0705

ISBN 1-879112-25-6

Printed in the United States of America.

DEDICATION

It is only love for my Lord that would cause me to neglect my responsibilities and relationships as a daughter, wife, mother, grandmother, sister, friend and to the beautiful, spiritual family of the church my husband pastors. So it is to Christ that I dedicate this work for whatever purpose he has for it.

I give heartfelt thanks to Paul, my beloved husband and faithful running partner. Would there even be a book without his constant encouragement? I have found with him the meaning of Solomon's words:

> Two are better than one; because they have a
> good reward for their labour. For if they fall,
> the one will lift up his fellow.

This book could not be written without God's faithful servants who themselves became flaming torches, who were imprisoned, who spent their weakened bodies to literally crawl to win one more soul, who neglected all those things that the world views as priorities, and forsook all earthly pleasure to simply burn out for their Master.

For it is about these faithful torchbearers who have finished their course that this book is written.

Oh, Lord, raise up from our generation more like them.

I write that I might introduce the lost to a Savior.

And I write that someone - perhaps *you* - will have enough courage to join the race and carry the torch through a neighborhood growing darker with each passing day.

Finally, I write with the hope that one weary, footsore and discouraged runner will be encouraged to press on until he crosses his finish line in triumph.

Acknowledgments

Thank you so much . . .

Tom LeBlanc, my publisher, who is himself a dedicated torchbearer.

Suzy Courtright, one of my beautiful daughters, who made the terrible chore of proofreading fun.

Jan Hicks, Alfretta Smith, and the more than one-hundred around-the-clock prayer warriors of *New Life In Christ Church*, who faithfully prayed me through this book.

Paul, my husband, my love, my very best friend, for stedfast support in whatever project I attempt for our beloved Savior.

All Scriptures are taken from the King James version of the Bible. I have taken the liberty to change *thee, thine, sayest, canst, etc.* to *you, your, say, can, etc.,* when verses are inserted into the story line.

The Torchbearers
Through the Centuries

70 to 156	Polycarp
Died in 258	Lawrence
316 to 397	Martin of Tours
354 to 430	Augustine
The 400s	Patrick
521 to 597	Columba
540 to 604	Gregory the Great
675 to 754	Boniface
801 to 865	Anskar
Died in 997	Adalbert
Died in 1012	Alphage
Died in 1045	Gerard
Died in 1079	Stanislaus
Late 1100s to 1217	Waldo
1334 to 1384	John Wyclif
1372 to 1415	John Hus
1452 to 1498	Girolamo Savonarola
1483 to 1547	Martin Luther
1494 to 1536	William Tyndale
1663 to 1727	Auguste Francke
1669 to 1742	Susanna Wesley
1700 to 1760	Count Zinzendorf
1703 to 1791	John Wesley
1718 to 1747	David Brainerd
1725 to 1807	John Newton
1780 to 1845	Elizabeth Fry
1789 to 1871	Charlotte Elliott
1792 to 1875	Charles Finney
1805 to 1898	George Mueller
Born in 1855	Annie Taylor
1902 to 1970	Gladys Aylward
Running in 1920s	Aged Woman
1910 to 1975	James Stewart
Today	Dave

Torchbearer:
1. One who carries a torch.
2. One who imparts knowledge and truth.

Funk & Wagnalls Standard Dictionary
International Edition

Dave, his relatives, his friends, and his acquaintances are fictional. All other torchbearers you will meet in the pages of this book are real - men, women, and children who are part of our rich Christian heritage. Included in their life stories are their quotations and teachings.

"Let your loins be girded about, and your lights burning."
Jesus
Luke 12:35

CONTENTS

Chapter 1

Dave
(Today)

Know ye not that they which run in a race run all, but one receiveth the prize? So run, that ye may obtain.
I Corinthians 9:24

The sudden silence of the crowd seemed even louder than the dull roar. Every eye was riveted on the taut bodies of the runners. The hush would last only until the blast of the gun shattered it.

The shot rang out and the race began.

Dave fought to shut out the noise and keep his mind wholly centered on the race, but it was impossible. His brain was cluttered with unbidden thoughts. He had lived for this moment for the past four years. The fact that the race would be all over in just a few minutes terrified him. The outcome of this race would judge those four pressure-packed years either a total waste or his most profitable.

He watched his teammate run, agony contorting his face, his mouth open wide in a desperate gasp for air. Dave's eyes dropped to the hand that gripped the baton . . . the baton that would soon be passed to him. But even as he watched, his mind remained a jumble of conflicting thoughts.

He was too excited to get a good night's sleep.

Could he win?

He had to win!

This was his last chance!

He couldn't let down his coach.

He needed to win for his country. There was so much antagonism right now against his nation.

He'd show the hateful press with their unrelenting insults that he could win.

Dave tried desperately to stop his thoughts. This was no time to dwell on the insults of the media!

1

Dave

One teammate was just about to pass the baton to another. He saw both their bodies stretched to their limit as the exchange was made. He stood staring at the runners encircling the track. It would be his turn soon.

The runners were closer now. Dave could hear their jagged breaths and panting groans. The news media was right. The team they had predicted would win was out in front.

"We aren't too far behind," Dave thought. But he didn't enter this race to be behind. Maybe others were satisfied with just the thrill of being in this race, but the thrill wasn't enough to satisfy him. Neither were the silver or the bronze. He was here for the gold.

His physical condition would never be better. If he didn't win today, he never would. He was all too aware of his weak areas - but the body was a complex structure. There would always be at least one muscle or tendon that was sore or in the process of recovering from being pushed or stretched to its limit.

He struggled to quit thinking and to focus on the race. He had expected his teammates to do better. Perhaps they too had trouble with the high of this race. None of his training had prepared him for this. *His training . . .*

He had kept running with his swollen foot protruding from his shoe. He had kept running when he was sure that his throbbing side would rupture.

He had kept going when his lungs ached for more oxygen, and his parched mouth hung open in a soundless scream for water. He had kept running when his whole body begged to collapse, and his mind shrieked for him to give up.

He had slowed to a crawl through bog, but he had not stopped. He had kept running through ankle deep mud, while lightning zig-zagged through the blackened sky, and rain smarted his face and stung his eyes.

He had kept running when every joint and muscle were in agony.

He had run while sick, with sweat streaming from his pores even as his body shook with chills.

He had kept running when the cheers of the crowd changed to jeers as he fell behind.

2

Dave

He was out running while other runners were sleeping and still others playing.

He had continued to run when everyone but his coach had told him there was no way this race was worth the sacrifice.

He had kept running to prepare for this one moment in time. How then could he now feel so totally inadequate and unprepared?

He had laughed off the ridicule of the press. Why now, of all times, did he suddenly believe the sneering newsmen were right? For who was he to be among the world's best athletes? Whatever had given him the idea that he was good enough to win?

He felt the icy claws of fear grip his heart.

He stood riveted, staring, unseeing, wanting to run, not in the race, but far away from the arena and the defeat of his dream.

It was nearly his turn now.

And it was not until just seconds before reaching out to grasp the baton that Dave's years of training rose up within him to meet the challange.

A barrier settled around his mind, blocking out all thoughts of panic.

Dave no longer could hear the dull roar of the crowd. He didn't hear the voices of those around him.

He was totally unaware of his stance or the tension building in his body.

He saw nothing . . . nothing but the baton in the hand of his teammate - the baton that was his to take to the finish line.

It no longer mattered who was ahead of him. He would simply pass them - for Dave had come to win.

Just before turning off his light, Dave looked up at the gold medal encased in glass on the shelf. And he lay back in bed, grinning foolishly in the night.

Would the thrill of snapping that cord against his rippling chest muscles ever wear off? Nearly seven months had passed since the race, but since then every day had ended and every night's sleep had started this very same way.

Dave

He could not sleep without first savoring his win. Night after night, he had felt all over again the triumph of victory.

His next memory was of the pain of his lungs screaming for air and hearing nothing but the sound of his own heaving gasps for breath and the booming thud of his heart.

He remembered becoming aware of people helping him in his struggle to sit up so he could breathe.

He recalled sensing, rather than seeing, the crowd on its feet, and then suddenly hearing again its thundering roar reverberating through his entire body.

He remembered how his eyes had slowly focused on his coach, kneeling beside him, roughly sponging his face. A huge grin split Coach's face.

He kept repeating the same words, and finally the sense of them came with their sound.

"We did it, Dave. We did it!"

He could still taste the thrill of victory coursing through his body, instantly expelling all weakness and pain.

Dave was no longer an Olympic runner. He was now an Olympic *Champion.*

Dave could still feel himself being lifted to his feet by his teammates. He saw pictures later of their hands clasped and raised as victors. They were smiling through their tears.

He never could remember their walk to the victors' platform. But he never would forget the feeling he had while standing there, surrounded by multiplied thousands of cheering people. Nothing in his life had even come close to the indescribable feeling of pride, awe and thanksgiving, all mixed up together, that he experienced at that moment. He had tried to sing his national anthem, but found himself instead alternately weeping and grinning.

And that was the moment when every pain-filled day and torture-wracked night, along with the four years of sacrifice and deprivation had paled into insignificance.

For he had won.

Dave fell asleep, still smiling.

4

Dave

He did not yet realize that this was the night he would
be called into yet more training . . .
> *by the unsurpassed Coach of all time*
> *to the race of all races*
> *for the greatest prize of all.*

Chapter 2

Dave

Ye did run well; who did hinder you that ye should not obey the truth? Now they do it to obtain a corruptible crown; but we an incorruptible.

Galatians 5:7
I Corinthians 9:25

Dave fumbled for the lamp switch and looked at his watch that lay on the bedstand. Two a.m. Why was he so wide awake? And why this sudden urge to read the Bible?

He turned the light off, and tried to get back to sleep. After tossing restlessly for a few minutes, he got up to search for his Bible. He finally found it on the bottom shelf of a bookcase. He sat holding it for a few minutes without opening it. He didn't have to open its worn cover to remember the inscription written inside.

To Dave, on the day of your new birth. May this book be a lamp unto your feet and a light unto your path as you begin your new life with Christ.
With my heartfelt love and fervent prayers,
Pastor Whyte

Dave realized he was gripping the book so hard his knuckles had turned white. How long had it been since he had devoured its truths? How many years had it been since he had knelt and talked to his God?

He recalled the nights he had prayed for the strength and power to be an effective witness to his family and friends. Pleasing Jesus had been all that mattered to him.

He hadn't consciously left Christ behind when he began training for the Olympics. But somehow, the race had become his all-encompassing goal and running had replaced Christ as his first love. God, like the Bible, had

6

been hidden away on the bottom shelf of his life. He randomly opened the book and absent-mindedly read a verse.

> **Wherefore seeing we also are compassed about with so great a cloud of witnesses, let us lay aside every weight, and the sin which doth so easily beset us, and let us run with patience the race that is set before us.**

The race . . .
Let us run the race . . .
Dave was instantly alert, his mind fully on the words he had just read, his eyes scanning them again and again.

Dawn was just breaking in the eastern sky when Dave finally rose from his knees. Consenting to enter the race had not been easy for him. He hadn't wanted to make the lifetime commitment that it demanded of its runners. He was tired of having someone else make his rules and plan his days.

He had, sometimes willingly and sometimes rebelliously, faithfully followed orders for the past four years. It was finally over, and he was looking forward to living his life as he chose. He hadn't been sure what to do with his life, but he had made one firm decision. He would answer to no one. The last thing he wanted was the constant discipline and unquestioning obedience a coach demanded.

Then Jesus had come, demanding not only his next four years, but the rest of his life.

Dave had fought bitterly.

"My whole life! It's too much for you to ask!"

"He that finds his life shall lose it; and he that loses his life for my sake shall find it."

"But why me? I am not qualified! You need someone smarter, full of wisdom, someone who is a great orator! Surely you don't need me!"

"God hath chosen the foolish things of the world to confound the wise . . . that no flesh should glory in his presence."

Dave grinned. "I guess I do qualify after all, when you put it that way."

Then he sobered.

"What will my family think? I've all but ignored them for the past four years, and am just now getting close to them again!"

"He that loves father or mother more than me is not worthy of me."

"Lord! Lord! It's not what I planned to do with my life."

"Why do you call me, Lord, Lord, and do not the things which I say?"

Dave had been careful not to address Jesus as Lord again.

"But my friends - what will they think when they see me running with your torch? This race is not a popular one right now."

"Whosoever therefore shall be ashamed of me and of my words in this adulterous and sinful generation; of him also shall the Son of man be ashamed, when he comes in the glory of his Father with the holy angels."

Dave literally groaned aloud.

"It's going to be so hard."'

"Whosoever will come after me, let him deny himself, and take up his cross, and follow me."

"I am weak in areas. You must know I am not good at public speaking. I would never want you to ask me to do that!"

"My strength is made perfect in weakness."

"Could I just try it for awhile, and if it doesn't work, I'll just go back to my plans?"

"No man, having put his hand to the plough, and looking back, is fit for the kingdom of God. Remember Lot's wife."

Dave felt almost crushed with the weight of the decision. He said, half to himself, "It would be easier if I didn't know what you're asking of me. But I do know what this means. It means giving up everything and everyone that means anything to me."

He hadn't expected an answer, but received a quick reply.

Dave

"Whosoever he be of you that forsakes not all that he has, he cannot be my disciple."

Dave thought of the friendships he had renewed in the past few months. He enjoyed having a good time, free at last from the responsibilities of training and running. He swallowed bitterly.

"My friends will no longer want to be around me. I'll be all alone."

"I am with you always, even unto the end of the world."

Dave was still for a few minutes, and then the full impact of the call made him speak once more.

"But I will never have all the things that I hoped to have!"

A question became his answer, and with it, Dave ran out of arguments.

"For what shall it profit a man, if he shall gain the whole world, and lose his own soul?"

Dave was silent for a long while.

Then he asked hesitantly, "Where do you want me to go?"

"Follow me."

So the Lord would chart the course. Who knew where it would lead? He thought of the path others had run, and shuddered.

"This race can be dangerous. Several have died running for you."

"Be faithful unto death, and I will give you a crown of life."

"What exactly is it that you want me to do?"

"Let your light so shine before men, that they may see your good works, and glorify your Father which is in heaven."

Dave pictured himself, holding high his flaming torch as he ran through a sin-blackened world. A small flicker of excitement stirred within him, as he realized how desperately the world needed light.

"And I will represent you?"

"You will be my ambassador."

Dave's voice was almost a whisper, but he had to ask one more question that was troubling him.

"What about my support? I have to eat . . . I have some bills . . . "

The words of the Lord interrupted him . . .

"Take no thought for your life, what you shall eat, or what you shall drink; nor yet for your body, what you shall put on. But seek first the kingdom of God, and his righteousness; and all these things shall be added unto you."

There were no more excuses. There was nothing else to say. The word of God offered man no alternative to total surrender.

The chair where Dave knelt became an altar. Dave offered himself as the sacrifice. His words at the end were simple. "Here I am, my Lord. Send me."

He was totally unprepared for what happened next. Electrifying joy filled him to overflowing. He had expected a misery to settle within him that would only be liberated by death itself. Instead, he was weeping and laughing both at the same time, thanking God for choosing him to run with the torch.

The thrill of winning the Olympics was nothing compared to this! It reminded him of the words King David had penned thousands of years before:

In thy presence is fulness of joy. At thy right hand there are pleasures for evermore.

This then was the blessing that came from surrendering to Jesus! He could feel His presence, almost see his outstretched hands and hear his cheerful words, *"Dave! Enter into the joy of the Lord!"*

Looking up, tears shining through his radiant face, he whispered reverently, "How I love you, my Lord. Forgive me for straying from you. Please help me to never again make anyone or anything my first love. I thought a commitment to you would bring pain. But I have never been as happy as I am right now."

"If you know these things, happy are you if you do them!"

Dave was silent, basking in the presence of his Lord.

Finally he spoke. "Lord, I hardly dare believe that I have made you happy by agreeing to run for you. But I know I have. Is it your pleasure that has made me so happy?   Lord, I never knew a happiness like this even existed.

"I love you. I give you my life, my strength. I give you my mind, my soul, my heart.   I present my body to you, a living sacrifice. I forsake this world, Lord, to choose you.

" Please make me a good runner. I ask for nothing but your continued pleasure. My Lord, I will run for you . . . and you alone."

The altar.
> *The sacrifice.*
>> *The fire.*

The three always go together.
Dave's torch was set aflame by the touch of God.

Chapter 3

Dave

*And the light shineth in darkness; and the darkness
comprehended it not.*
John 1:5

It was often a lonely run.

Perhaps Dave remembered too well the thrill of the
Olympics, with its massive arena, thousands of fans,
deafening cheers, news reporters competing with one
another for an interview . . .

Dave hadn't realized how different this race would be.
There were no reporters, no cheering fans. Not even the
members of his own family showed interest in this race.

When Dave had mentioned his new race to some of his
family and friends, they had laughed and scoffed. Only
one great-uncle had clasped his hand with approval.

"Dave, you will find your new life to be one of total
commitment. You will also find this an unpopular race.
But there is nothing you can do with your life that will be
more profitable to you in the long run. Nothing."

He was silent then, and Dave began to speak. His
uncle interrupted in a low voice that broke with emotion.
Dave leaned forward, straining to hear his words.

"Dave, the Lord called me to this race when I was
about your age. I was afraid to tell him, 'No. I refuse to
run.' So I just ignored him.

"The years of my life have passed so quickly. All the
time, in the back of my mind, I thought maybe someday I
would answer the call of God. But I never did. I just
drifted, busy with the day-to-day affairs of living.

"Now my life is nearly over. I should be looking
forward to meeting Christ. Instead, I wonder what I am
going to say to Him. What concerns me more is
wondering what he will say to me. I would love to hear,
'Well done, good and faithful servant.' But I will never
hear those words."

He looked up, tears filling his eyes.

Dave

"Don't concern yourself with the opinions of your family. You have made the decision I should have made, but didn't. I wasted my life."

Dave was relieved when Uncle Joe had walked away, for he hadn't known what to say. What words could ease the pain of an unanswered call, a squandered life?

He was the only relative who had spoken favorably of Dave's race. Dave hadn't expected his family to be excited about his decision, but neither had he expected their bitter reaction. Some had responded with a curse, some with disgust, some with a lecture, and some with total disinterest. They now avoided him when possible.

He would have to run alone, misunderstood and criticized by both friends and family. This run was proving to be far different from the one that began in Olympia of ancient Greece.

He remembered beginning his training for that race. He could still hear the lecture of his coach. "Dave, you must be single minded! You have to have one goal, and only one. All these other concerns and ambitions of yours have got to go."

So, one by one, they went. His family had grown used to Dave's absence at things they considered important. His girl had dropped him in disgust after just a few weeks of training. While his friends were out enjoying life, getting the good jobs, the pretty girls, the fast cars and having fun, Dave was training. He had tried to slip off now and then to look up his old friends, but Coach had reminded him in no uncertain terms of his priority. His family and friends had scoffed at his rigid lifestyle, but he knew secretly they were all pulling for him. They wanted him to make the Olympic team, and when he had, they talked of nothing else. No one could have asked for more enthusiastic supporters.

This time it was different. Again they were scoffing at his rigid lifestyle. But they weren't pulling for him now. They were embarrassed when their acquaintances learned he had entered the race. He remembered his brother's sneer.

"You don't look like a runner for God."

Dave had answered with a question.

"What are God's runners supposed to look like, Bro?"

His brother hadn't bothered to answer.

Dave had been so proud when they had all gathered around enthusiastically to see his Olympic medal. They had passed it around almost reverently, awed by its six grams of gold. It seemed strange to Dave that they were not in the least bit interested in a place where gold was so abundant that it was used to pave the streets.

The Lord had forewarned his runners of the difficulties of this race. He had clearly informed them in advance that there would be conflict with their families.

What could be clearer than, *"A man's foes shall be they of his own household"?*

And yet it was painful. However, no amount of pain inflicted by the world could ever overshadow the joy of pleasing Jesus.

Joy in the presence of Christ had caused John to leap while still in the womb!

John. What a runner!

Dave grinned.

"Bro has some preconceived idea about what runners should look like," he thought. "He would have been shocked if he could have seen John!"

Then he sobered. John's race had not ended in a blaze of glory. What hurts had he experienced? Had loneliness plagued him? Was he misunderstood . . . forsaken by those he loved?

"I think I will take a look at the great runners of the past," he thought. "It might be interesting."

He decided to begin that evening. He didn't realize that his search through the centuries would introduce him to mass murderers, desolate slaves, prosperous merchants, destitute failures, aged men, fearless professors, courageous women, helpless invalids, elderly women, sharp lawyers, drunken teenagers, hardworking housewives, dying men, respectable counts, sneering agnostics, vile blasphemers, despised priests . . . and these were just a few of God's torch bearers!

He would meet runners of distant lands, of other times, discovering them in slave ships, hog pens, battlefields, prisons, Indian teepees, mansions, orphanages, forests and dungeons.

His search began that evening with the simple words,

14

Dave

"There was a man sent from God, whose name was John . . . "

Chapter 4

John

Behold, I will send my messenger, and he shall prepare the way before me . . .
Malachi 3:1

The *Jordan River.* Could there be a stranger place to run the race? It was the lowest in the world - and probably the ugliest. Its swirling waters and threatening currents made its crossing a challenge.

No wonder Naaman had cringed at the thought of his dip in the Jordan River. The trek to it was anything but pleasant. He had to fight his way through the dense, half tropical jungle, inhabited with wild boars. Nearer the clay banks, poisonous reptiles and tormenting insects hid among wild grasses and reeds.

By the time a person reached the dirty, yellow waters, he was bitten, scratched and filthy.

The river bed did not invite waders. Mud seeped around the ankles, making each step a chore.

A strange river . . .

A stranger runner . . .

His beard was full and untrimmed. His eyes were fierce, and fixed straight ahead. He was not only covered with his own hair, but was clad in garments made of camel hair.

There were a few people nearby the day he made his appearance. They stared as the man emerged from the wilderness and half walked, half slid down the river bank. John waded into the river without hesitation, then suddenly turned and stared straight at them. Their conversation and gestures ceased abruptly.

His eyes blazed. They jumped when they heard his piercing words, "Repent! Repent! Repent, you sinners! The kingdom of heaven is coming! The Lord is coming! Get rid of your sins and get ready for him!"

Little children ran to hide behind their mothers and the teenagers just sort of eased themselves backward to stand with their families.

John

The wild man continued to rant about their sins, and the people fled the area. In a short time, the news had spread.

Speculation ran wild.

"Who is he?

"Where did he come from?

"Could he be a prophet?"

"Do you think he is still there?"

Some men of the area got together and went to see.

He was there. He was still standing in the river, yelling at one lone fisherman to repent.

They all listened to him intently, transfixed by his eyes. Then they began to listen to his words. The longer they listened, the more sense he made.

"Come in and get baptized and confess your sins," he shouted.

After listening for about an hour, one young man broke away from the group. He ran down the embankment and waded out to John.

John watched as he came, his eyes never leaving his face. When the man almost reached him, John stopped him with the command, "Confess your sins, Man. When you've confessed them all, I will baptize you."

The young man began to confess his sins to God . . . one by one. Midway in his confession, tears were streaming down his face. His heart was heavy with shame. He felt naked before a holy God.

He finally lifted his head, and looked again into those blazing eyes of the savage man.

And he stared. The eyes that had looked so harsh just minutes before had softened and were radiating love. John reached out to him. His fear was gone as he was almost compelled to John's side. John dipped him into the river and lifted him up.

Waves of relief swelled through him. "My Lord!" he prayed. "I feel clean for the first time in my life!"

He turned and made his way back to the river bank, up through the tangled brush, to his friends.

They stood staring at him. "You look different," one of his friends finally said.

"I feel different - clean - and great!"

17

He wanted to run, shout, dance and leap for joy. He was free! Free from a load that had been piling up and weighing him down since birth!

He didn't understand what had happened to him. He only knew that the guilt was no longer there. God had done a work.

It was the unconcealed joy on his face that caused two of his friends to warily approach John for the same experience.

When they later made their way back home, their wives and children tried to sort out their words.

So he *was* a messenger from God. Prophets were no strangers to Jews who knew their history. Yet . . . it was so much easier to believe in the prophets of old than to be confronted with a live one!

The following day, the men took their neighbors, families, and friends to the river bank, hoping and praying that John would be there.

He was sitting on the bank of clay, eating locusts when they arrived. When he saw them coming, he dipped his finger into a comb of honey and then sucked it. Then he waded into the river and again began shouting.

It was about an hour before the men convinced their families to get into the river and approach him. But his message, coupled with their transformed husbands and fathers, finally motivated them to be baptized. When they waded from the river, their faces radiant with joy, other families made the trek to John.

The word spread. Daily more people arrived. They came seeking God's message by hearing his messenger.

The Jordan, for centuries the violent boundary that divided the holy from the unholy, now became the dividing of the old ways from the new.

Men joined John in the task of baptizing the crowds.

The crowds . . .

The priests were losing control. How dare God send his messenger without their permission?

"Stay away from the river! Stay away from the man! Ignore his message," they warned. But the people were replacing death with life, and they took no heed to their bitter counsel.

John

The day was hot, heavy with humidity. Mobs thronged the area. Suddenly, there was a stir. Fingers pointed and voices whispered. The priests had arrived, their robes snagged, the hems soiled.

The peoples' eyes shifted from the priests to John. There would surely be a confrontation now.

John didn't seem to even notice them, but continued to baptize.

Then with a swift movement, he faced the priests. The crowd gasped. The eyes that they had seen filled with love just seconds before were now blazing with fire. He stared into the eyes of each of their leaders. One stared back defiantly, but the others lowered their heads or turned away. He waited silently until every eye was back on him. A hush came over the crowd. Even the children stared at this John they had almost learned not to fear.

Everyone jumped as his shout penetrated the silence.

"You *snakes!* You *vipers!* You *serpents!* What are you doing here? If you do not bring forth good fruit, you will be cut down by the axe of God and cast into the fire!"

The men stared at him. Who did this man think he was? How dare he speak to them like this, especially in front of their people? And he wouldn't quit! His voice continued to rave. They turned and nearly ran from him.

John turned to the crowd as they were leaving. "There is someone coming who will lead you," he said gently. "I'm not even good enough to untie his shoes. I can only baptize you with water. He will baptize you with the Holy Ghost and with fire."

Then his voice stopped abruptly. His eyes left the crowd and he stood staring at a man who came walking toward him.

His face that had so recently changed from anger to compassion was now filled with awe. He seemed to shrink before the one who made his way closer.

He turned to the spectators. "Look," he said, pointing at the man approaching him. "This is the Lamb of God, who will take away the sin of the world. This is the one I've been telling you would come."

The crowd glanced at the one coming, but then turned back to stare at John. Where was the John they knew - the one who fearlessly exposed sin and condemned sinners? John had been intimidated by no man. He had rebuked the king, challenged the soldiers, and denounced the priests.

But now . . . now he stood trembling before this one who had reached his side. They peered closely at the stranger. They could see nothing in him that would inspire such deference in John.

"Baptize me, John."

John's head dropped.

"I can't," he answered. "I'm not worthy to baptize you."

The crowd was shocked at his answer.

"Now," the man answered.

John hesitated, then reached out to baptize him. He didn't even ask him to first confess his sins, as he had demanded of everyone else. He simply baptized him.

The crowd rose to their feet as this stranger rose from the water. He literally radiated light!

Suddenly a dove swooped from the clouds and flew directly toward them, and then settled upon the stranger's shoulder.

A voice thundered from the heavens "This is my beloved Son, in whom I am well pleased."

It was a day earth would not forget.

Things changed for John after that day. He had begun his race with vigor and uncompromising boldness. He ran hard, and the crowd was amazed at his stamina. But after that day, he simply slowed his pace. What had been the greatest day of his life also seemed to be the beginning of a decline. Some of his best helpers left him that day. They just turned and followed the man who had been declared by a voice in the heavens to be the Son of God.

Most of the people left too.

Some stayed.

"Why is everyone leaving the river, John?" some asked him.

"I told you I was not the one to follow. I was just the one sent here to announce his coming."

John watched, as more of the crowd left.

John wasn't sad that they were leaving him. He knew that he had come to prepare people for the coming of God's Son, and he felt good about having done that. He felt something like the best man in the wedding. It was great to be a part of the wedding, but it wasn't his big day! The groom was the one with the bride!

He looked at the stragglers still on the bank, and smiled one of his rare smiles that lit up his face.

"He must increase, but I must decrease," he told them. "I am a man from this earth. He is a man who has come from heaven. God has sent him to you and filled him with his Spirit. God is his father, and he loves his Son, and has given him all power and all authority. If you will believe and trust him, you will have everlasting life. If you reject him, God's wrath will be toward you."

He turned and made his way out of the river, up the bank and into the woods. He was still smiling.

John entered a dark area in his race then, so tangled and thick that no sunlight could penetrate. It began with his arrest. He was accused of speaking against the king. He had only spoken the truth, and even as guards shackled and dragged him to prison, he denounced the sins of the king. "King Herod has broken the law of God! He too needs to confess his sins! He is living with his sister-in-law! She is married to his brother, Philip, and he has no right to take her!"

Herod and his wife were infuriated when they were told of John's denunciation! The King confessed to no one!

"Kill him!" Herod ordered.

"We will have an uprising if we kill him, Your Majesty," one of his subjects advised. "The people believe he is a messenger from their God. They refer to him as a prophet."

"Then lock the man up!"

This part of John's race was the toughest yet. It was too dark in the musty cell to see the rats, but he both heard and felt them. His wrists, waist and ankles were shackled with chains that were embedded in the stone wall. They prevented him from stretching out or sitting, except in a crouched position.

His former helpers came when they could, making their way down the musty corridors. He identified them by their voices at the small, square opening to his cell.

They prayed with him, and kept him informed of the news.

As time dragged on, John became bitterly discouraged. He had trained for this race as far back as he could remember. From his earliest childhood, he knew this race was his destiny and could hardly wait for it to begin.

But it had come to this. He was told about Jesus and the crowds that were beginning to follow him. The news was good. So why was he abandoned and forgotten?

Was his race over? The weeks dragged on. Insects filled John's matted beard. Rat bites covered his weakened body.

One morning - or was it evening - he heard a voice telling him more about Jesus. He listened eagerly.

Jesus. Just the mention of his name brought hope and a surge of strength. Another voice interrupted. There were two men at the door, both excitedly describing the crowds, the miracles, the Master.

John's ravaged body ached with pain. He spoke with an effort.

"Ask Him . . . ask Him . . . "

He paused. Dare he ask the question that plagued him in the black, lonely hours? Yes. For he had to know the answer. It seemed so long since that day when the heavens opened and the sign of the dove was given.

"Ask him . . . tell him I have to know for sure that he is the one. Or is there another we should look for."

He heard the messenger gasp. "John! You *know* he's the one! You yourself told us he was the one! You saw the dove light on him! You heard God's voice speak from heaven!"

John sighed heavily.

"Please ask him for me . . . and hurry back to give me his answer."

Exhausted with the effort of speech, he closed his eyes.

How many hours, days, or weeks passed before the answer finally came? He didn't know. In this place of blackness, days and nights all blended together.

"John!

"John! We told Jesus what you said! Do you want to hear his answer?"

22

"Yes! Oh, yes. Tell me - quickly!"

"John! Jesus told us to come and tell you what we are hearing and seeing. Blind people are seeing for the first time in their lives! People who have never walked are walking and jumping and running! He has healed lepers with just his touch! Deaf people are hearing! John, even dead people are coming back to life! Jesus is preaching the gospel to the poor!

"And, John . . . "

"Yes?"

"Jesus said everyone would be blessed who is not offended because of him."

They waited for his answer.

"My Lord," he prayed silently. "Don't let me be offended by this prison cell."

"Did he say anything else?" he asked when he was able.

"John, he began telling the crowd what a great man you are. We didn't stay to listen to all that he was saying about you. We did hear him say you were a messenger sent from God. We left then, and came running to you with His answer."

"Thank you. Thank you," John whispered.

Hours after they left, he still lay thinking about their message. If this Jesus was raising the dead and healing lepers, he could surely release him from prison. He undoubtedly would be out of this wretched place soon. He slept peacefully for the first time in weeks.

Things continued as they were, but John was no longer troubled. It helped so much just knowing that Jesus remembered him. Jesus had praised him to the people as a great runner. It was enough. If God should choose that he never preach again . . . if he should finish his race in the stench of this hole . . . then he would die at peace. For he had done his work faithfully, announcing the Christ to all who awaited his coming.

A few evenings later, he heard the feet of soldiers outside his cell. Suddenly the door burst open, and John looked up expectantly. Three soldiers stood over him, one with his sword drawn. Another soldier placed his shoe on the head of John, crushing the side of his face into the floor. His hoarse scream, the final reaction of his tortured body, ended abruptly as his head was severed from it.

The Herods of this world esteem neither the race nor its runners. This race is only in, not of, this world.

And while earth derides, heaven applauds.

An angel had announced John with the message: "He shall be great in the sight of the Lord."

And he was. The Lord himself had paid him his highest compliment:

"Among them born of women, there has not risen a greater than John the Baptist."

Chapter 5

Dave

Thine ears shall hear a word behind thee, saying, This is the way, walk ye in it, when ye turn to the right hand, and when ye turn to the left.
Isaiah 30:21

Dave's heart was pounding as his thoughts returned to the present . . . his time, his call, his race.

"Oh, God," he breathed. "I don't know if I can survive this race! What if the course you set for me takes me where you took John? I don't think I can go through what John did! And God, if John was so great, why did you let his race end in such a violent death?"

The words of Jesus reverberated through his mind, answering his question as He so often did, with a question of His own.

"Dave, do you seek the glory of men - or do you seek to fulfil *my* will for your life?"

Dave didn't answer until he had searched his heart.

Then his quiet answer came. "I seek only your will, my Lord."

Was not that what John had sought? He did not seek approval from man!

Had not his race ended in a blaze of glory? For what greater glory could a man have than the stamp of approval given him by the Master he had lived to please?

Dave recalled the way the Lord had described John to the people.

What went ye out into the wilderness to see? A reed shaken with the wind?

But what went ye out for to see? A man clothed in soft raiment? behold, they that wear soft clothing are in kings' houses.

But what went ye out for to see? A prophet? yea, I say unto you, and more than a prophet.

For this is he, of whom it is written, Behold, I send my messenger before thy face, which shall prepare thy way before thee.

Verily I say unto you, Among them that are born of women there hath not risen a greater than John the Baptist . . .

"Oh, Lord," Dave sighed. "Let me live my life as John did."

A Bible verse he had memorized when a teen suddenly came back to him.

Thy word is a lamp unto my feet, and a light unto my path.

The words had never meant much to Dave. But now their message filled him with joy and relief. The Bible would light his way, beaming its rays upon the course he should run! He didn't have to worry about this race. He would just simply follow the light, as other runners had before him. If a prison cell or a sword were in his future, then so be it. He, like John before him, would be concerned only with pleasing his Lord.

He picked up the Bible from the table beside him. Opening it randomly, he read:

Looking unto Jesus the author and finisher of our faith; who for the joy that was set before him endured the cross, despising the shame, and is set down at the right hand of the throne of God.

Look to Jesus, the author . . .

There was no doubt about Jesus being the author of his race. He surely would never have decided on his own to run!

And Jesus, the finisher?

The Lord obviously wouldn't start something he didn't intend to finish. Dave would trust his leadership one day at a time, one step at a time, until he crossed his finish line.

Look to Jesus, Dave. Look to Jesus . . .

Chapter 6

JESUS

(From Eternity to Eternity)

*His lightnings enlightened the world: the earth saw,
and trembled.*
Psalm 97:4

Earth had never seen a runner like Jesus. He did not just carry a torch. He was THE TORCH.

His race began with an explosion of light. Angels left the heavens to announce his birth to shepherds. The night air lit up with their awesome presence, and the shepherds followed their directions to the stable to welcome God's lamb.

Wise men from the East followed the same path, lit for them by a star, and worshiped at his crib.

His mother knew he was destined to run the race, and she spent many of his childhood hours watching him, contemplating his future in the privacy of her heart.

At twelve years of age, he was already in training, announcing to whomever cared to listen, "I must be about my father's business."

He was thirty when God himself announced him to this earth as his chosen runner. Those at his baptism trembled at the introduction. "This is my beloved son, in whom I am well pleased," God reverberated from the heavens. And his race began.

He ran until he was exhausted, but not once faltered in his run. Crowds gathered and stared at this runner, transfixed. The dead came off their funeral biers and out of their graves when he spoke their names. Lepers crept from their caves, and at his touch, were no longer lepers. The brilliance of his presence penetrated blinded eyes, and the first sight they gazed upon was his face. The stooped and bent straightened to attention when they heard his name. The crippled ran, danced, and leaped. Demons screamed through their human cages, but were silenced by his rebuke.

27

JESUS

He ran past a cemetery, freeing a tormented lunatic from over four-thousand demons. Demons, terrified at being evicted from their home, clawed their way into a herd of three-thousand swine. Even pigs chose to drown themselves, rather than face life inhabited by these filthy creatures. Jesus, for his act of compassion, was begged by those whose only concern was with the loss of their hogs, to continue his race elsewhere. He ran from their coasts, leaving behind him a new runner, holding his torch so high that it emitted rays of light over ten cities!

He preached fearlessly as he ran, the deaf listening raptly. The hearing stopped their ears.

As he ran through the multitudes, sinners discovered their Savior, the righteous their sin.

Everyone and everything touched by this TORCH were forever altered. Those who ran to him were themselves transformed from darkness to light. Those who fled his presence found themselves groping in unimaginable, horrible blackness. Water became wine when lit by this TORCH. A lad's small lunch became food for five-thousand hungry men.

Howling winds grew silent at his command for peace, and the sea lost its power to pull man to its depths, as he ran nonchalantly across its surface.

The religious leaders came to question, sneer, and scoff, but fled from him, trembling with rage and fear. His friends tried to stop his race, calling him mad. Scribes, Priests, and Pharisees, fueled with envy, incited the mobs to push him from cliff edges as he ran. He escaped their fury and kept running.

"Vipers! Serpents!" he shouted vehemently to jealous leaders.

Then his eyes would invariably leave theirs, and turning tenderly to the sick, lame, possessed, hungry, thirsty, and needy, he gently called them his lambs and his little children.

He ran into Jerusalem's temple, shocking those in attendance, as he drove out both the moneychangers and their customers with a whip, dumped their money on the floor, tipped over their tables, upended their cages of doves and threw out their sheep and their oxen. By ridding the temple of its profiteers, he further incurred the rage of his enemies.

Earth was not prepared for a runner such as this. His light was blinding, exposing man's weaknesses, frailty, faults, and sins. The world never regarded this race or its runners, but men particularly despised this one. He entered and ran through the world as someone more than human, and men realized they would either have to bow to him or kill him. They chose death, not realizing it was the path he himself chose.

Earth's cry gained volume in one mighty crescendo: *Stop this runner!*

Men tried desperately to stop him. He was praying one evening in the solitude of a hillside olive garden. The peace was suddenly shattered by the noise of a multitude. They advanced with torches and lanterns, but what were they in the presence of Light?

Man approached his creator armed with swords, but as he walked toward them, simply declaring, "I am he," they fell backward, their bodies and their useless weapons littering the ground.

His trial was a mockery. Running in this race was not unlawful, and everyone involved knew it. He submitted meekly to his creation, stretching his body out on a tree he had made. He winced as hands he had formed wielded the hammer, driving nails through his hands and feet. His cross was set on a hill he had shaped.

He looked upon his hovering army of angelic warriors awaiting his nod to advance and destroy. Then he stopped his troops with a shake of his head and hung in agony as every drop of blood streamed from his wounds.

God turned the lights of heaven off, and the earth turned black, as it heaved and trembled.

The crucifixion of Christ was man's worst hour . . . but God's best. Only matchless mercy stayed the avenging hand of a loving God.

"It is finished," Jesus cried in his agony, and the veil in the temple separating unholy man from holy God ripped in half, from its top to its bottom.

The terrified officer and his men could only say, "Truly this was the Son of God."

The runner of all runners was down. The race was over. The runners who had been in training to carry the torch wept in defeat. Satan and man had together succeeded in extinguishing the light that had lit a sin-blackened world. Satan and demons howled in glee. They had won.

But Christ lay only in a borrowed tomb. He had no plans to remain there. Because how can LIFE be killed? And how can LIGHT be darkened? And how can RESURRECTION be buried?

Satan, his devils, and his human agents would soon learn that they had attempted the impossible and failed. They had claimed their victory prematurely.

For the race of Jesus was not over.

He was on a journey and his destination was the abode of the doomed. He arrived, an unexpected and an uninvited guest, for LIGHT blazed into hell that day, shattering darkness. Demons shrieked as Jesus advanced triumphantly through earth's bowels. Satan cringed with terrible comprehension.

LIFE had blazed a path through Death.

All that remained of the war then were the final skirmishes. Satan had lost.

A vicious hatred boiled up within him. He may have received the death blow, but he would fight to the end. He would use every cunning wile, every deceitful lie and every evil torture he could devise to drag one man, woman or child to hell with him. His scream of rage became a battle cry that echoed throughout the universe. No follower of Jesus Christ would get to heaven without a vicious warfare!

Jesus ignored both him and his cowering demons. Traveling through the corridors of darkness, LIGHT ran. His brilliance lit up paradise. Prisoners of war, held in the black bowels of death, squinted and shielded their eyes as LIGHT marched toward them.

"O Lord! My strength! My Redeemer!" the Psalmist cried.

"He has come to get us at last," John sighed, as he looked at his Deliverer.

A mighty crescendo of shouts merged with his. Their hopes had not been in vain! He had come to liberate them! Satan shuddered as praise and applause for Jesus met somewhere between heaven and earth.

Fire leaped from the serpent's eyes as his avowed enemy led the redeemed to their new home in the heavens. He could imagine their homecoming. He had been evicted. Now mere humans were being ushered in with a celestial welcome.

There was nothing he could do about them. They were home safe. But he vowed he would do everything in his power to prevent any more people from getting there. He glared at the screeching demons surrounding him. They were beginning to comprehend the awful purpose of Christ's death and their impending doom. A snarl twisted his features. He would use them to fill the earth with sin and misery until the end. He would have to hurry. He didn't have long.

Jesus was oblivious to his empty threats and hopeless schemes. He was even now alone with his Father in the most holy place. No human being had ever dared to approach the throne of God. Jesus, the son of man and the son of God, now knelt before his Father, presenting to him his own blood as the ransom for the souls of fallen man. His offering was received. Man's debt was paid in full.

"How I despised the shame of the cross," he thought. "But, oh, the joy, the joy that I have now!"

He looked at Noah, Abraham, and Moses savoring heaven's beauty. He smiled upon David, as he sat caressing his tiny son, stolen from him by sin and death. And *John*. He was freed from man's prison at last. Jesus didn't want to leave them even for a second. But he still had work to do on earth. He must meet with his torchbearers.

God dispatched an angel from heaven and he arrived as a streak of lightning at the grave site. With a touch of his finger, he removed the stone, not so Jesus could get out, but so man could get in. For we all needed to know that his tomb was empty.

Arriving back on earth, he ran to the seashore to find his men out fishing in the sea.

"Children," he called, "Have you any meat?"

"No!" came the weary reply from the ship. They had fished the whole night, but had caught nothing.

The creator of the sea, the fish and the men, shouted back, "Cast the net on the right side of the ship, and you shall find!"

The words sounded familiar. But more concerned with the business of catching fish than remembering the words of their former Master, the disciples cast their net. And then struggled with its weight. John stared at the swarming net, then at Peter.

"Peter! It's the Lord!"

Peter's eyes grew wide in wonder. Then, grabbing a coat, he dove overboard and began to swim ashore.

Jesus had a fire going before the ship landed. "Bring the fish!" Jesus called. It took all of them to drag in their catch.

Jesus set out the bread and grilled the fish. When the meal was ready, he invited, "Come and dine!"

They were still stunned. Even Peter was tongue-tied. No one dared to approach either Christ or the food. Jesus looked upon these rugged men. He knew they were fearful and embarrassed. Had they not hidden from the murderous mob and left him to face his torturers alone?

He divided the bread and the fish and served them. They could feel his love as they ate together.

"Peter," he said after they finished eating.

Here it was then. The reproof. The shame.

"Feed my sheep, Peter.

"Feed my lambs."

Peter immediately lost all desire to do anything else.

The crowd leaned forward, listening intently to his final instructions.

"Don't leave Jerusalem. I will baptize you with the Holy Ghost and with fire."

Then he had just stood there, gazing with a tender love upon his people.

And as they gazed back, they realized their eyes were slowly lifting to the heavens. They stared in awe, as their champion runner rose in the air. A cloud enfolded him. He was no longer visible.

And still they stood, staring into the heavens, stretching for just one more glimpse of him. It took a voice to call them back to earth. Two men, clothed in snow white garments, asked them, "Why do you stand here gazing up into heaven?"

Why? Why!

Jesus had come!

They had watched him die!

He had been resurrected!

And now he was gone again!

They all turned and stared at the two angels, taking their presence at this scene for granted. One question was written on all their faces.

Will he come back?

The angels answered their unspoken question.

"This same Jesus, which is taken up from you into heaven, shall so come in like manner as ye have seen him go into heaven."

They sighed in pleasure. He would come back. That promise would keep them going to their finish line.

Peter was already running in place, anxiously waiting for his baptism of fire.

Chapter 7

Dave

*Let us run with patience the race that is set before us,
looking unto Jesus the author and finisher of our faith.*
Hebrews 12:1-2

Dave knelt before Jesus.

"Lord," he prayed softly. Don't ever let me lose sight of you. You are the Author of this race. And you alone are the finisher of it. If I ever get proud of my accomplishments, Lord, please remind me that all is darkness without you, for you are the light. And remind me that all is death without you, for you alone are life."

Dave paused, thinking about the runners down through the centuries who had run with the torch. There were so many . . . and they were so different. The Lord never seemed to choose the ones you would expect him to pick. There were the old ones and the young, the weak ones and the strong, the poor ones and the rich, the educated and the uneducated, some wicked and vile, and others pompous and arrogant.

"Lord," he said aloud. You gave strength to the weak and weakness to the strong. You made the poor rich and the rich poor. You renewed the old and matured the young, gave knowledge to the uneducated and a child's faith to the educated. You made the wicked righteous and the arrogant humble.

"You have always had runners carrying the torch, through every generation, in every century. During the blackest hours, you had your light on earth. Though all the forces of evil gathered together to stop the race, you have always kept someone running with the blazing torch. And when his race was over, you had another ready to take his place.

"What an awesome race! It never quits, and it never will, until your shout of triumph echoes throughout the universe. When you fill all of heaven and earth with light, the need for a mere torch will be eliminated."

Dave felt small and unworthy as he thought about the runners who had preceded him. Who was he in such a company? But then . . . who were any of them without Christ?

What could the great prayer warriors have accomplished without one to pray to? And what would the renowned preachers have preached, if God had not given the message? Could the famed revivalists convict a sinner or create a new heart?

"All of us are but men," Dave said softly. "From the greatest to the least. Only Christ can hold our universe together, send the sun across the sky, prevent the oceans from overflowing, grow a harvest from a seed - and anoint a runner with his awesome Spirit."

Dave wondered where his race would lead him. He knew it wouldn't be easy. He had been studying the lives of the past runners, and not one had an easy race. All the forces of hell were determined to stop the smallest flicker of light that threatened the darkness that enveloped the earth.

But the enemy wasn't what really bothered Dave. His main concern was himself. He was all too aware of his weaknesses. Would it be his explosive temper that would defeat him? How many times had it gotten him into trouble!

"Lord," he prayed sincerely. "Are you sure you want me in this race? If you are going to make a runner out of me, you have lots of work to do."

Dave sighed, and picked up his Bible. He read: "The spirit indeed is willing, but the flesh is weak."

And then he began to read about the runner called Peter . . .

Chapter 8

Peter

And the Lord said, Simon, Simon, behold, Satan hath desired to have you, that he may sift you as wheat: But I have prayed for thee, that thy faith fail not: and when thou art converted, strengthen thy brethren.
Luke 22:31-32

Peter could not believe he was sitting in this room waiting for the fire of God to light his torch so he could begin his race. He thought he had forfeited his right to run. He had left the training field, cursing Jesus to anyone who cared to listen to his ranting. He had even claimed that he never knew him to a maid who questioned his friendship with Jesus. Jesus had warned him it would happen.

"Peter, this night, before the cock crow, you shall deny me thrice."

Peter knew Jesus had missed it this time. There was no way he would ever deny his master. Ever. And then, with soldiers pressing thorns into the head of Jesus, sneering at him and brandishing their swords, he had. He had denied him, not once, but three times. The rooster crowed, even as he cursed. The sound of a rooster crowing to this day sent shudders of shame reverberating through his body. In fact, the crow of a rooster not only reminded him of his failure to stand for Jesus, but reminded him of himself, strutting around in his pride, believing he could get through anything, with or without God's help.

It had been a heady experience being with Jesus. From the time Jesus had called him from his Dad's boat, his ego had steadily inflated. No other apostle had walked on water. Sure, he had begun to sink, but he had done it, while the others stood gaping from the ship.

He recalled the day he had fished the whole night and had caught nothing. Then Jesus had told him to go back out in the lake and let down his nets. Peter had boldly argued with him. Jesus was no fisherman. He was a carpenter! Who was he to tell Peter, one of the best fishermen in his time, how to fish?

He had argued, but then had decided to pacify Jesus. "I'll let down the net," he sighed. "One net," he muttered as he headed back out to sea.

If he had let down both nets that day, as Jesus had instructed, he would not have a broken net and two boats sinking!

He could only fall at the feet of Jesus when he finally reached the shore, saying, "I am a sinful man, O Lord."

He should have realized Jesus knew all about fish. How else could he have sent Peter to the sea with a pole and hook with a promise that the first fish he caught would have money in his mouth?

Jesus had certainly proved to him in no uncertain terms that he knew more about the sea and its fish than mere men ever knew. If Peter wanted to be a successful fisher of men, he would have to go to his Creator for help!

He had been the one with the revelation of who Christ really was, and Jesus had commended him for it. His pride had been deflated a few minutes later though, when he began to lecture Jesus about the prophecy of his untimely death. Jesus had turned to him with eyes of fire commanding sternly, "Get behind me, Satan! You are an offence unto me!"

Peter had stayed in the background for a few days, but then Jesus had asked him and James and John to climb a mountain with him. He hadn't asked the others to go along, so Peter knew he was still in the Lord's favor. He would never forget that mountain scene. Jesus had told them that he was the light of the world, but that day Peter saw Jesus literally transformed into light itself. He knew for certain then that Jesus was no mere man.

He was brighter than the sun, and his clothing was almost blinding in its brilliance. As he stood there glistening, Moses and Elijah appeared and the three of them talked together. Peter remembered with embarrassment how he had blurted out the suggestion that three tabernacles be built right there on the mountain top: one for Moses, one for Elijah, and one for Jesus.

While he was still babbling, without the benefit of much thought, the voice of God Himself interrupted his with the announcement: "This is my beloved Son, in whom I am well pleased; *hear him!*"

Peter recalled falling on his face, trembling with fear. He stayed on his face until Jesus touched him, saying gently, "Arise, and be not afraid."

He and the two brothers, James and John, had gotten unsteadily to their feet, not knowing what they would see. When they looked around, only Jesus stood with them. Moses and Elijah were nowhere to be seen. Peter now realized that he had been out of order suggesting three temples be built. The law, represented by Moses, and the prophets, represented by Elijah, had both been fulfilled in the person of Jesus Christ. God Himself had thundered from the heavens to point this out to him.

Thinking back, he wondered how Jesus had put up with his brashness.

He had been so patient. Peter had reminded Jesus that he and the other apostles had forsaken everything to follow him. Then he had come right out and asked him what they were going to get out of their sacrifice. Jesus had calmly reassured him that they were not following him in vain.

He thought back to the time he had vehemently stated, "Though all men shall be offended because of you, yet will I never be offended." He had been so arrogant while he trained for his race. "I'll die with you before I would deny you!" he had insisted to Jesus. Jesus had warned him to pray for strength, as he was too weak to face the battle to come. But he had been so sure of his spiritual strength, that he had slept the evening away. He had slept when just a few feet away from him, Jesus was agonizing in prayer. An angel had come to his aid. When Judas had come leading the soldiers to arrest Jesus, he had jumped to his feet, whipped out his sword, and cut off the ear of Malchus. Jesus hadn't even glanced his way, as he stooped, picked up the ear and gently placed it back on Malchus' head.

His arrogance was inconceivable to him now. He was so sure of himself, but he shortly discovered he couldn't even stand strong against a maid.

Peter

"I recognize you!" she said loudly! "You were with Jesus!"

He was immediately the center of attention in the room full of people.

"I don't know what you are talking about," he yelled.

She had no sooner left, then another maid spotted him.

After staring for a moment, she turned to the crowd and announced shrilly, "This fellow was also with Jesus of Nazareth!"

"I don't know the man!" Peter cried.

Peter noticed a group of men staring at him after being pointed out the second time. Finally they came over to him.

"You are one of them! We can tell by your speech!"

Peter had begun cursing and shouted, "I know not the man!"

It was then that the rooster had crowed.

He looked quickly over at Jesus, and just then Jesus turned and looked - not just at him - but into the very depths of his soul. Never had he felt such shame. He ran from the hall, sobbing bitterly.

He never wanted to face Jesus again. Never! But just a few days later, Mary Magdalene had run to him and the rest of the apostles with the two words that forever changed his mind and his life. Mary was so electrified from her experience at the sepulchre, that she could hardly relate the angel's message for them.

She finally had settled down enough to tell them what the angel had said.

"Go your way, tell his disciples *and Peter. . .* "

And Peter.

And *Peter!*

Those two words would thrill him to his dying day.

The angel had singled *him* out.

There was hope that he was still eligible to run the race! When he went to eat with Jesus on the seashore later, Jesus had drawn him aside and asked, "Do you love me?"

Peter assured Jesus of his love.

Jesus simply answered, "Feed my lambs."

Jesus then asked, "Peter! Do you love me?"

Peter replied, "Yes, Lord! I love you!"

"Feed my sheep."

The third time Jesus's words pierced his very soul. "Do you love me, Peter?"

"You *know* I love you," Peter had said, hurt in his voice.

He pondered that conversation for days. Had Jesus questioned his love one time for each time he had denied knowing him? He determined in his heart to run his race well. He would spend the remaining days of his life to feed the lambs and the sheep of his Lord's pasture.

He waited now in this upper room. He didn't know what was supposed to happen. So far nothing had, and he was getting restless.

Suddenly the room grew still with an unearthly hush. Something supernatural was about to happen, and Peter could feel it.

A strange noise filled the heavens and a mighty wind surged through the room. Tongues of fire appeared as if from nowhere and settled on each one present. Peter was aware of an awe-inspiring Presence in the room, and for once in his life, though his mouth opened in amazement, he had nothing to say. Then he realized he was speaking - but in words he did not even recognize.

Peter's torch had been set aflame by God himself.

And he began to run.

He ran down the steps and out the door. He preached with power and authority. Peoples' hearts were filled with guilt, and they cried out, "What shall we do?"

The beginning of Peter's race was explosive. Three-thousand people repented of their sins and were baptized the first day.

Peter ran to the temple to pray, and found a man over forty years old who had never walked. Peter lifted him to his feet, boldly demanding, "In the name of Jesus Christ of Nazareth, rise up and walk!"

He didn't just walk! He leaped, jumped, and bounded into the temple, praising God!

Religious leaders, believing they had stopped the race at last, raged in fury at another miracle, another runner. They fumed as they saw Peter's torch held high, and made their devious plans to kill this ignorant man. They arrested him, but Peter ran to his cell with joy. He was celebrating! Five-thousand more people had now turned to Jesus.

Those who conspired to stop the race threatened Peter, but dared not stop him by force yet. He was surrounded by too many cheering spectators. They could only release him, knowing he would just run harder and faster.

Peter ran in the newly formed church, rebuking Ananias and Sapphira fearlessly for their shameless lies, watching them fall dead at his feet.

He ran through the streets and crowds thronged him, carrying their sick friends and relatives on stretchers to lay them in his shadow. All were instantly healed.

He ran through Joppa, pausing long enough to listen to the mournful wails around the cold and lifeless body of Tabitha. He knelt to pray, and then summoned her back to life with two words, *"Tabitha, arise."* He ran from the room, where ashes had become beauty, mourning had become joy, and the spirit of heaviness was clothed with the garment of praise. He ran, laughing with delight.

Then he changed his course.

"No runner has ever run there," spectators called.

But Peter had received a vision from God and began to run among the Gentiles. God alone charted his course.

He paused in his race only momentarily, as a bystander called out to him some shocking news. "Herod has killed James! He is determined to stop this race! He is searching for you!"

Peter's pace slowed, but only for a moment, before committing his life to the race anew. He had backed down in the face of death previously. With God's help, he would never back down in fear again. He realized he would one day be stopped. But until that day, he would run with all the strength God gave him.

He thought it was all over the day he was arrested by sixteen of Herod's soldiers.

That dark night, he lay sleeping. Yes, he was chained to two cruel soldiers. Yes, guards stood alert at the prison doors to prevent his escape. Yet his sleep was sweet, because his race, its course, and its length were all in the hands of his master.

Peter

He awoke with a jerk as he felt a smack on his side. He looked up to see the prison lit up as day. A stranger was reaching down to lift him to his feet. He urged, "Get up quickly!"

Simultaneously the chains locking him to the soldiers fell from his hands.

"Get dressed, Peter! Put on your shoes! Follow me!"

Peter got dressed in a daze, convinced he was dreaming.

They hurried from the prison. The locked iron gate swung open of its own accord before they even reached it. Peter thought of Isaiah's words, "I will go before thee! I will break in pieces the gates of brass, and cut in sunder the bars of iron!"

He looked up to grin at the stranger. He wasn't there. Peter stood alone in the middle of the dark city.

Peter trembled as he realized an angel of the Lord had been dispatched from heaven to deliver him from his prison cell and certain execution by Herod.

He was even more fearless after that day.

He ran through Asia, holding his torch high.

He ran valiantly, crying, *"Christ left us an example! Follow his steps!"*

He ran until his enemies, intent on stopping his race, came upon him violently.

Even as they sought to forever extinguish his light, he cried to those watching his race, "If you suffer for righteousness' sake, happy are you! Be not afraid of their terror, neither be troubled! If any man suffer as a Christian, let him not be ashamed; but let him glorify God on this behalf! Wherefore let them that suffer according to the will of God commit the keeping of their souls to him in well doing, as unto a faithful Creator!"

Then one day he penned these words: "Shortly I must put off this my tabernacle, even as our Lord Jesus Christ has showed me."

He realized he was about to cross the finish line. He was tired. He had run hard and well. He remembered Jesus had warned him that in his old age he would be carried to a place he would not go of his own accord. He had often wondered about that. Perhaps he would be crucified, suffering the death his Lord had suffered. Even as he quaked at the possibility, he determined in his heart that if he was to be crucified, he would request to be hanged upside down. He was unworthy to even die the same death as his precious Lord.

One thought gave him peace of mind. Jesus had assured him that he would glorify God in his death. Jesus had then gently repeated the same two words that he had spoken to call him into this race: *"Follow me."*

He had been faithful.

When the time came for Peter to cross his finish line, he was untroubled. All he could think about was his excitement of being with Jesus again. As life ebbed from his body, and the torch fell from his limp hand, Peter was still smiling.

Chapter 9

Dave

Except the Lord build the house, they labour in vain
that build it: except the Lord keep the city, the
watchman waketh but in vain. It is vain for you to rise
up early, to sit up late, to eat the bread of sorrows: for so
he giveth his beloved sleep.
Psalm 127:1-2

Dave leaned back in his chair, grinning.

"Wow! Lord, you really did it with Peter, didn't you? Somehow you made a mighty runner out of him! He went from chopping off a man's ear to being led meekly to his execution!

"He went from cursing you to singing praises to you!

"He didn't even have enough faith to let down his nets - but you gave him enough faith to lift up that crippled man!

"You took a coward who had denied you before a maid and made him into a fearless runner who lit up the darkness wherever he ran!

"Do it for me too, Lord! Make a faithful runner out of me. Turn my temper into gentleness. Turn my weakness into strength! Help me to be faithful to the end, even if it means my death!

". . . and Lord . . . I just now remembered who you said you are. You said you are the beginning - and the end! So, I think I'll just call it a night, and leave the end of my race in your hands! Good-night, Lord."

* * * * * * *

Dave dreamed he was back in high school. He hadn't studied the night before and the teacher had just asked him for a synopsis of the chapter he should have read. Then the bell rang. It kept ringing . . .and ringing. Dave finally woke up enough to realize it was the telephone. He reached for it, and muttered a halfhearted "Hello."

"Dave, this is Rev. Norton. We have never met, but I would like to change that. Could you come to my church office today at 4:30?"

Dave assured Rev. Norton he would be there, and spent the rest of the day wondering why Rev. Norton would want to talk to him. His church was huge. Dave had attended his cousin's wedding there.

Someone must have told him he had entered the race. Perhaps he had a place in his church for Dave to serve. This day could be the beginning of a great ministry!

Dave wondered how he had gotten his name - who had told him that he had dedicated his life to the race? No one that Dave knew seemed even remotely interested except Uncle Joe. He surely wouldn't have discussed Dave's race with Rev. Norton.

Shortly after four, Dave arrived at the church. He looked up at the huge pillars that seemed to dwarf men as they entered. He was shown into an office area by a polite secretary, who instructed him to wait. Exactly at 4:30, she came back to lead him to Rev. Norton's office.

Dave felt awkward in the presence of this distinguished man, but the noted preacher greeted him with a smile.

"Dave," said the man. "Please be seated. Someone close to you is very concerned about your welfare, and asked me to talk with you."

"Concerned?" Dave asked. "May I ask who requested that you talk to me, Sir?"

"That is confidential information, Dave. I will tell you that their concern is that you may be heading in a wrong direction. Could you tell me your thoughts about the Bible and how it relates to your life?"

Dave's eyes lit eagerly. Here was a subject he was glad to talk about!

"Rev. Norton, I was not raised in a Christian home. My family never went to church. We had a family Bible in our library, but none of us ever read it. Then I met Jesus Christ, and . . ."

"Dave, please forgive me for interrupting you, but I feel I must. How is it that you *met* Jesus Christ?"

45

"Sir," Dave answered, smiling, "I learned that Jesus had shed his blood on the cross of Calvary for me, and that He wanted to be my Savior. I knelt before Him . . ."

"Did you see him, Dave?"

"No, Sir, not in the same way I see you. However, I did see him, and I asked him to be my Savior and to come into my heart . . ."

"Dave!" Rev Norton said firmly. "I must again interrupt your tirade and inform you that you have been mislead and deluded by the uneducated and ignorant. It is little wonder that those close to you are concerned about your mental welfare. I have only listened to you a few minutes, and realize that you are not rational in your thinking."

"Sir, don't you believe the words that Jesus Christ himself spoke in John 1:12 . . ."

Rev. Norton momentarily lost his poise. His face reddened and he slammed his hand on his desk. His features struggled to regain control. Then he smiled, but his eyes remained cold.

"I will ask you to refrain from quoting Bible verses to me, Young Man!" he said in a stiffly controlled voice.

"Sir, you opened this conversation by asking me to tell you my thoughts about the Bible!"

"Yes, David, I did," Rev. Norton answered coldly. "I was referring to your thoughts about the book itself, not to your uneducated interpretation of specific verses. You see, Dave, the Bible is a valuable book for its history and many of its beautiful passages of poetry. It is hardly a book relevant for today or for your life. Many people make a grave mistake by assuming the Bible is a book they can base their lives upon. These are people who border on the edge of fanaticism. Now the advice I have for you is . . ."

Dave stood to his feet, his eyes flashing.

"I am sorry to interrupt you, but I will not listen to you or your lies another minute. You can tell those who are so concerned about me to consider instead their own eternal destiny and their own relationship with God."

Dave hurried from the stifling office, swept past the startled secretary and out of the church. He tried to slam the door, but it eased shut behind him.

Dave

He walked for a couple miles at a brisk pace, until he finally began to cool off. How could a man like that stand behind a pulpit Sunday after Sunday? He could think of no reason why anyone would attend such a church.

"I'm surely glad I'm not like that man," he muttered.

Then he frowned, as a verse of Scripture filled his mind:

> The Pharisee stood and prayed thus with himself. God, I thank thee, that I am not as other men are . . .

"That verse surely doesn't pertain to me," Dave mumbled.

All the high hopes and peace of the day were gone. Finally, he turned toward home. He avoided the Bible. He was afraid that if he tried to read it, it would open right to the verses dealing with anger and wrath - or even self-righteousness.

Self-righteousness? Could that describe him? Well, he just didn't want to think about it right now. He would get his mind on other things. But nothing he did stilled his troubled thoughts.

Finally he picked up his Bible and opened it to the passage that kept churning in his mind. He remembered reading just yesterday about the Pharisee and the sinner who had gone to the temple to pray. He dreaded reading it, but knew he would have no peace until he did.

> "And he spake this parable unto certain which trusted in themselves, that they were righteous, and despised others . . ."

"All right, Lord. I admit it. I don't like that man. I also don't appreciate my family insinuating that I am mentally unstable."

He set his Bible down and looked around the room for a job that would keep him too busy to think. How could today be so miserable when he had gone to sleep so peacefully? He felt so close to the Lord just last night!

He slammed around the house, completing various chores he had put off for months, but his accomplishments brought him no joy.

He stood looking out the window for some moments, thinking. Which one of his family members or his former friends called Mr. Norton? Could it have been his own parents? There was no doubt that they were upset over the direction his life had taken, but it hurt him more than he cared to admit that they would consider him mentally unbalanced.

Finally he turned and went into his room. Kneeling by his bed, he opened his Bible again. His eyes grew wide as he read and reread the words before him.

> And when his friends heard of it, they went out to lay hold on him: for they said, He is beside himself! For neither did his brethren believe in him.

"Jesus! Your family didn't believe in you? Your friends thought that you were beside yourself? I didn't realize that you went through these same things!

"Lord, I am so sorry. Just yesterday I told you I would go with you to death. Today I am slamming around and all upset because someone close to me cannot understand the race and my call to it. Please forgive me for my unwillingness to suffer persecution for you. I need your help if I am going to run this race right. Please change me, Lord!"

He felt a little better, but still something was standing between him and the Lord.

"What is it, Lord?" he whispered.

Then he knew.

"Lord, I can't love that man! I know your word tells me to love my enemies and pray for those who despitefully use me. How do I pray for him? What can I say? Dr. Norton is too proud to turn to you for salvation! How could that man ever be part of your race? He is so sure of himself, even while he is leading people away from salvation! He belittles your runners and doesn't even believe in you or your word! He wraps himself up in religion and calls himself a spiritual leader!"

Dave

Dave knew his praying wasn't getting him anywhere, so he turned off his light and went to bed. He tossed restlessly, and finally he turned his light back on and picking up his Bible, began to read words that Paul had penned centuries ago . . .

". . . after the most straitest sect of our religion I lived a Pharisee. I verily thought with myself, that I ought to do many things contrary to the name of Jesus of Nazareth. Which thing I also did in Jerusalem: and many of the saints did I shut up in prison, having received authority from the chief priests; and when they were put to death, I gave my voice against them.
And I punished them oft in every synagogue, and compelled them to blaspheme . . . "

Dave closed his Bible with a groan. So Paul, a religious man, took pleasure in getting Christians to blaspheme their Lord.

And did *anyone* ever run a better - or more exciting - race than he ran?

Dave wondered what it must have been like to be smuggled out of a city in a basket.

Paul - what a runner . . .

Chapter 10

Paul

He is a chosen vessel unto me, to bear my name before the Gentiles, and kings, and the children of Israel: For I will shew him how great things he must suffer for my name's sake.
Acts 9:15-16

The evening calm was shattered as a messenger burst through the door into the room where Paul sat visiting with disciples of Christ.

"They're waiting to capture Paul when he leaves Damascus!" the messenger cried. "They've posted guards around the clock at every gate of the city!"

Everyone talked at once, grasping at wild ideas for Paul's escape. Paul's thoughts were racing too, but every suggestion that was presented would only result in his capture and execution.

"Oh, God," he half prayed and half sighed, "Is my race to end so soon?"

Out of the tumult, he heard from the corner, "Yes, that just may work."

He pulled his chair nearer to the two men. As they discussed the pros and cons of the plan, Paul interrupted them. "What might work?"

"Paul! We were just coming to see if you would be in favor of us letting you down the city wall in a basket tied to a rope."

A few hours later, under the cloak of night, Paul climbed gingerly into the basket. He looked anxiously at the rope, hoping and praying that it would hold his weight and the men would hold the rope!

And to think he had once thought this race would be dull! He relived his experience on the road into this city repeatedly. His encounter with Jesus Christ would be forever etched in his mind. He had started his trip to Damascus with great expectation. He despised followers of Jesus. Someone had to stop their lies, and if no one else would do it, he would. His whole life was fueled by his hatred. His very breath exhaled threatening. Christians were a plague in the streets and in the synagogues, and he would not rest in peace until they were all exterminated from the earth.

His craze had compelled him to appear before the high priest, begging for authority to arrest them. He then would bring them to Jerusalem to be tried for their blasphemous heresy. He planned to capture them, dead or alive, child or adult, man or woman, infirm or healthy, old or young. The thrill of the hunt to come made his journey seem longer than usual.

Then it had happened. One second everything was normal. The next, a blinding light enveloped him and he literally crashed to the earth with a thud.

Out of the light, a voice spoke, ringing with power and authority.

"Saul, Saul, why do you persecute me? It is hard for you to kick against the pricks."

Paul remembered trembling in fear as he asked, "Who are you, Lord?"

The next words sent terror through him. "I am Jesus whom you persecute."

Jesus. Jesus, whom he hated. Jesus, whose followers he wanted to massacre. Jesus, whose church he was determined to destroy. Jesus, who had lit up the whole area, knocked him to the earth with an unseen hand, and was now demanding to know why Paul was persecuting him.

"Rise! Stand upon your feet!" Paul leaped to his feet. He still saw nothing but blinding light, far brighter than the sun itself. He squeezed his eyes shut, but still the light penetrated his body and soul.

Jesus continued speaking. "I have appeared unto you for this purpose, to make you a minister and a witness . . . I send you to the Gentiles, to open their eyes, and to turn them from darkness to light, and from the power of Satan unto God, that they may receive forgiveness of sins, and inheritance among them which are sanctified by faith that is in me."

The light left as abruptly as it had arrived. Paul remembered opening his eyes, and then shutting and opening them again and again, but still he saw nothing.

He reached out, groping, until he felt the arm of one of his fellow travelers.

"Did you see the light? Did you hear the voice?" Paul asked in a voice still shaking with terror.

It was several seconds before the voice of the man whose arm Paul gripped answered weakly. "I heard a voice. I saw no man."

"I still see no man," Paul said. "I see nothing."

Paul remembered how the men had gathered around him. They took his hand gently and led him like a child to Damascus.

Paul had remained in a room in the house of Judas for three days. He refused to eat or drink anything served to him. He recalled pondering all that had happened to him. Jesus, famous for making blind eyes see, had appeared to him, making his seeing eyes blind. Why? He recalled the message over and over again that Jesus had given him.

"I will make you a minister. I will make you a witness. I will send you to the Gentiles to open their eyes, to turn them from darkness to light, to turn them from Satan unto God."

There was no way to misunderstand that message. He himself would be a runner in the despised race. He had no choice. He would carry the torch.

Three days later, Paul heard his door open and someone walking toward him. Then he felt a hand on his head and the stranger spoke in a strong, clear voice. "Brother Saul, the Lord, even Jesus, that appeared unto you in the way as you came, has sent me, that you might receive your sight, and be filled with the Holy Ghost."

Paul could almost feel that strange sensation all over again, as scales cracked and peeled from his eyes. As they fell away, his sight was completely restored.

Then God lit his torch, and Paul began to run.

He ran first to the synagogue of Damascus, not to arrest disciples of Jesus as he had planned, but to announce himself as a runner.

He ran throughout the city, confounding the Jews everywhere, proving that Jesus is the Christ.

And now he was climbing into a basket to escape certain death.

Paul

"God be with you, Paul," one spoke, as the basket was lifted carefully over the wall to begin its descent. The basket swung against the wall, jarring Paul, but finally hit the ground with a thud. Paul was out of it almost immediately, running.

He ran in and out of Jerusalem, then on to Caesarea and on to Tarsus.

He ran tirelessly, holding his torch high. He ran along the seashores, in cities, in streets, in houses, in synagogues, in churches. He was chased from cities, but, shaking the dust from his feet, ran on to others.

He ran out of Iconium to escape being stoned, and ran into Lystra. He ran past a cripple, and as he passed by, shouted, "Stand upright on your feet!" He scarcely paused to watch as the man leaped and ran behind him.

A crowd, witnessing the wonder, chased him, desiring to worship him. He turned and ran among them, his cry ringing, "Worship God!"

They turned on him, hurling stones as he ran. His pace slowed and then stopped, as he crumpled to the ground. They dragged his limp body outside their city, and left it there to rot.

Other runners of the race stopped their dash long enough to gather around him. Their torches cast light upon his bruised and bleeding body. Paul stirred and, jumping to his feet, began to run again. He ran through the city, leaving a trail of his flabbergasted murderers behind him.

He ran toward Bithynia, but God redirected his course to Troas. There Paul saw in a night vision a Macedonian, pleading, "Come over into Macedonia, and help us!"

Paul ran to Macedonia, down by a river side, then on through the city. He was followed by a girl, out of whom he cast an evil spirit. A multitude chased him, magistrates caught him, beat him brutally, and cast him into an inner prison. Enemies of the race thrust his feet in stocks, cruelly bringing his race to a standstill.

Paul's back was bruised and bleeding. The dirt hole stank with dung, and rats moved in the darkness. Paul reflected on his experience. He was not bitter. He gloried in his adversities. No matter how many afflictions he suffered, they would never wipe out the scene that came back to him in the night hours.

"Oh, Stephen. Stephen. God, I'm so sorry about what I did to Stephen."

Would he ever quit seeing that young man, radiating with life and power, yet cut off just as his race began? Paul squeezed his eyes shut, but he could still see him. He had been so serene and calm during the mockery of his trial, even while being accused of blasphemy. His face itself had become the torch, lighting the entire room with unnatural light.

The men, crazed with their lust to murder, took their coats off and laid them at Paul's feet. Paul not only consented to the death of this valiant runner, but exulted in it. Would the next scene never be erased from his mind? Paul tried to will the memory away, but he looked yet again at the blood pouring from Stephen's eyes, his nose, his ears, until his wrenching body had finally stilled, his race finished.

If only he could forever wipe away his triumphant smile of pride. If only he could never again recall his arrogant determination to incite a mob to stone every runner and extinguish every torch.

Paul shook his head, and his thoughts returned to the present.

"I will glory in my infirmities," he resolved in his heart. "I am glad I was beaten! I will take pleasure in this prison!"

It was pitch black. Paul saw nothing. But he heard Silas, his fellow runner, softly moaning.

"Silas," Paul whispered, "Are you okay?"

"I'm sore all over, Paul. And you?"

"Yes. But Silas - we're alive! We're alive! Yes, we suffered for Jesus! But he suffered for us! Yes, we've been persecuted! But Silas, we're not forsaken! Can this persecution separate us from the love of Christ? No! We are more than conquerors through him!"

"You're right, Paul. Surely we will be killed in the morning."

"To be absent from the body, is to be present with the Lord, Silas. And if we suffer, we shall also reign with him."

"Yes," Silas breathed.

Paul was quiet for a few minutes, then he spoke again. "Silas, let's pray. And then, sing with me."

Before Silas could respond, Paul began praying softly, his love for God pouring from his heart.

His prayer soon turned into a sweet song of praise. Silas joined him after a few words, and the two sang weakly at first, then their voices gained both strength and volume. They sang their worship, unaware that prisoners listened intently.

Never had singing been heard in this prison. Prisoners crept nearer the sound at the midnight hour, listening, wondering.

Suddenly the song was interrupted by the screams and curses of the inmates, as the building began to quake and the floor to heave. The doors of every cell swung open with a crash, and chains, shackling the prisoners, snapped.

The inmates, released from their bonds, were held captive by fear.

Paul, leaping to his feet, ran to the doorway, and saw the keeper of the prison staring wild-eyed at the scene. Then he slowly drew out his sword to kill himself.

"Do yourself no harm! We're all here!" Paul prevented his suicide with a shout.

Paul prepared to run again, pausing long enough to explain his race and his torch to the jail keeper and his family. The keeper, notorious for his cruelty, knelt to wash the caked blood from Paul's back. Then kneeling before Jesus, he asked him to wash away his sins.

Paul, after baptizing the family and being released by the city's magistrates, lifted high his torch and ran.

He ran to Thessalonica, to Berea and then on to Athens. He ran past their idols, into their synagogues, through their market places. He ran on to Corinth, where Jesus encouraged him during the night hours. *"Be not afraid, but speak, and hold not your peace: for I am with you, and no man shall . . hurt you . . . "*

He ran past the sick, leaving them well, past those chained to darkness, now lit by the light of his torch.

A spectator called out as he ran, "Paul, did you hear about the fire? Jews and Greeks of Ephesus turned to

Jesus and have burned Satanic books and symbols worth fifty-thousand pieces of silver!"

Paul laughed as he ran on. Yes, this race was a difficult one, but the world was not as black now. More and more runners were joining the race, their torches penetrating its darkness. As for Paul, his life was complete, his spirit at peace. He found this race exhilarating!

He ran into Ephesus, through a crowd of people who worshipped the goddess, Diana. Demetrius had presented the image he created to the ignorant, claiming the idol had fallen to earth from the planet Jupiter.

As Paul ran, scattering the crowd, a riot erupted. The Ephesians despised Paul and his torch. His light exposed them, leaving them naked without their cloak of darkness.

Crowds thronged the sidewalks, screaming, "Great is Diana of the Ephesians!"

"There are no gods made with hands," Paul yelled above the din. It took the townclerk to restore peace to the city.

Paul then turned toward Jerusalem.

"Paul!" he was warned repeatedly. "Don't run in that direction! Your life is in danger!"

"None of these things move me, neither count I my life dear unto myself," he dismissed their warnings with a shrug. "I'll finish my course with joy!"

Who were men to set his course? His route was determined by God Himself!

He ran to Jerusalem, was stopped by an angry mob, and was beaten unmercifully. A chief captain strode into the tumult, bound him with chains, and carried him away. But the howling mob followed, chanting, "Away with him! Away with him!"

Paul quieted the multitude with a sweep of his hand, telling them why he was now running this race. He preached fervently and fearlessly, and when he finished, they cried as one enraged voice, "Away with such a fellow from the earth! It is not fit that he should live!"

The captain, fearing Paul would literally be pulled in pieces by the mob, carried him to a castle for refuge.

Paul

Jesus was already there. He came to Paul's room that night. "Be of good cheer, Paul! You have testified of me in Jerusalem, so must you bear witness also at Rome!"

Paul slept peacefully, his lips forming a smile.

Over forty Jews vowed they would neither eat nor drink until they had killed this runner. They either broke their vow or died of starvation. That night the captain smuggled Paul to Caesarea. He was accompanied by two-hundred soldiers, seventy horsemen, and two-hundred spearmen.

Paul ran past governors. He carried his torch before kings and queens!

He was thrown on a ship full of convicts. An angel of God was aboard, waiting for the runner. Paul gripped his torch as a hurricane roared, tossing the ship like a match and breaking it in half. Paul swam to an island, his torch still held high, its fire still burning.

Paul ran on the island. He shook off the deadly snake that attached itself to his hand, intent on breaking his hold on the torch. Flinging the viper into the fire, Paul continued to run, passing those who lay dying and diseased, his life-giving torch restoring them to health.

He ran into Rome, still clutching his torch, shouting in triumph, "If God be for us, who can be against us?"

Paul ran to the point of exhaustion. Laying on the ground, he panted, "Christ shall be magnified in my body, whether it be by life, or by death. To me to live is Christ, and to die is gain."

He lay still a moment, then whispered his wish. "I desire to depart, and to be with Christ."

He lay limply, listening, looking up at the heavens. The sky was full of beautiful, snow-white clouds, drifting, drifting . . .

The clouds slowly transformed into the faces of previous runners who had finished their course and were now watching him, all their expectations fixed on him.

There was Abel. Abel, who, prompted by his thankful heart, had offered God the best of his flock. Abel, who had enjoyed the pleasure of his God, but had incurred the wrath of his brother, and become the first victim of murder.

Paul

"Lord," Paul whispered. "I understand how it was with Abel now. I have been in perils by my own countrymen, my own people. I have been threatened by false brethren. And their hatred hurts. I am tired."

He recognized another face, the face of Enoch. Enoch, who had simply been translated to heaven, without taking the death route that other men travelled. Enoch had pleased God. "I want to please you too, my Lord," Paul breathed, as the face faded from view.

Was that Abraham? Yes! Abraham was there, watching him intently. Abraham, who had run his race without wavering, his eyes fixed on the finish line and beyond the finish line, looked steadily toward the city, whose builder and maker is God.

"Abraham reached it - and I can too," Paul thought.

He searched the other faces.

"Moses, is that you?" Paul asked, as he recognized Moses in the stands, viewing Paul's race with rapt attention. Paul felt tears filling his eyes, as he sensed Moses's love and concern for him.

Who was he to be cheered on by Moses? Moses had walked away from all of Egypt's treasures to endure suffering and hardship as he ran the race for Christ!

The faces of the crowd of spectators were too many for Paul to even contemplate individually. He had so often felt alone, not realizing that while the race was being run on earth, the heavens were filled with a multitude of spectators, watching, cheering, sometimes weeping, often breaking into a thunderous applause.

Paul felt new vigor and a faint stirring to get up and continue in spite of his weariness. For wasn't he being watched and applauded and urged on by a vast company of those heroes who had finished before him? They had not quit! Dare he?

They were drifting from his view now. He strained to identify others. Gideon, Samson, David and Samuel were all there. Daniel was in the stands, a champion who had faced lions on their own home turf, and had been lifted from their den, praising the Lord for victory over every foe, be it man or beast!

There were spectators he didn't know, but he heard their shouts of victory.

Paul

A woman he could not identify spoke to those near her in a triumphant voice. "If only the runners will keep their faith! I saw the dead raised during my race!"

Another group came into focus.

"We were tortured!"

"And I stoned!"

"We were killed with the sword!"

A man called out in a voice ringing with victory, "I was sawed apart!"

After a sudden hush, a father said almost gently, "I and my family were cast out of our home. We wandered in mountains. We lived in dens and caves. We wore skins of sheep and goats. But, by faith, we kept running."

Their voices then seemed to blend into one mighty crescendo, as they worshiped their Savior and King.

Paul knelt below, weeping. My Christ, the sufferings that I have endured are not worthy to be compared to the glory that will be revealed in me when I finish my course! This light affliction, which is but a moment, will win me a reward of eternal glory!"

"My God," he continued, tears streaming down his face. "I didn't realize I was surrounded with this huge cloud of witnesses! I didn't know so many spectators were watching this race! Lord, help me to run even better! Help me to rid myself of all weights that slow me down! Free me of every sin! Give me patience to run this race well!"

A peace settled over Paul, as he lay thinking about all the trials that champion runners before him had endured. His race, like theirs, had not been an easy one. He had endured one trial after another. His body was scarred by the one hundred and ninety-five vicious lashes of the brutal scourge. He had been beaten sadistically with rods, not once, but three times. Angry mobs had hurled stones, bruising his pain-wracked body, their wrath unspent until he lay at their feet as dead. He had survived three shipwrecks, and had spent a night and a day in the open sea. He had run on dusty, hot roads, his parched mouth craving water. Thieves had robbed him of all but his faith. He was hunted as a common criminal by his own people. He had run until his body was worn out, and he often had wondered how he could keep going. He recalled days of gnawing hunger, cold nights when he lay shivering without shelter, the shameful time when he had been stripped even of his clothing.

But he had kept running.

For through it all, Jesus was there. Jesus had told him right at the beginning that he would never forsake him. And he hadn't.

"Jesus," Paul whispered, "tribulation, distress, persecution, famine, nakedness, peril, the sword - none of these things have ever been able to keep me from running for you. I have felt your love through them all!

"I am now persuaded that death, life, angels, principalities, powers, things present, things to come, height, depth, or any other creature will never be able to separate us!

"Yes, I've been troubled on every side - but I'm not in distress. I have been perplexed - but you have kept me from despair! I have been persecuted - but you have never forsaken me! Men have cast me down, but you have kept them from destroying me! In all of these things, because of you, Jesus, I have been more than a conqueror!"

Paul remembered the sneers and ridicule of his friends, as he walked away from the world and its riches to run this race for Christ, and he laughed aloud. "All this world has to offer is dung!" he proclaimed to anyone who cared to listen. Few did.

Paul felt strength displace his weakness.

He looked up to the heavens and spoke, even though the spectators were no longer visible.

"They finished. And I will too. I will run until my Lord says my course is finished. Until that final day, I will press toward the mark for the prize of the high calling of God in Christ Jesus!"

Paul rose to his feet, renewed vigor surging through his body. He knew the time of his departure was at hand. He also now knew that he would continue to run, teaching and committing to the next runners all he had learned about this race, preparing them to carry the torch.

Paul

He ran, even while imprisoned, writing, *always writing*, the fire in his torch transformed to words that would burn their way into the hearts of his readers down through the centuries.

Paul's body weakened steadily, but his spirit thrived with power, and as he fell across the finish line, he expended every ounce of energy left in his spent body to shout, so all in the stands could hear,

"I have fought a good fight!

"I have finished my course!

"I have kept the faith!

"Lord! I am coming for my crown!"

Paul laughed as he faced his executioner. He had just one more thing to say before he crossed his finish line. The sword was stayed as Paul's cry pierced the silence with words that would echo down through the ages to runners of this race.

"O death, where is thy sting? O grave, where is thy victory?

"The sting of death is sin; and the strength of sin is the law!

"Thanks be to God, which gives us the victory through our Lord Jesus Christ!

"Therefore, my beloved brothers, be stedfast, unmoveable, always abounding in the work of the Lord! Your labour is not in vain in the Lord! I have not run in vain!"

His shout of triumph was severed with the sword. Paul's words would themselves fan the flames in the torches carried by future runners.

Runners like Dave . . .

Chapter 11

Dave

*Whosoever shall smite thee on thy right cheek, turn to
him the other also. Recompense to no man evil for evil.*
Matthew 5:39
Romans 12:17

"**I** want to be able to make the same claim that Paul
did when my race is over, Lord," Dave prayed. "I too want
to fight a good fight. And I want to finish the course you
have set for me."

Dave dreaded tomorrow, for he knew what he had to
do. He was not going to let anyone - even Dr. Norton -
point to his temper to discredit the message of the gospel.

The next morning, Dave prayed that God would give
him wisdom both to speak and to keep silent.

"Lord, you know how that man aggravates me. Please
help me to see him with your eyes of mercy and your
heart of love."

The pillars seemed even bigger than before as Dave
walked into the church.

The secretary's eyes seemed to narrow as she watched
him enter the office.

"Yes?" she asked.

Dave smiled, but her expression remained cold.

"I am here to see Dr. Norton. I need only a couple
minutes with him."

"Do you have an appointment?"

"No, Ma'am. But I will wait."

"Yes, you will," she answered, turning back to her
work.

Dave was finally summoned after nearly an hour and a
half had passed.

"Lord, give me courage," he prayed silently, as he made
his way to the office.

Dr. Norton was barely civil as he greeted him.

"Dr. Norton," Dave said, "I have come to apologize for
the anger I displayed yesterday. I was rude and . . ."

Dave

"David," Dr. Norton interrupted coldly. "Are you trying to say that you have considered what I said and have come to your senses?"

Dave smiled.

"No, Sir. Jesus Christ gave his life for me, and I could do no less than give my life back to him. And I will base my life and stake my eternity on his holy word . . ."

"Then why are you here? We have nothing to discuss. You are wasting both my time and yours."

"As I said, Dr. Norton, I have come to apologize . . ."

"You are repeating yourself, David. If that is all you have come for, you may leave."

Dr. Norton pressed a button to summon his secretary. The door opened so swiftly that Dave decided she must have been listening at the door.

"Send in my next parishioner, Doris."

Dave extended his hand, but Dr. Norton ignored it, and began rearranging papers on his desk.

"Thank you, Dr. Norton. God bless you," Dave said as he turned and left the office.

He caught himself whistling even before he reached the massive doors of the church. He looked up at the pillars as he went down the steps. They didn't look so big after all! Above them floated beautiful, fluffy, snow-white clouds. Above them was the endless blue sky. And above the sky the sun shone, sending its blazing light and warmth to the earth. But what was the sun compared to the Son, who sent his brilliant light and warmth into the hearts of men? For far above the universe was the heaven of heavens, where the Creator of it all reigned over his vast creation. It was to him that Dave spoke, and by faith he could see the tender love in the eyes that gazed straight into his heart.

"I feel so good, Lord! I never would have dreamed that apologizing to someone could make me feel like this. Guilt is a heavy load to carry. Why do I let it weigh me down, when with just a few simple words, I can be free of it? Dr. Norton didn't accept my apology, but what does that matter? For you did, Lord. You did. And you know, that's beginning to be all that really matters!"

Chapter 12

Dave

*Withhold not good from them to whom it is due, when
it is in the power of thine hand to do it.*
Proverbs 3:27

Dave could hardly wait to begin the day. He didn't often sing aloud as he ran. He had tried it a few times. Those who had the misfortune of hearing him said he sang off key more often than on. But today was made for singing! Hadn't God made the crows to caw as well as the nightingales to sing? He figured God must make just one big symphony out of it and somehow enjoy the sounds of his creation.

"Please guide my steps today, Lord," Dave prayed. "Lead me to people I can serve."

Dave felt like shouting praises as he began his run. He just knew that the Lord had tremendous victories in store for him.

Then he stopped abruptly and slowly retraced his steps. He stood looking at the dark house before him and sighed deeply.

"All right, Lord. I'm here, because you told me to come back. I don't know exactly what you want me to do, so please direct me."

Dave looked at the neglected lawn as the doorbell echoed in the house. Finally the door opened just a crack, and two fearful eyes peered out.

"Mrs. Arnold, I am your neighbor from across the street. My name is Dave. I've heard your husband is very ill. Could I just come in and visit him for a moment?"

She opened the door just wide enough for him to squeeze into the dark foyer. He looked into the living room beyond and saw the wasted body of an old man lying on a bed.

Dave walked over and picked up a gnarled hand.

Dave

"Mr. Arnold, I am your neighbor, Dave. I have come to visit with you and your wife and to see if there is anything you need."

He thought he saw a flicker in his eyes, but wasn't sure. Had he even heard?

"Mrs. Arnold, may I pray for your husband?"

He hoped the barely imperceptible movement of her head meant yes, and began praying.

"Lord, you are needed here. Please come and strengthen and encourage Mr. and Mrs. Arnold. Bless this home, in Jesus' name, Amen."

Dave laid the limp hand back on the sheet and turned to Mrs. Arnold.

"Mrs. Arnold, I am a follower of Jesus Christ. Is there anything I can do for you?"

Her sagging chin lifted and the eyes in her wrinkled face flashed.

"There is nothing we need, young man. We are getting along fine." As she talked, she walked to the door and opened it wide, making sure Dave would have no trouble leaving.

As Dave left, he said, "God bless you, Mrs. Arnold. Please feel free to call on me if you need anything."

As he resumed his run, he prayed silently.

"Lord, I don't think I accomplished much there. At least I did what you told me to do."

Then the Lord's voice penetrated Dave's heart.

"It is *you* who are needed in that home. It is *through you* that I choose to bless the Arnolds."

Dave couldn't believe what he was hearing.

"Lord, I told them if they needed anything to call me!"

"Did you see any needs?"

Dave recalled the broken porch step and the overgrown lawn.

"Yes."

He knew the conversation was finished. Again he turned around, and this time he went back home. Minutes later he came out of his driveway dressed in old work clothes and carrying a rake.

He chuckled. "This is hardly the high hopes I had for today, Lord."

Dave

Hours later, Dave wiped the sweat from his eyes. He hadn't realized how bad this yard was. He wondered how many years the leaves, branches and debris had been accumulating. He hadn't seen Mrs. Arnold, and he was sure she hadn't seen him either. Her drapes remained tightly closed.

He would have to make arrangements to haul the piles of trash away. He surely wouldn't get this job done all at once, but if he kept at it a little bit each day he would eventually see some progress.

Dave looked across the street as a car pulled up to his apartment. It was his aunt. Why would she visit him? She never had.

He called out to her as she got out of the car.

"Aunt Marie? I'm over here. I'm coming!"

She looked at him critically as he approached.

"David." she stated firmly, then continued stiffly, "I wasn't aware that you had been reduced to yard work."

Dave laughed.

"Come on in, Aunt Marie, while I wash up."

He didn't have long to wonder why she had come. As usual, she got right to the point.

"David, your family is very upset with the direction your life is taking. You are bright, and we all have had high hopes for you. Now look at you. We were told you had entered some new kind of race, but raking lawns hardly seems like a respectable race to me. What kind of nonsensical race is this?"

Dave breathed a silent prayer before he answered.

"Aunt Marie, I cannot expect you to understand the change in my life. No one can, unless they are acquainted with my Lord. I have given my life to Jesus Christ. He tells me how to live, and if he directs me to rake the lawn of my elderly neighbors, then that is all part of my new life."

"What is all this about a race?"

"Aunt Marie, you watched my relay race on television. You saw the runners carrying the torch through the host nation before the Olympics began.

"The race I am now running is a spiritual race. Down through the ages, in every century, there have been men, women, and even children who have carried the torch for

Dave

Christ in their generation. I have been called to carry it in mine."

Dave could see his aunt was unimpressed, and her next words verified his conclusion.

"It all sounds very noble, David, but the fact of the matter is that you are standing in front of me in old work clothes, covered with dirt from a neighbor's yard. I hardly think you are making much of an impact on your generation.

"If you refuse to think about yourself, then consider your parents, David. They have made many sacrifices so you could obtain a good education and have a financially stable life. It is time you repaid them with some common sense."

She was gone before Dave even realized she was leaving. He stood by the window for a moment, contemplating her mission. Then he prayed quietly.

"Lord, thank you for my family. My parents *have* made many sacrifices for me, and I thank you for Dad and Mom and the home they provided. *You* alone are the one who made the ultimate sacrifice on the cross. You bought me with the price of your own precious blood. My life does not belong to my family, or even to myself. I belong to you, now and forever."

Dave lifted his head and grinned.

"Even if I have to spend my days raking yards!"

Dave cleaned up and ran toward the park. Maybe there would be some boys there playing basketball. He'd seen them before, but hadn't stopped to talk to them.

There were six boys there, about ten or twelve years old. Dave stood and watched them for a few minutes, and then he grew restless. He never had been good at watching others play. He wanted to get out there and play himself.

"Do you mind if I join you, Fellows?"

They stopped and stared, but one finally shrugged.

After several minutes, he finally got the ball and sent it through the net. They made sure he didn't get the ball again.

The game ended, and Dave sat down on a picnic table near the boys. Two girls walked by and before they were even beyond hearing distance, obscene filth poured from their mouths. They laughed and joked, and then looked at Dave. Their grins changed to scowls as they noticed he wasn't laughing.

"Hey, what kind of guy are you anyway?" one asked.

Dave looked at each boy steadily before answering, and then he spoke directly to Tom, the boy who seemed to be the leader of the others.

"I am glad you asked me that question . . . because I *am* different. You see, I am a follower of Jesus Christ. You must know who he is, for you have referred to him consistently in your conversation. Do you realize that he is God? I have heard you ask him to damn one another, but Jesus didn't come to earth to damn anyone. He came instead to save you from your sins, and to give you eternal life."

The boy in front of him underwent a transformation right before Dave's eyes. His eyes narrowed to slits and filled with a hatred and rage that Dave had seldom seen even in an older person. Vile blasphemy, curses and threats poured from his mouth.

Dave knew he was no longer listening to the words of a twelve year old boy, but to a deranged demon, whose hate-filled eyes looked out from a lad who desperately needed deliverance.

Dave looked fearlessly past the venomous devil and into the heart of the captive boy.

"Jesus loves you, Tom. And I love you too. Jesus Christ alone can deliver you from the bondage of Satan and save you from your sins and eternal death. The devil is a loser. The precious blood given on the cross of Calvary by Jesus Christ caused the devil's defeat.

"Tom, I want you to know that I will be praying for you - every single day."

Dave left the deceptively peaceful park, and the screams of profanity that filled the air. He was heartsick.

"My Lord," he cried. "What has happened to our children? What has Satan done to this generation?"

He was still heavy-hearted when he entered the door of the church. He was a little late, and when he slipped into a pew, people were already singing.

It took a few minutes for the music to penetrate his soul. He looked around at the people as they worshipped the Lord in singing. And then his eyes settled on a young boy, about the age of the boys he has just left. Dave noticed tears glistening on his face, as he lifted his voice in song,

Let the temple be filled with his glory.
Let the courts be filled with his praise.
Let the people sing praises in the holy of holies,
Zion rejoices again!

"My sweet Lord," Dave prayed. "There is hope for this generation - but only in you. Please help me to somehow reach Tom with the life-changing message of the gospel. And Jesus . . . I want to tell you how much I appreciate this beautiful church and these beautiful people. Thank you for my pastor who encourages your runners and so faithfully teaches us your word. Thank you for my brothers and sisters in Christ.

"This race is not easy. In fact, it seems to get harder each day. You knew how desperately we would all need to meet together in your name and encourage and strengthen one another. It is so refreshing to come out of the world of darkness, hatred and profanity, and enter into this place of light, love and worship. "

When the service was over, Dave told his pastor how much the church meant to him.

"Dave," the pastor said. "Thank you for appreciating your church family and our ministry to the believers. You said that it is harder today to run this race than at any other time. This race, Dave, has never been easy for God's true people. The apostles faced constant persecution. God's prophets were killed. The blood of Christian martyrs has been spilled throughout the world in every generation.

"I often think of one of the most beloved pastors who ever lived. He did not waver in the heat of the battle. He left his congregation not only an example of righteous living, but an example of facing death with dignity and courage. Let me tell you about a pastor who has been an inspiration to me . . .

Chapter 13

Polycarp
(About A.D. 70 to 156)

*I will give you pastors according to mine heart, which
shall feed you with knowledge and understanding.*
Jeremiah 3:15

The world succeeded in purging itself of the twelve
apostles and Paul, hoping to forever end the despised
race. But for every drop of blood planted by faithful
martyrs, a crop of new runners grew. Their courage and
joy, even when facing torture and death, caused many to
pick up the torch. Ignited by the fire from God's censor,
runners carried light throughout the earth.

Polycarp, born about A.D. 70, was one of many who
ran gallantly, casting light in dark places.

Polycarp had spent hours, days, even weeks, with the
Apostle John, drinking in his every word and facial
expression as he talked about Jesus. Others sat with
them, but Polycarp was the last to leave, never tiring of
hearing about his master.

When John's voice would grow hoarse and his body
tired, Polycarp would urge him to tell him more.

John smiled tenderly at the eager face before him, and
said, "Polycarp, Jesus did so many things! If they were
all written, I suppose that even the world itself could not
contain all the books."

Polycarp thirsted to know more and more of Jesus. He
had fallen in love with him when he was only nine years
old.

The dark day came when John was gone, captured by
the enemies of the race and banished to Patmos, the
island of convicts.

It was then that Polycarp realized it would never be
enough to just hear about Jesus from another. So he
himself reached up to the hand of his Lord, and with
great trembling and much humility, took the torch that
Christ held out to him.

Polycarp

The fire of God coursed through his body, burning, filling him with light. He had not known a touch from the Master would be like this! All that John had told him could not compare to this one touch! He was totally and unexpectantly consumed with a love he had never known. He loved everyone. He was thrilled to be part of the race and wanted to share with the world the news that Jesus lives and Jesus saves!

He ran to Smyrna, gathering together slaves and aristocrats alike, loving them all fervently, helping them to love one another.

He pastored this flock, leading his people gently, pointing them always to his Savior.

His congregation grew until all Asia Minor watched in horror as the fire spread. The dreaded light radiated throughout the entire area. It seemed that no family was exempt from its influence. Hatred began to ferment in the hearts of men.

"This man is an atheist," they ranted. "Don't listen to him!" The mob responded with a cry of fury.

"Polycarp, the destroyer of our gods, must himself be destroyed!"

He paid no attention to the wrath of his enemies.

And that enraged them the more.

"There is only one way to stop this race! Polycarp cannot be allowed to run! His preaching must be silenced! His writings must be banned! We cannot allow him to produce more torch bearers! Even members of our governor's staff have joined his church!"

The voice grew louder, as Polycarp continued to run. When he was eighty-six years of age, and still running strong, the voice became deafening.

It was then that his adversaries decided he would be allowed to run no longer. The Roman Governor sent guards to seize him, but they searched for him in vain. Polycarp lay in an upper room of a cottage, nourished by his concerned congregation.

"We need you. Please hide for our sake," they had pleaded. Out of his love for them, he had conceded.

When his friends warned him that mounted police were on their way to search the cottage, he refused to be moved to another farm.

Polycarp

"The will of God be done," Polycarp said.

The police found him there and gathered around their prey. Polycarp rose to his feet, speaking calmly to his captors.

"Would you be my guests at dinner?"

The Roman guards joined their prisoner for a feast. As they ate, they glanced questionably at their host. He gazed back at them, love in his eyes. Never had they been this close to one carrying the torch. They felt naked in its light.

When they finished eating, Polycarp rose to his feet. "Please give me one hour to talk to my Lord."

They looked at one another, shrugging, then nodded.

While they sat watching him intently, Polycarp looked upon the face of his beloved Friend and Savior, totally absorbed in his conversation with him. For one hour, he prayed passionately.

As the guards sat in the glow of his torch, listening to the prayer of this condemned, aged man, they cursed themselves for having captured this brave and loving runner. They now had no choice but to carry him to the governor. They found themselves dreading his fate.

The governor was thrilled, and yet troubled, when Polycarp was brought to him. For what should he do with such a renowned prisoner? Would his execution stop other runners? Or would they just lift their torches higher, as in the past, and run with renewed vigor?

He realized that victory would be his, only when Polycarp himself chose to extinguish his torch. He must persuade him to reject Jesus and embrace Caesar.

He faced Polycarp.

"Save yourself!" he demanded. "Admit that Caesar is Lord!"

"Jesus is my Lord," Polycarp answered.

"Offer incense to Caesar! Carry your torch for him!"

Polycarp calmly shook his head.

"Have respect for your age," the governor pleaded. "Swear by the divinity of Caesar! Repent!"

All his begging availed nothing.

Polycarp's reply remained unmovable. "Jesus is, and forever will be, my Lord!"

It would take more than begging to break this runner.

Polycarp

He called soldiers to drag him into the stadium. A blood-thirsty crowd sat waiting impatiently to be entertained by the sport of murder.

The governor noticed Polycarp looking at the crowd.

"Take the oath of Caesar!" he implored. "I will still let you go!"

Polycarp turned toward him, his face set, his heart fixed. His torch still lit the darkness around him, exposing all those in its path.

The governor grew impatient. He hated standing in this cursed light. And he despised the one who dared to carry it. He determined to extinguish it by any means. How much better it would be if Polycarp would lay down his torch! He would try just once more.

"Polycarp, curse your Christ. I have the authority to set you free!"

Polycarp looked upon him with pity, and then his eyes rested on the restless crowd. Men, women, children - all eyes were upon him, eagerly waiting his execution.

He shook his head wearily. His race was nearly at an end, and he would finish on the run, his torch held high.

He turned again toward the anxious governor.

"For eighty-six years," he said in a strong, firm voice, "I have been his servant. Christ has never done me wrong. How can I blaspheme my King who saved me?"

The governor stared at him. Polycarp's eyes bored right back into his, unwavering. The governor stood trembling, but Polycarp calmly awaited his sentence, no fear in his eyes. It made the governor boil with anger.

Polycarp would run to the end. Then let the end come.

"I have wild beasts!" he yelled viciously.

Polycarp stood unmoved.

"If you make light of them, I will have you destroyed by fire!"

A hush had settled over the crowd. Even the children were still, as Polycarp answered. His gentle eyes seemed as fire as he shouted in a voice that echoed throughout the stadium.

"The fire you threaten burns for a time and is soon extinguished. There is a fire you know nothing about - the fire of the judgment to come and of eternal punishment - the fire reserved for the ungodly!"

He continued to look at the crowd who sat, unconcerned, unmoving. Then he turned toward the governor.

"Why do you hesitate? Do what you want to me."

The governor stared at this valiant runner.

He could not gaze long into his eyes. Turning abruptly, he shouted, "Crier! Go to the center of the arena and announce three times: 'Polycarp has confessed that he is a Christian!'

The crier ran with his message.

Polycarp has confessed that he is a Christian!
Polycarp has confessed that he is a Christian!
Polycarp has confessed that he is a Christian!

The crowd seemed to writhe with anticipation as adults and children alike thundered in one mighty voice, "Burn Polycarp alive!"

Soldiers tied him to the stake, piling wood around his feet.

He stood unresisting, praying to the Christ he knew would soon enfold him in a welcoming embrace.

His prayer was heard by all in the arenas of both earth and heaven.

"O Lord God Almighty, the Father of your beloved and blessed Son Jesus Christ, by whom we have the knowledge of you, the God of angels and powers, and of every creature, and of the whole race of the righteous who live before you: I give you thanks that you have counted me worthy of this day and this hour, that I should have a part in the number of your martyrs, in the cup of your Christ, unto the resurrection of eternal life."

He smiled as he spoke his last *"Amen".* The crowd stared in horror as flames encircled his body like an arch. He stood untouched, unburned, in their midst.

"Pierce him with a sword!"

The executioner obeyed the order but leaped back as so much blood flowed from Polycarp's body that the fire was instantly extinguished.

His remains were burned, but the mob was in turmoil. Many realized that they had not only witnessed, but also had participated in the grisly murder of one of the world's most gallant runners. Unanswered questions began to echo in men's minds.

What race was this, that its runners would embrace death with gladness, rather than throw down their torch?

What caused these runners to be unmovable and fearless before the powerful rulers of the world?
How could this race ever be stopped with such runners sprinting throughout the entire earth, leaving more runners, more torches burning in their wake?

There had been no joy in the execution of Polycarp. His death had brought no victory for Rome.

Many people, inspired by this faithful runner, held their torches aloft to be lit by heaven's fire.

Polycarp, now one of heaven's witnesses to earth's race, remembered the words spoken to him by his beloved friend, John. It was both a prayer for those still carrying the torch and a victory cry of his own.

"Whatsoever is born of God overcomes the world: and this is the victory that overcomes the world, even our faith. Who is he that overcomes the world, but he that believes that Jesus is the Son of God? The world passes away, and the lust thereof; but he that does the will of God abides for ever."

Chapter 14

Dave

Now ye are the body of Christ, and members in particular.
I Corinthians 12:27

There was silence as Dave stood quietly thinking about Polycarp's life and death. Then the pastor spoke.

"Dave, I like to look back at the lives of previous runners. Many of their lives have challenged me to new heights. What a blessing it is to learn that God has never failed one of his own. I can count on *every one* of his promises. I have never had to face torture, but I know God gives courage and grace to face even death as a martyr. I have read that Stephen smiled while being stoned. Many runners down through the centuries have faced both life and death victoriously. Their triumphant entry into the courts of heaven overshadowed their painful exit from this sin-sick world.

"Polycarp is an inspiration to me as a pastor because he was a single minded shepherd over his flock who chose to love his people. His people in turn chose to love him. As he faced arrest, he chose to love his enemies. Even as he was given the choice of saving his life by denying his Savior, he chose to love his beloved Lord unto death.

"Dave, you will face many challenges during the course of your run. Only one Runner has ever run the perfect course and left us the perfect Example. That is Jesus himself. But his runners, who have carried the torch before us, can be a great inspiration for those of us who carry it today. Many ran a triumphant race, their sole purpose to please their Lord."

He sighed and shook his head. "We do not have enough runners today whose lives challenge us to new heights in Christ."

He smiled gently at Dave, then said earnestly, "I pray, Dave, that you will become one.

"Let me leave you with one thought before you leave this evening. I may not get another chance to share with you a lesson I have learned during my race."

"I appreciate the time you are giving me," Dave answered. "And I value your counsel."

The pastor smiled and continued.

"Dave, our Lord treats us all as individuals. He will make a unique runner out of each one of us. We only need a glance at his creation to see that truth. God has filled this earth with millions of species of fish, birds, animals, plants, flowers, and even insects.

"Billions of snowflakes fall to this earth, remain for a short time, and then melt. Each is a marvel of God's handiwork. Wilson Bentley dedicated forty-six years of his life to photograph snowflakes. He lived alone in a shack battling the fierce Vermont winters, but he never tired of his work. Each snowflake was a fresh and beautiful new design.

"Billions of people inhabit this earth, but each one is unique. Every individual can be identified by just his fingerprint. You too are unique, Dave. There is only one *you*. Don't pattern your life or your race after another's. Simply let our Master Designer make you into his own special design for his service.

"As you run, you will meet other runners, each one unique in our Master's plan. Just like the snowflake, each one, though different, is beautifully designed by the master Creator. God values each one and speaks of his people as his precious jewels. The church will renew its first love when we value and love one another as our Lord loves us.

"Let me tell you about an early runner whose name was Lawrence. He was a runner with a message for the people of his day - and of ours."

Chapter 15

Lawrence

(258)

A book of remembrance was written before him for them that feared the Lord, and that thought upon his name. And they shall be mine, saith the Lord of hosts, in that day when I make up my jewels.
Malachi 3:16-17

Lawrence enjoyed his race. He ministered to the flock of God faithfully, caring for both their physical and spiritual needs. He knew his race would be short, for he ran when running was forbidden.

Valerian, the emperor of Rome, had ordered in the year 258 that all bishops, priests, and deacons be executed, and that the laity and civil servants lose their privileges and be reduced to slavery. Then he added the order that excited Marcianus, who managed the Roman government for Valerian: all church property was to be confiscated!

Marcianus was a ruthless and cruel man, who enjoyed killing the runners he despised. But he searched in vain to locate the treasures of the despised sect.

He knew there had to be a treasury. How else could the Christians continue to eat and stay clothed? The government had made every effort to crush them, but still their needs were supplied. Someone, someplace had to have a vast storehouse to continuously supply the Christians with their needs.

He asked questions, sometimes discreetly, often by torture. The answer was always the same. *Lawrence.* For Lawrence, men claimed, was the runner in charge of distributing goods to the poor. He could lead him to the church's treasure. Marcianus longed to capture Lawrence, not only to rid the earth of one of its faithful runners, but also to take for himself the wealth of the Christians.

Lawrence was running, his torch held high, when he was approached and halted by Marcianus. Lawrence looked with pity upon the cruel countenance of the one standing before him, seeing in him both hatred and raw greed.

"Lead me to your treasures," Marcianus demanded coldly.

"Marcianus," Lawrence answered calmly, "it will take me three days to gather the treasures of the church in one place. I will meet you then and show you our treasures."

"Three days then," Marcianus answered curtly.

Lawrence didn't even waste a moment to watch Marcianus and his attendants leave.

He knew he had only three days left to run.

He ran throughout the city, the hillsides, the market place.

Then his three days were spent.

He went to meet the ruthless persecutor and thief.

Marcianus marched to the appointed place, surrounded by his guards.

He found not one runner, not one torch, but many runners, many torches. He cringed in the light.

"What is this?" he demanded of Lawrence.

Lawrence smiled, then turned to those he had gathered together. He looked gently upon the poor of the earth, the despised, the persecuted, those tossed away by the world as its refuse.

He walked over and joined them, stretching out his arms, and turned back to Marcianus.

"These, Marcianus, are the precious treasures of the Church.

"These are the treasures indeed, in whom Jesus Christ has his mansion place.

"What more precious jewels can Christ have, than those in whom he has promised to dwell?

"What greater riches can Christ our Master possess, than the poor people in whom he loves to be seen?

"These are truly the precious treasures, in whom the faith of Christ reigns!"

Marcianus was mad with fury! He stomped; he glared; he literally foamed at the mouth!

Lawrence looked upon him with pity.

Lawrence

This mere servant of an earthly emperor saw only rabble standing before him.

And at the same time, the King of Kings and Lord of Lords looked down from his throne of gold, and with love in his eyes, saw priceless jewels.

Lawrence would love and serve King Jesus unto death.

Marcianus turned his bulging eyes back to Lawrence.

Then he turned toward his guards.

"Kindle the fire!" he cried. "Has this villain deluded the emperor? Away with him, away with him! Whip him with scourges, jerk him with rods, buffet him with fists, brain him with clubs, ye tormentors!"

Lawrence looked upon this maniac and prayed, "God, help him."

He thanked God that he was the persecuted, not the persecutor. He thanked God that he was the one hated, rather than the one full of hatred. He thanked God that he would be the martyr, rather than the murderer.

He would soon be ushered before the King of Kings and Lord of Lords, who looked upon his followers, not as just part of a worthless mob, but as the priceless treasures of his kingdom.

Those who watched his hand finally grow limp and his torch fall to be picked up by another, said later that Lawrence did not seem consumed by pain, but merely at rest in the everlasting arms of the King, for whom he had joyfully run.

Chapter 16

Dave

*See that ye love one another with a pure heart
fervently. If any man defile the temple of God, him shall
God destroy; for the temple of God is holy, which temple
ye are.*
I Peter 1:22
I Corinthians 3:17

The pastor paused, then said, "Dave, there aren't many Christians like Lawrence who see God's people as God sees them. If God's people are his precious jewels, as indeed they are, then don't ever handle his priceless treasures without the utmost care. As you see your sisters and brothers in Christ as God sees them, they will become precious to you also."

He sighed.

"Dave, if the church today could just learn what Lawrence knew back in the year 258 . . ."

Tears filled Dave's eyes as the pastor gripped his hand and prayed that God would bless his race.

As Dave left the church, he prayed, "Lord, if the church today could have more men like Polycarp, like Lawrence, and like my pastor - men who really love your people - what a church it would be!"

He stopped and lifted his hands and face to the heavens.

"My Lord," he breathed. "Please give me love for each one of your precious jewels! May I never treat one carelessly. Help me to realize your people are your temple, and value each one as you do."

Chapter 17

Dave

For every one that doeth evil hateth the light, neither cometh to the light, lest his deeds should be reproved.
John 3:20

Dave was running down a side street when his face broke into a huge grin. Two of his old friends from school were approaching him, laughing and talking together. Their laughter faded abruptly when they saw him. One stared at Dave's torch, then cursed. They ignored his warm greeting and passed by without a word.

It hurt.

What a contrast that encounter was to meeting a fellow runner! The fire leaping from two torches mingled and created a warmth . . . even among strangers.

Dave smiled, thinking about the boy he often met on another sreeet. He felt close to him, even though all he knew about him was that his name was Jack. He guessed he was about seventeen years old.

Dave stopped suddenly. He hadn't seen Jack the last four or five times he had run through the area. He turned around and slowly retraced his steps. He walked down the street he had just left gazing at the houses. He remembered seeing Jack come out of one of them a couple times. They all looked alike to him.

"Lord, if you want me to find Jack, please lead me to the right house," he prayed.

A door opened at the house just in front of him, then quickly closed. A figure had started out, seen Dave, and then ducked back in.

"Thank you, Lord!"

Dave knocked a long time before Jack came to the door.

He looked different. The friendly grin was gone. His eyes were dull, his shoulders slumped. His hand held his barely flickering torch loosely. It looked ready to drop.

He grudgingly motioned Dave to follow him inside.

Dave

The conversation was strained. Actually there was no conversation. Dave just kept talking and Jack answered with a barely perceptible nod now and then.

Finally Dave bluntly asked, "Jack, I see your torch is about to drop. Why?"

For the first time Jack looked into Dave's eyes.

Then a torrent of pent-up frustration poured from him.

"Do you know what it is like to have your whole family turn against you? Do you know what it is like to have your parents wish you would get out of their life? Do you know how hard it is to stay close to Christ in a house filled with cursing, filth, blasphemy, drunkenness, drugs, and constant screaming and fighting?

"Do you know how hard it is to keep smiling when everyone shuns you and ridicules you? Do you know what it's like today to carry the torch in school? The school I attend denies God, ridicules his Word and forbids our prayers. Oh, the name of Jesus Christ is spoken of often - constantly, in fact. But the only ones who can freely speak of him without censure are those who curse his name.

"Can you even imagine, Dave, how they despise my torch? Even the teachers and coaches who were my friends will have nothing to do with me. The custodian won't even speak to me!

"My cousin stayed around me for awhile. He sneers with the rest now. Dave, I just don't think I've got what it takes to finish this race! I *hate* being hated!"

Silence filled the room.

Finally Dave said, "Jack, I know only a little bit of what you are going through. I've been shunned and ridiculed by my family and cursed at by my friends. But my answer to your questions is no. I haven't been through all the things you face in your home and school. I can tell you about one who has.

"His name was Martin. He's gone down in history as *Martin of Tours* . . .

Chapter 18

Martin
(316 to 397)

My son, if sinners entice thee, consent thou not.
Proverbs 1:10

Martin tried to keep from overhearing his parents' conversation. His Dad, as usual, was shouting. His mother's voice was raised in anger too. The fury of both was directed at Martin.

". . . ever since he joined these Christians, he has changed! He refuses to sacrifice to our gods or join our festivities. He's always wanted to be a soldier like me - but not now! Oh, no! The Roman soldiers are too brutal for him! I can feel his disapproval when I curse in my own home! The boy is only ten years old, and I have lost control of him! We have to keep him away from Christians! Without their influence, he'll get back to normal."

Martin sighed. He would never be able to please both Christ and his family. He hated causing his parents pain. But they had been furious when he denounced their pagan gods and received both salvation and his torch from Jesus Christ. He was forbidden to mention his name at home. But everyone else was free to curse him.

The years passed slowly. As Martin grew in the Lord, the tension grew in the home.

He was only in his mid-teens when his Dad forced him to join the Roman army.

"My Lord," Martin prayed the night before he had to leave. "Deliver me! I cannot become a Roman soldier! You have called me to give people life, not death!"

His prayer, as usual, ended in desperation. "Christ, what am I to do?"

He hoped for deliverance, but the answer he received was, "I am with you always. I will never leave you, nor forsake you."

It was enough.

Martin of Tours

Martin was dressed in the uniform of Rome. A sword was thrust into his reluctant hand. He hoped and prayed he wouldn't be forced to use it.

His Dad was relieved. He was an officer in the army, and he knew it wouldn't take long for his son to forsake Christ in the company of the blaspheming soldiers.

He smiled in relief. "And he is finally away from those horrible Christians," he muttered. It wouldn't be long before he had his son back.

Martin was miserable. Fellow soldiers despised both Martin and his torch. Curses and obscenity colored the very atmosphere. Christ and his followers were mocked. Martin was ridiculed for refusing to treat people with cruelty.

The years dragged by. Martin's parents had little hope for their son now. The dreaded torch was still in his hand.

Martin petitioned the Roman Emperor to release him.

"I am Christ's soldier," he said simply. "I am not allowed to fight."

The news of his request spread among the soldiers.

"Coward," they yelled fiercely, knowing there was nothing cowardly about him. For years he had stood alone, one Christian in their midst. They had never heard him curse, but they had heard him pray. They had never seen him treat anyone cruelly, but they had watched him share his food, his clothing and his money with the needy. While they roughly shoved children out of their way, they could see him stooping down before them, smiling kindly, speaking gently. They had tried everything in their power to reduce him to their level. But still he continued to serve the Christ they hated.

Their failure to corrupt him filled them with rage.

Their voices swelled into one mighty shout.

"Coward! COWARD! COWARD!"

Martin faced them all head-on. There was a sudden hush as he spoke in a firm voice.

"I will be glad to stand in front of the battle line with all of Rome's soldiers lined up against me. My only weapon will be the cross."

Martin of Tours

They turned away in defeat. As far as they were concerned, he and his cross could both leave the army. Rome had no use for a soldier who refused to fight.

He was thrown into prison. Even there, his light exposed darkness. They discharged him in disgust.

His family turned away from their disgraceful son. They too had lost the battle.

Martin was finally free to do what he was called to do. He ran to the Balkan Peninsula to evangelize there.

"You came to preach Christ? We already follow Christ!" he was told. But no one held a torch. "We believe Christ is one of the prophets," they explained.

"Jesus Christ is not merely one of the prophets," Martin replied. "Jesus Christ is God!"

But the doctrine of Arianism had preceded him here. He was expelled from the country.

Undaunted, Martin ran to Italy, and then on to Gaul.

There he founded a monastery. He had faced loneliness all his life. He knew how desperately torch-bearers needed fellowship, strength, encouragement, and a place to study the Scriptures together. Many weary and footsore runners stopped by for rest and renewal.

Martin was used to being alone in a crowd. So he ran to places where people had never heard of Christ. He demolished pagan shrines and idols with an ax.

Then a smile lit his face as he preached about the Love of his life, and his great salvation. He ran throughout the French countryside, spreading the gospel wherever he went.

And he left behind an example of courage for the one with the torch who stands alone

in the home
in the classroom
at the place of work . . .
among family
among classmates
or among soldiers.

Chapter 19

Dave

I have somewhat against thee, because thou hast left thy first love. Remember therefore from whence thou art fallen, and repent.
Revelation 2:5

Jack sat with his head bowed.

The room was quiet.

Dave finally spoke softly.

"Jack?"

Jack ignored him and began talking softly to God.

"Jesus," he began. "I am so sorry for the way I've been acting. It's been so long since I've even talked to you. I was feeling so sorry for myself. I forgot . . . I forgot how it used to be before I knew you. I was always lonely then. I had friends - but I was so empty inside.

"Lord, I told Dave that I hate being hated.

"I want you to know that I love being loved by you more than I hate being hated by people. No one ever cared for me like you have."

His voice broke, and there was a long pause. Finally he continued his prayer.

"I love you, my Christ. Please help me to be brave like Martin. Keep me company during the lonely times.

"And Jesus . . . thanks so much for sending Dave to get me back on track."

He looked up. His brilliant smile was back, shining through his tears, lighting his face. Flames leaped from his torch.

"You know, Dave, I didn't get lonely when I stayed close to Christ. I talked to him constantly. He spoke to me as I read the Bible. We ran together.

"Then somehow, I just quit talking to him and spending time with him. That's when I got lonely. I realized when I was praying . . . I wasn't really lonely for my friends or my family. I was lonely for my Jesus."

Dave clasped his shoulder.

"Jack," he said quietly. "I suppose most runners have gotten their eyes on their troubles and on people, instead of keeping them on the Lord. Peter sure did when he ran across the water!"

Jack nodded soberly. "Yes. And Peter started to sink too."

Dave nodded. "You're right, Jack, he did start to sink - but only low enough to jolt him into looking up!"

He chuckled.

"Peter was the only one who started to sink, because he was the only one brave enough to get out of the boat."

Dave was already running down the street, when Jack called out, "Hey, Dave! I'm going to look up that Martin when I finish my race!"

Dave turned around with a grin and a wave.

"Jack," he called back, "I think you and Martin are going to spend your eternity surrounded by friends!"

Chapter 20

Dave

*Keep that which is committed to thy trust, avoiding
profane and vain babblings, and oppositions of science
falsely so called: Which some professing have erred
concerning the faith.*
I Timothy 6:20-21

Dave gripped his torch tighter as he ran onto the
university campus. The darkness was oppressing. Light
from his torch was only able to penetrate a small area of
the thick blackness. He ignored the many jeers as he
made his way to the dormitory to visit Phil.

"Phil!" Dave cried, glad to see his childhood friend
again.

Phil glanced at his roommates, embarrassed to have a
torchbearer coming to visit him. Sure, he and Dave had
gone to church together as kids, but he had left his
childish friends and beliefs behind years ago. He glanced
warily at the torch Dave carried. It made him uneasy.
His friends laughed scornfully as Phil introduced Dave.

"This is great, Dave! We've heard about this race, but
have never met a runner our own age!"

They looked him over, a sneer on their faces. They
seemed especially amused by his torch.

"Tell us, Dave, how can you be so naive? Do you
seriously believe that Bible you carry is the Word of God?
Don't you realize it's full of outdated principles? This is a
new day! The so-called *Word of God* you live by is nothing but antiquated mythology and fables! Modern
knowledge has taken us far beyond its teachings."

Dave smiled at them, then looked at Phil. Phil looked
quickly away, and Dave knew his old friend no longer
believed in Christ. He turned back to Phil's friends.

"Do you really believe this is a new day?"

Without invitation, he sat on the nearest bed. His eyes
seemed to look into the past.

"Let me take you back to another time . . . another
place . . . "

Chapter 21

Augustine
(AD 354 to 430)

Wherewithal shall a young man cleanse his way? by taking heed thereto according to thy word.
Psalm 119:9

It was a day made for the young and their pleasure. The rigid restrictions that had bound their parents and grandparents were no longer binding this generation, and the young people enjoyed their freedom to live their lives as they pleased. Fornication and adultery were included in most everyone's life style, and few labelled them sin. Teenagers revelled in lust and bragged openly of their conquests. Young men and women simply lived together, delaying marriage to pursue their careers. Unplanned pregnancies and unwanted babies were terminated by means of abortion. The divorce rate was skyrocketing.

Teens and adults alike lived for pleasure. Sports were the craze. To maintain their popularity they had to become ever more brutal.

Complaints were heard continually about the excessive spending of the extravagant government. No one was willing, however, to make the necessary sacrifices to curtail increasing taxes.

Resentment was brewing throughout the world against Rome and its powerful, long-reaching tentacles. Vast amounts of money had to be spent to build gigantic armaments for protection.

The people chose the guidance of astrologers rather than God, for astrologers did not demand a holy life of their followers.

There were the few voices warning that the enemy that would finally destroy the powerful nation lay within, rather than without. Modern men had decided that both God and his laws were obsolete. Anyone who cared to look could see that with the removal of God from their nation, a deep moral decay had set in. Rome was in the process of rotting.

Restless vandals, dissatisfied with their station in life, set fire to cities, laughing as men's houses and livelihoods turned to ashes.

Christianity, the religion many claimed, but few lived, was attacked both physically and intellectually.

Into this world, in the year 370, marched a brilliant sixteen year old youth. All his teachers were impressed with his superior intelligence. But if a subject did not come easily to Augustine, he dismissed it as unworthy of his attention. There was no way he was going to waste his teen years studying. For he, like his peers, was caught up in the pursuit of pleasure. Unbridled lust gripped him. Since he had no wish to be loosed, he surrendered himself completely to its control. His father was amused. His mother, a Christian who clung stubbornly to the old-fashioned values of the Bible, was troubled.

He cared nothing about her disapproval of his life style. If she chose to live by the laws of God, let her.

"It's a new day, Mom," he laughed, as she tried to reason with him. "This is *The New Morality!*"

His mother wept, praying that her son would one day see that this so-called new morality was nothing more than the old immorality.

Augustine mocked her Christ and the Bible she faithfully followed, with its warnings of sin and judgment. He found a perverse pleasure in doing whatever was forbidden in the Scriptures.

"The Bible is merely a book of fables," he jeered.

A wealthy pagan watched this brilliant young man closely, listening to his bold defiance of God.

"I wish Augustine to be my protege," he remarked to his friends. "This young man, with the right training, could very well become the philosopher Rome needs to turn its Christians back to paganism!"

His parents were not wealthy, but no financial sacrifice was too great to send their son to the best of universities.

Augustine left home, without a backward glance, to attend college at Carthage. When he was eighteen years old, he looked forward to college life with great anticipation. What young man wouldn't be excited? Carthage was the most sophisticated and worldly city in North Africa!

He was on campus only a short time when he met a beautiful woman and fell hopelessly in love.

"I mean to have her!" he declared to his friends.

They laughed at him.

"Augustine! She is not a suitable wife! You know she is beneath your social standing! She would do nothing to further your career!"

"Oh, I don't plan to marry her," he laughed. "I realize she would hurt my career! But I do plan to take her as my mistress!"

And he did. He lived with her for the next thirteen years. She bore him a handsome son.

He had no shame about his relationship with her. Most of his friends had mistresses. After all, it was a new day . . .

His career flourished, and Augustine became a popular college professor. The brightest of his students became his faithful followers. He consulted astrologers to guide his every decision.

He lived life to the fullest. He loved his mistress and their son. Even though he was now a success and had reached many of his career goals, he realized she would still be a detriment to him socially if he were to marry her. He vowed to do nothing that would damage his career.

He lived in Rome, esteemed by the elite of the city as a great man of influence. He had carefully formed friendships with senators and others who had political status in Rome. He envied their status and became obsessed with the desire for their powerful position.

He was even willing to claim their pagan gods as his own. Rome considered itself a Christian nation, but an altar to the *Goddess of Victory* still stood in the Senate chamber. Romans were willing to include Christ in their worship, but had no wish to exclude their gods. Many of Augustine's Senator friends worshiped Jupiter and Juno. Most of them didn't take their worship too seriously, but didn't want to take a chance on offending any god.

Augustine

Augustine willingly worshipped whatever god was popular with the crowd he longed to impress.

Steadily he climbed the ladder of success. He was in constant contact with Valentinian II, the young Emperor of Rome. He finally managed to win his favor. Valentinian was impressed with the brilliant young professor and asked him to become his speech writer. Augustine was thrilled! To write speeches for the Emperor was beyond his wildest dreams!

* * * * * * *

Dave paused. The silence in the room made the students uncomfortable.

Finally one said, "Life was really like that back in the fourth century?"

Dave smiled. "Did you really believe that this generation had invented a new style of living? Have you not read the words penned by King Solomon, the world's wisest sage?

He wrote:

The thing that hath been, it is that which shall be; and that which is done is that which shall be done: and there is no new thing under the sun. Is there any thing whereof it may be said, See, this is new? it hath been already of old time, which was before us. Ecclesiastes 1:9-10.

Phil looked down. One of his friends said, "Well, Dave, you've got us sort of interested in this Augustine. You may as well tell us the rest of the story. I'm sure it doesn't end there, right?"

"No, his story doesn't end there. If it had, we would know nothing of him today. He would be just another one of the men in his generation who lived and died and was buried under mountains of rubble and forgotten through the centuries of time.

"But something happened to Augustine that changed his life . . . "

* * * * * * *

Augustine finally felt secure enough in his career to marry. His mother arranged a marriage with an heiress.

Augustine

He watched as his mistress left her lover of over thirteen years and listened to her sobs as she hugged her beloved son good-bye. It had been a simple legal maneuver for Augustine to get custody of him. He would miss her, and he knew she would desperately miss her son. But life must go on.

Life go on? Augustine panicked at the thought of living alone until he was married. Then he grinned. He knew exactly what he would do! He would find himself another mistress and ask her to move in until his wedding day! And he did.

He tried to get excited about his fiance and wedding, but he was depressed.

His career was flourishing, but his personal life was a shambles. He was restless, engaged to marry a woman he did not love, and deeply troubled. He could no longer sleep nights. The success he craved had brought him neither peace nor joy. His gods had not calmed his endless mental torment. Astrology had not brought him the assurance that his decisions were the right ones.

He had to get out of his house. Just before leaving, his eyes fell upon a Bible. He picked it up, almost without thinking, and left for a walk.

He wandered aimlessly, finally stopping in a garden. There he faced the fact that he was one of the most miserable men who had ever lived. Why was he so unhappy? Would nothing or no one bring him contentment? Was he to spend his entire life dissatisfied and with this emptiness within him? Was anything or anyone worth living for? Was there to be no peace of mind for him?

Peace of mind . . . He would doubt there even was such a thing, but then he remembered his best friend.

Again the scene he had tried to forget replayed itself in his mind. Could he never erase the memory?

Their friendship began when they were both children. They had grown up together, and as they neared manhood, they found a perverse pleasure in ridiculing Christ. They had fun thinking up new ways to mock Christianity with its denunciation of so-called sin.

Augustine

Then the dark day had come when his friend had been struck with a sudden sickness, and fell into a coma. Augustine was devastated.

He remembered rushing to his room, and then stopping short as he viewed the scene before him. His friend lay perfectly still, his eyes wide and unseeing. A priest was leaning over him - baptizing him!

Augustine stared, and then rushed up to the bedside.

"How dare you baptize him?" he raged, shaking with anger.

"He wants nothing to do with your Christ! Now that he lays in a coma, unable to stop your foolishness, you dare to baptize him!"

Augustine turned and hurried from the room.

The following day, he was called to his friend's room. He dreaded seeing his friend in his comatose state.

He entered the room slowly, and then a huge smile lit his face. His friend greeted him with a grin. He had miraculously recovered! Augustine rushed to his bed, laughing.

When he had greeted him, he joked, "Can you believe a priest baptized you while you were in your coma?"

The smile on his friend's face immediately vanished. "I received Christ and his atonement for my sins, Augustine," he answered, a new sincerity ringing in his voice.

Just two weeks later, Augustine stood weeping, as his friend again began his journey through death's unknown valley. Augustine was in turmoil, but his friend faced death without fear. He seemed to be filled with a strange and beautiful peace. He drew his last breath effortlessly and passed beyond Augustine's reach.

The vivid memory still haunted Augustine. He and his friend had mocked and blasphemed Christ and his offer of salvation so many times. Christ had come with his offer of peace when he needed it most. What did Augustine have to offer his friend as he lay on his death bed, facing eternity?

Augustine forced himself to answer the question he had avoided all these years, for he knew he had nothing to offer anyone, himself included, in the face of death.

He was unable to calm the inner storm of unrest that raged within him and could no longer ignore it.

Finally he threw himself prostrate under a fig tree, his body wrenching violently and uncontrollably with sobs.

Augustine found himself crying out to God, "End my uncleanness, O Lord! End my uncleanness!"

Between his praying and weeping, he heard the voice of a child in a nearby house begin to chant, "Take up and read! Take up and read!"

Augustine remembered the Bible he had brought with him. With shaking hands, he opened it in obedience to the voice of the unseen child. He read:

Not in rioting and drunkenness, not in chambering and wantonness, not in strife and envying: but put you on the Lord Jesus Christ, and make not provision for the flesh, in concupiscence.

Not in rioting and drunkenness . . .
He had partied since the days of his youth.
Not in chambering . . .
He had lived a life of fornication and fathered a son outside of marriage.
Not in wantonness . . .
His mind was a filthy pit of unclean thoughts.
Not in strife and envying . . .
He spent his whole life striving for power and status. He envied everyone in a higher position than he held.
Put on the Lord Jesus Christ.
He had done nothing but mock and jeer the only one who loved him enough to die for him.
Make not provision for the flesh.
He had cared for nothing or no one, but was concerned only with his own fleshly and self-centered desires.
In concupiscence . . .
His whole being was saturated with lust.

His inner core of rottenness was exposed by the light of God's Word. He had never seen himself as he really was. He cringed at the stench of vile filth within him. For the first time in his life, he stood alone, naked in spirit, before the piercing gaze of a holy God.

Augustine

"Oh, my God! End my uncleanness! End my uncleanness, O Lord!"

And God opened a fountain for cleansing sin and uncleanness, the precious blood of his only begotten Son. Augustine became a new creation in Christ.

Light literally blazed into his heart, driving out darkness and all other gods with its presence.

"Oh, my Christ," Augustine prayed in wonder and awe. "Let me live the rest of my life only to please you."

Men stared as Augustine ran from the garden, his face lit from within, his torch held confidently.

"I have no need to ever consult another astrologer," he cried. "Yes, I consulted these impostors, but Christ is and forever more will be my guide!"

All his craving for worldly success was gone. The esteem of men meant nothing to him. Why should he marry an heiress he did not love? He broke his engagement. He resigned his position as professor and retreated to a country villa to write.

Shortly after beginning his new life, his restlessness returned. He turned to the Scriptures for help, and daily grounded himself in the Word of God. And the restlessness was again replaced with a beautiful peace.

Within a few months, his mother, his son, and one of his best friends died. But death no longer held him in its grip of fear and bondage. He had met the one who holds the keys of death, and found him faithful even in life's most trying hour.

Men had accepted the pleasure-mad, lustful, ambitious Augustine. He was one of their own. But men recoiled from this new Augustine. They plotted to murder him.

A group of people were gathered around him when one of the group called out, "Augustine! Did you know that men who used to be your friends are planning to kill you?"

Augustine was unconcerned about their plans. He was ready and willing to both live and die for Christ.

"But why, Augustine?" he was asked. "Why must a Christian endure these persecutions? Why are Christians so hated? Why does God allow so many to be killed?"

"Many Christians were slaughtered and put to death in a hideous variety of cruel ways," he answered. "Well, if this be hard to bear, it is assuredly the common lot of all who are born into this life! Of this at least I am certain, that no one has ever died who was not destined to die sometime. They who are destined to die, need not inquire about what death they are to die, but into what place death will usher them!"

"So many Christians have lost all their possessions," another voice stated. "Why would a loving God allow His people to lose everything?"

Augustine answered without hesitation.

"Our Lord's injunction is, *Lay not up for yourselves treasures upon earth, where moth and rust corrupt, and where thieves break through and steal.'*

"Oh, the joy of those who, by the counsel of their God, had fled with their treasure to a fort which no enemy can possibly reach . . .

"The tragedy is not the loss of one's possessions, but the love one had for the possession in the first place. If in losing them one no longer loves them, he has received a significant net gain!

"You say that they lost all they had? Did they then lose their faith? Their godliness? The possession of the hidden man of the heart, which in the sight of God is of great price? Did they lose these? For these are the wealth of the Christian!

"The Scriptures contain no promise to Christians of all-comfortable lives nor freedom from suffering. And who is so absurd and blinded as to be audacious enough to affirm that in the midst of the calamities of this mortal state, God's people, or even one single saint, does live, or has ever lived, or shall ever live, without tears or pain?"

A cultured voice filled his pause.

"Do you then have an aversion to wealth?"

The crowd turned to stare. The man and his servants stood a little apart from the rest. Everyone knew they required space. His servants were clad better than they. He was dressed in a tunic of fine silk, embroidered with a border of spun gold. His girdle was inlaid with gems. Matching bracelets encircled his arms and ankles.

No one was surprised at his question.

Augustine

Augustine looked upon the poor among the crowd, then turned back to him with his answer.

"That bread which you keep, my friend, belongs to the hungry. That coat which you preserve in your wardrobe, belongs to the naked. Those shoes which are rotting in your possession - give them to the shoeless. The gold which you have hidden in the ground, distribute to the needy."

"Augustine!" a listener challenged. "How is it that *you*, a mocker of Christ, now claim to understand scriptural truth?"

Augustine smiled.

"To understand scriptural truth, my Friend," he answered, "You must have faith. You are not required to understand in order to believe, but to believe in order to understand! And I now believe in Christ and the Scriptures."

"Our priest," a woman stated in her cultured voice, "tells us that we will enjoy only peace and prosperity if we have faith. We will not have problems and setbacks!"

Augustine's face clouded with sternness.

"May the Lord deliver his church from the eloquence that prophesies falsehood, yet inspires the priests to clap their hands and the people to love their words. May this madness never happen to us!"

"What about abortion, Augustine?" a young woman asked. "Is a baby a human being at the time of its conception?"

Augustine slowly shook his head. "I can't assuredly say at exactly what point human life begins."

A pained expression then crossed his face.

"But anyone who looks upon the cut-up remains of an aborted baby, as I have, has to recognize that this has been a human life."

A doctrinal dispute arose in the group. Voices increased in volume as each claimed to belong to the only group that was right.

Suddenly they were aware of a silence, and looking at Augustine, saw his eyes, black with anger, boring into theirs.

"The essence of the church is in the union of the whole church with Christ, not in the personal character of certain select Christians. The house of the Lord shall be built throughout the earth; and these frogs sit in their marsh and croak, 'We are the only Christians'!

"I bring against you the charge of schism, for you do not communicate with all the nations of the earth, nor with those churches which were founded by the labor of the apostles."

"But Augustine, did not Christ call Peter the rock?" a youth inquired.

"Christ did not name Peter the rock upon which he would build his church," Augustine answered. "Our Lord said, 'On this rock I will build my church,' because Peter had said, 'Thou art the Christ, the Son of the living God.' On this rock, therefore, he said, which you have confessed, I will build my church! The Rock is Christ!"

"You apparently forget that Peter alone was given the promise of the keys!" a church leader argued.

"Peter represented the universal church. Tell me, Sir," Augustine said. "Did Peter receive those keys and Paul not receive them? Did Peter receive them, and John and James and the rest of the apostles not receive them? Peter was symbolically representing the church, and what was given to him singly was given to the entire church!"

"Augustine," a woman questioned. "Why did you not marry your mistress?"

Augustine looked down for a moment, then lifting his head, answered truthfully, "I was not so much a lover of marriage, as a slave to lust."

He paused, thinking quietly about his promiscuous life style as a young teenager, his mistress of thirteen years, his engagement to an heiress for the sake of convenience, and the mistress he took while waiting for his wedding day.

"From a perverted act of my will," he confessed, "desire grew, and when desire was given satisfaction, habit was forged; and when habit passed unresisted, a compulsive urge set in.

"The arrogance of pride, the pleasure of lust, and the poison of curiosity are movements of a soul that is dead - not dead in the sense that it is motionless, but dead because it has forsaken the fountain of life and is engrossed in this world and conformed to it.

Augustine

"My heart was always restless, until it found its rest in Jesus Christ.

"You see, God's being is in himself: man's being is in God. Foolishly, man tries to be like God and find rest in himself. He cannot."

"Do you believe we are saved by our works?" a quiet voice spoke from the crowd.

"God surely does not save us by good works," Augustine responded, "But remember this. Good works are *always* present in those who believe!"

"Augustine," an authoritative voice questioned. "Is it not true that Rome is falling because so many Romans have offended the pagan gods by turning to this Christ?"

The speaker looked at the group of people, an arrogant smile on his face.

Augustine waited until the speaker looked back at him, then answered sharply.

"Rome's vulnerability has come from internal decay and moral decadence, not some pagan god's rebuke for not being worshipped. No nation can stand. No nation will ever stand! Only the City of God will stand forever!"

"Augustine," a young man inquired. "If God is a God of love, as you teach, why is there so much evil in this world?"

"Young man, sin is the corruption of God's very handiwork," Augustine explained. "You see, evil is a hopeless parasite. It does not exist in its own right, but only as a corruption of something good.

"You ask me about the love of God. Even the life and vital power of wicked angels and wicked people depend on the continuing gifts of God.

"There are two cities, made by two loves. The earthly city is built by the love of self unto the contempt of God. And the heavenly city is made by the love of God unto the contempt of self.

"The city of God is inhabited by God's people, whose citizenship is determined by a personal relationship to God, through Jesus Christ.

"The earthly city is inhabited by sinners who reject God.

"They are combatants in the age-old struggle between righteousness and wickedness.

101

Augustine

"The founder of the earthly city was Cain. Overcome with envy, he slew his own brother, who was a citizen of the eternal city and a sojourner on earth. As were the relations in the beginning, so will they be even unto the end. The church will continue to go forward, amid the persecutions of the world. God knows who are citizens of the one city, and who are citizens of the other. An unmistakable and eternal barrier shall be set up between them at the day of judgment."

A moment's silence, as the crowd pondered his words, was broken by a shrill voice.

"Is it right to worship deceased persons whom we consider saints?"

"Let me assure you," Augustine answered quickly, "that by the **Christian Catholics**, no deceased person is worshipped!"

"Augustine, you are always telling us to give," an elderly woman said. "What should we give?"

The crowd turned to stare at her. Her appearance made it obvious that she had little to give. They turned back to Augustine, as he began to speak.

"Give alms to the poor.

"Give forgiveness freely to all who wrong you.

"And," Augustine said, a smile warming his face, "Give to your own self what you need most - Christ."

Augustine turned to walk back home.

A young man caught up to him and walked beside him.

"Augustine, please answer just one more question that is bothering me! What should I do about the sins I have in my life?"

"Confess your sins before God, Young Man! Never let sin become comfortable in your life. Struggle with it!

"Seek God, and God alone! Be not conformed to this world. Restrain yourself from it. The soul's life is in avoiding those things which are death to seek!"

Augustine turned into his villa and resumed his writings. He wrote for a short while, and then paused for a moment, remembering how proud he had been as he wrote speeches for the Emperor of Rome. He had been the envy of every writer.

Augustine

But when he had met Christ, he turned from the Emperor and fame without a backward glance.

Men mocked his decision, but Augustine rejoiced at his promotion. For he now wrote for the King of kings and Lord of lords!

Augustine died at the age of seventy-six, leaving for us seven-hundred fifty-eight songs and poems and two-hundred forty-two books that would bless multitudes down through the ages. People have studied Augustine's teachings for over sixteen-hundred years. But does anyone remember even one word spoken by Emperor Valentinian II?

＊＊＊＊＊＊

Dave looked at each one in the silent room.

Then he said softly, "You give your lives for the pursuit of earthly success, wealth, position, pleasures.

"Worldly pleasures cease the instant you draw your last breath.

"Every possession you have accumulated will be owned by another.

"The position you have strived for will be filled by another.

"Are these things really worth giving your life for?

The Bible you ridicule says it best:

For what is your life? It is even a vapour, that appears for a little time, and then vanishes away.

For all that is in the world, the lust of the flesh, and the lust of the eyes, and the pride of life, is not of the Father but of the world. And the world passes away, and the lust thereof . . . "

Dave paused, and then continued quietly, "You mock the race and its runners who carry the torch. Do you believe that Augustine wasted his life? Do you consider me a fool?

"Anyone with any foresight at all knows that this world passes away from the grasp of every one who lives and dies. But Friends, God's Word says that . . .

He that does the will of God abides for ever."

Dave stood to his feet.

"Goodbye, Phil," he said quietly, and nodding at the others, he left the room. He was already outside when he heard Phil call out to him.

"Dave! Dave!"

He turned.

"I just wanted to say good-bye. I don't understand this race you're in. And I'll admit your torch puts me on edge.

"But don't quit running, Dave. And who knows? Maybe someday I'll join you!"

"Someday," Dave thought, as he left the dark campus.

How many people, both young and old, had he met who gambled their eternal destiny on the uncertainty of a tomorrow?

A beautiful peace seemed to descend and literally fill him with its presence.

"My Lord," he breathed.

"Sometimes this race gets lonely. There are times I feel so far away from you. And I confess I get tired of the jeers along the way.

"But seeing Phil and his friends tonight, Lord, made me realize that without you, the life of man is meaningless.

"I just want you to know, Lord, that there is nothing I'd rather do than carry your torch!"

Chapter 22

Dave

Bless them that curse you. For if ye love them which love you, what reward have ye? Therefore if thine enemy hunger, feed him; if he thirst, give him drink.
Matthew 5:44 & 46
Romans 12:20

The sun had not yet risen, but Dave, unable to sleep, knelt by his bed, his Bible open before him.

He had read the same words over and over:

Love your enemies.

Bless them that curse you.

Do good to them that hate you.

Pray for them which despitefully use you,
and persecute you.

"Who is it, Lord?" Dave asked simply.

He knew immediately.   Sometime today he would check the park and see if Tom was there.

"Now."

"But Lord, surely Tom will be in bed!   Everyone probably is but me!"

Dave got back in bed, but sleep was out of the question. Throwing back the covers, he got back up. The sun was just rising when he began his walk to the park.

The birds were welcoming the new day, the only sound in the otherwise silent park.   There was no noise of a basketball bouncing, no curses, no shouts. The park was empty.

Dave turned and started back home, feeling foolish. Then he stopped and walked slowly back into the park. He would find a bench and begin his day here in prayer.

Suddenly he stopped and stared. A boy was curled up on the bench in front of him.   His head rested on a wadded up sweatshirt, and his thin arms were wrapped around his chest, trying to keep warm.

Dave

It was Tom. Dave stood looking down at him. There were no obscene sneers now - just a pitiful, skinny child, alone and cold in the park. Why wasn't he home in bed?

Dave left quietly. A few minutes later, he sat down at a table near the bench where Tom still lay. Noisily, he opened a sack. Out of the corner of his eye, he saw Tom spring to his feet. Dave turned toward him just in time to see insolence settle over his face.

"Oh, hello," Dave said, as he laid the contents of his sack on the table. "I came to meet someone here. As you can see, no one is here but you and me. Do you want to help me eat all of this food?"

Tom neither spoke nor moved. Dave placed half of the food on the other side of the table. Then ignoring Tom, he began eating. He was nearly done, when Tom picked up the food and sauntered over to a tree and leaned against it, eating.

By the time Dave finished his last few bites, Tom had finished his meal and was walking away.

"Tom!" Dave called, following him.

The boy turned, his eyes cold with a challenge that Dave could plainly read. "Don't you dare ask me if I live in this park. Don't you dare."

Dave smiled and said softly, "I just wanted to say God bless you. I want you to know that I am still praying for you. If I can ever do . . . "

His words were cut short by a vicious curse, and Tom was gone.

Dave slowly made his way home, thinking about another time . . . another torch bearer . . . one whose race took him straight into the land of his enemies . . .

Chapter 23

Patrick
(The 400s)

*For by thee I have run through a troop; and by my God
have I leaped over a wall.*
Psalm 19:29

Patrick was not quite sixteen years old when the
wild raiders from Ireland invaded his town. They shackled him and dragged him from his home near the west
coast of Britain to Ireland.

Patrick looked at the other young boys who had been
captured along with him. He saw raw fright in their eyes,
and wondered if his eyes looked the same. He realized
they must, for he was nearly wild with fear. Where was
he being taken? And what would happen to him when he
reached his destination?

He was prodded rudely by one of the raiders as he
stumbled along with the rest.

They finally reached Ireland where brutal men herded
the boys to the town's center. Men gathered around
them. One grabbed him roughly, and he realized with
horror that he had been purchased by him. Patrick was
now a slave, no longer free to live the life he would
choose, but owned by another.

When he reached his master's farm, he was taken to
the pig pen. As he realized that his new job was herding
and feeding swine, all the hopes and ambitions for his
future were lost in hopeless despair.

Patrick made his home with pigs for the next six years.
He often thought back to his Christian home and his
godly parents. Time after time, they had told him about
their Savior, but Patrick had no faith in God and no
desire to make the acquaintance of His Son.

And now, like the prodigal son Jesus had referred to,
he was reduced to feeding hogs in a far country.

Finally, with all hope gone, Patrick, like the wayward son of old, came to himself in the pig pen. And it was there that he found his Lord.

Years later, he would write of his experience, "The Lord opened the understanding of my unbelief so I would remember my faults and turn to the Lord, my God, with all of my heart."

Though he was still a slave of man, he was now gloriously set free from sin. Patrick's days were now joyful ones, spent in intense and persistent prayer. He was no longer alone. "God strengthened and comforted me there as a father does his son," he recalled later.

It was when he was twenty-two years old that God helped him escape. It was night and Patrick lay sleeping on the hard ground. He awoke suddenly, hearing his Lord's voice.

"I will help you escape from here. You are to leave and run to the sea. I will have a ship waiting to take you home when you arrive at the Port.

Patrick jumped up and, in the cloak of night, began to run. When he reached the port, he found a ship prepared to sail to France. Its cargo was filled with hounds. Patrick was welcomed aboard. Someone was needed to care for the dogs!

He returned to Britain, praising God for His deliverance.

"My Lord set me free!" he testified to all who would listen. "He told me exactly how and when to escape!"

Friends and strangers alike looked at him skeptically when he claimed he heard the voice of God. Patrick was amazed that they doubted his testimony.

"Have you never read the words of Jesus?" he cried. "For He said, 'My sheep know my voice!'"

Patrick knew the voice of his Shepherd. He had heard his voice often while serving pigs!

"Jesus," he whispered, surrounded by his cynical friends. "I am so glad I know your voice! Thank you for setting me free!"

He shrugged off the opinions of men, and continued to find comfort in his Lord.

Then God spoke to him once again. This time he was sleeping when God spoke to him in a dream. He saw a man coming toward him out of Ireland,a bundle of letters in his hands. He handed one to Patrick, and as he opened it to read, he suddenly heard the voices of many people near the western sea, calling out, *"Please, holy boy, come and walk among us again!"*

Their cry pierced his heart, and he woke from his sleep, trembling.

"My Lord, what does this mean?" he prayed. "Am I to go back to the land of my captivity and preach your gospel?"

As he lay pondering the message of his dream, he remembered a similar vision given to the Apostle Paul. Patrick found the account in the book of Acts and read.

"A vision appeared to Paul in the night; There stood a man of Macedonia, and prayed him, saying, Come over into Macedonia, and help us!"

Patrick's heart began to pound. He read on.

"After Paul had seen the vision, immediately we endeavoured to go into Macedonia, assuredly gathering that the Lord had called us for to preach the gospel unto them."

Rising from his bed, Patrick knelt before the Lord he loved.

"My God," he prayed. "Could you be calling me? I am not well educated! I am not fit for such a task!"

And finally, "I will go."

God reached down into that humble home that night, and lit the fires of the torch of the young man who had come to know Him in the pig pen.

Patrick ran to Ireland. There he found a people bound in paganism. They were worshiping the sun, moon, wind, water, fire and rocks. Their faith was in the good and evil spirits that they believed lived in the trees and the hills. They were obsessed with magic. They not only sacrificed animals to pacify evil spirits, but also regularly sacrificed humans.

Patrick looked upon the druids and the priests and the demonic rituals these blind leaders were performing to deceive their blind followers.

They looked back at this one who had dared to run into their territory, and they hated him, his message, his torch. Frantically casting their evil spells and enchantments against him, they tried to force him to leave Ireland.

Patrick faced the druids fearlessly, and it was they who began to tremble as he cried, "Jesus said, *'All power* is given unto me in heaven and in earth!'

"My Lord said to His followers, 'Behold, I give unto you power to tread on serpents and scorpions, and over *all* the power of the enemy: and *nothing* shall by any means hurt you.'"

The druid chiefs, like the Egyptian magicians who used their magic in their struggle with Moses, found they were up against a greater power than they possessed.

Many Irishmen, watching this power struggle, were amazed that their powerful druid chiefs could not stop one runner armed only with a torch. Many turned away from the druids and their dark religion and were born through the blood of Jesus Christ into the kingdom of light. Eventually, even some of the druid chiefs made their way to the cross, and knelt there.

"God," they cried. "We come to you in the name of your only begotten Son, Jesus, the Christ! Set us free from sin and from Satan's dark kingdom! We receive Jesus as our Savior and our Lord!"

Patrick established a church for the new Christians, and then moved to new areas that had never heard the gospel.

"I have not come to turn you to an organization!" he proclaimed. "God has sent me here to make you disciples of Jesus Christ!"

By 447, after fifteen years of preaching, much of Ireland was evangelized by Patrick and the converts who had found Christ through his ministry.

Enemies of the gospel despised him and determined to kill him. He was kidnaped and held for two weeks, before escaping his captors and certain death. Twelve times God miraculously spared him from being murdered.

He boldly kept running. He established 200 churches and baptized 100,000 converts. Then, working diligently with these new Christians, he founded them in the Scriptures with intensive training.

"You must grow in Christ!" he counseled them. "And *you* must become involved in the ministry. God is calling *you* to bring light to this dark world!"

He lived a simple life, totally unselfish in his devotion to the race. He was amazed that God had called him. So many others, with their education and learning, were better suited for the job.

Just before he crossed his finish line, he left us this document:

Composed in Ireland by Patrick the sinner, an unlearned man to be sure. None should ever say that it was my ignorance that accomplished any small thing which I did. But let it be most truly believed, that it was the gift of God.

Chapter 24

Dave

Beloved, let us love one another: for love is of God;
and every one that loveth is born of God, and knoweth
God.
I John 4:7

"**I**f Patrick could serve the people who left him in a pig pen for six years, I guess I can feed people who curse at me," Dave thought.

Before his study, he had known only two things about Patrick. He knew he was Catholic and he knew he was Irish. He smiled to himself.

"Since my study of him," he thought, "I've learned two new things.

"What Patrick *wasn't* . . . was Catholic or Irish!

What Patrick *was* . . . was a fantastic runner who lived out his Lord's words:

Do good to them who hate you, and pray for them
which despitefully use you and persecute you.

Dave's Ireland would be the park.

* * * * * * *

Dave was absent-mindedly running along the outskirts of a city when the words of Jesus began to trouble his mind.

I was in prison, and you visited me not.

Dave did not even have to ask his Lord what he meant. He just turned around and began running back toward the prison he had passed about thirty minutes earlier.

"Do you have a lonely man I can talk with?" Dave asked the guard. The guard looked closely at Dave, at the torch, then at Dave again.

"I'll bring Sam," he decided. "He hasn't had a visitor in twenty-three years."

Dave

He motioned Dave to follow him and led him to a small room, the steel doors clanging shut behind him. Dave breathed a prayer for wisdom, wondering what this Sam would be like.

The door opened and a huge, burly man shuffled in. Dave put out his hand, but the man ignored it.

"Sam, I'm Dave," Dave began. "I have come to bring you good news. You can be set free!"

Sam looked at him, but quickly lowered his head, not willing to look a torch-bearer in the eye.

Dave began telling Sam that God loved him so much that he had sent Jesus to set him free. Sam began to shake his head vigorously.

"No," was the first word he spoke to Dave. "Heaven is not for me. If there is a hell, that's where I'm headed. This jail has been my home for over twenty-three years, and will be my home until I die. I'm in for murder."

"Sam," Dave said. "Just let me tell you about three of the greatest men in the Bible who are now in heaven! There was Moses, who killed an Egyptian and had to flee for his life to the desert! Then there was King David, a man who plotted the death of a beautiful woman's husband so he could marry her! There was Paul. Before Paul met Jesus, he was full of hate. He encouraged the stoning and slaughter of many Christians! But God forgave and received every one of them, and even used them in the ministry!

"And Sam, let me tell you about a man named Columba."

Chapter 25

Columba
(AD 521 to 597)

*The way of the wicked is as darkness: they know not
at what they stumble. Let us cleanse ourselves from all
filthiness of the flesh and spirit.*
Proverbs 4:19
II Corinthians 7:1

King Brude did not want to look out the window as
he walked past, but his eyes just seemed to turn that
way. And there he was. Did the man never sleep?

Ever since he had forbidden Columba to enter his city,
the persistent man had come every single day to the city
gate. He spent his days on his knees, obviously praying
for the king to change his mind. King Brude was finding
it more and more difficult as the days passed by to put
the kneeling figure from his thoughts.

Columba claimed to have some message to give to his
people about someone called Jesus. His people surely
wouldn't be affected by whatever he had to say. What
harm could he do anyway?

He motioned to his servant.

"Tell Columba I have decided that he may come into
my city and preach whatever message it is that he has
come to preach."

The news was carried to Columba and he leaped to his
feet, a smile lighting his face and, lifting his hands to
heaven, praised his God.

King Brude shook his head as he watched from the
window. "Strange fellow," he murmured as he walked
away. "I wonder who this Jesus is anyway."

Reports of converts to Jesus began to be heard
throughout his kingdom from that hour. His disgruntled
servants were smiling now. People he had known all his
life were somehow transformed. They were literally
radiating joy, love and peace.

Columba

And then the day came that Columba requested an audience with King Brude. The King consented to see him the following day. He was anxious to hear what he had to say, but it was always good not to appear too anxious. When Columba was brought before him, the king assumed an uninterested expression.

Columba opened the Scriptures and began to preach the gospel of Jesus Christ to the king.

"He is the only begotten Son of the Living God!" Columba declared. "He is Life! Only through receiving His blood as atonement for your sins will you be justified before God!"

The gospel message penetrated the heart of the king, and he turned to Jesus Christ for cleansing from his sin and salvation for his soul.

Columba was thrilled as he left the presence of the King. But as always, his joy was shadowed by his memory of another king, and he remembered the home he had been forced to flee . . .

Columba was born in Ireland in 521. His countrymen were in the midst of revival fires that had been burning ever since the days that Patrick had run through the land with the torch. He was raised among Christians whose entire lives were spent in serving their beloved Savior. They had been gloriously liberated from the dark practices of the druids, and were now dedicated to telling everyone about Christ and His salvation. They feared no danger and believed that no hardship was too much to suffer for the Lord they loved. They willingly followed him whenever and wherever he led them. Columba heard about those who had left Ireland and were running with their torches throughout Europe, as far north as Iceland.

Columba decided that he too would run in this thrilling race. He began to preach from the Scriptures. The Word did its work, and many who heard his message turned to Christ.

But there was a part of Columba that he was unable to control and unwilling to yield to God. For lurking like a coiled serpent, in the deep recesses of his heart, lay a dark and vicious temper. He tried to subdue it, but it seemed to always get the best of him. It had gotten him into one fight after another, and his testimony was ruined time and again by his outbursts of wrath.

"He is both a saint and a fighter," some said of him. All who knew him were very careful not to offend this huge and powerful man. Even strangers kept their distance when they heard his mighty voice. When and where would this man erupt next? Everyone was surprised when his temper lashed out to strike a king.

Columba never had any respect for King Diarmuid, but slowly a hatred began to grow within him. It first simmered, then began to boil, and finally exploded in Columba's determination to kill him.

He fueled hatred in others against the king, and the day came that Columba, leading a gang of seething men, marched to fight with him. A vicious and bloody battle was fought. When it was all over, five-thousand men lay dead. Columba, his anger spent, stared in horror at the corpses littering the battle field.

Then, leaving the devastation, he found a place to be alone with God.

"My God!" he cried. "What have I done?"

He was victorious in battle with the king, but would there never be victory over his violent temper?

He finally realized that this battle could never be won in his own strength and, crying out for mercy, gave his temper to God to conquer. At last he arose, cleansed and set free in Christ, a torch now in his hand.

He realized he would never again be respected by those in Ireland. He left his home country in 563, weighted down with the burden that his uncontrollable temper had caused the death of 5,000 men. Yes, his gracious God had forgiven him for his terrible sin, but he had a determination burning in his heart. He knew that he would never rest again until he had won 5,000 souls to Jesus Christ.

He ran to Britain, where the powerful druids fought him fiercely. He faced them fearlessly, challenging them openly with the power of God. They backed away as they saw the miracles that accompanied his ministry, and many of their followers found their way to the old rugged cross.

Columba

He made his home in Iona, a barren island just off the coast of Scotland. Most days his home was enveloped in fog and, throughout the year, the small island was battered by the pounding waves of the sea.

Columba, along with his twelve followers, dedicated his life to fasting and prayer and study of the Scriptures. He trained evangelists and sent them out to preach the everlasting gospel of Jesus Christ. He and his followers diligently translated and copied portions of Scriptures and hymns and distributed them among the people.

Columba kept careful count of those who turned to Christ.

He left his island home often to run throughout the land. Then one day, he ran into the Scottish highlands to bring the gospel to their inhabitants, the Picts.

It was there that he had been stopped by King Brude.

And now . . . now King Brude himself had turned to Christ for salvation! Columba knew he could never atone for his past. Only the blood of Jesus could blot out that dark stain. He praised his Lord as he left the palace that now glowed with the Light of the world.

"Thank you, my Lord. Thank you for bringing King Brude into your heavenly kingdom through my ministry. My temper caused a king to be alienated from You, but now another king has come to you. My temper caused the death of 5,000 men, but Lord, I will come before your throne bringing at least 5,000 precious souls with me."

Columba spent his life living Psalm 126:6: "He that goes forth and weeps, bearing precious seed, shall doubtless come again with rejoicing, bringing his sheaves with him."

He had left his homeland weeping, had faithfully scattered the precious seed of the Word of God, and as Columba crossed his finish line, he was rejoicing, bringing an abundant harvest of many more than 5,000 souls to his merciful master.

Chapter 26

Dave

The darkness is past, and the true light now shineth.
I John 2:8

The shouts and curses echoing throughout the prison could be clearly heard, but there was an unearthly stillness in the room with Dave and Sam.

Sam sat with his head bowed, while Dave silently prayed. Then he looked up, and the light of Dave's torch fell upon his face.

"Then there is hope for me. I can be set free from my sins and my guilt. I too want this Jesus."

Together Dave and Sam knelt on the cement floor. Sam poured out his heart before God, tears streaming down his face, often stopping in his prayer because he was too choked up to continue. When they rose to their feet, Dave stared at Sam. Sam was glowing from within, and a brilliant smile lit his face.

Dave reached out to shake his hand, but Sam gripped him in a powerful bear hug, thanking him for coming to visit him.

Dave had been tired as he turned into the prison. But now he felt renewed vigor surging through him, as he ran again down the highway, singing praises to his God, thanking him for once again reaching down to set a lonely captive free.

Chapter 27

Dave

*Let this mind be in you, which was also in Christ
Jesus: who, being in the form of God . . . took upon him
the form of a servant . . .*
Philippians 2:7

Dave was just about to cross the street to work on
the Arnolds' lawn when he noticed a blue Ford coming
toward him. He waved and grinned, and the car slowed.

Uncle Joe rolled down the window and pumped his
hand vigorously. His family seldom came to see him so
that made this visit special. Perhaps Uncle Joe was just
driving through the neighborhood instead of coming to
see him.

"I was just driving through the neighborhood, Dave . . .
No, I'm kidding. I came to see how you are doing!"

His eyes went to his torch and he smiled. "I see you're
still running the race!"

"Come on in, Uncle Joe! I'll tell you about my race,"
Dave invited.

His uncle shook his head.

"I don't want to keep you from doing something
important. Where were you headed when I arrived?" he
asked.

Dave pointed to the Arnolds' house.

"I was just going over to work in their yard."

"Did they hire you for the job?"

Dave grinned.

"No . . . but God did."

"Well, go ahead. We'll talk while we work."

Uncle Joe made the time go by quickly. Dave had
never spent time alone with him. The family was always
around when they'd been together.

"You've tackled quite a job here, Dave," he commented.

"You're right about that!"

They worked on in silence.

Finally Joe stood erect, wiping his brow with his
sleeve.

Dave

"Dave."

Dave looked up.

"What exactly did you mean when you said God hired you to clean up this yard? Does he ask his runners to do jobs like this?"

Dave leaned on his rake. "You know, Uncle Joe," he answered, "I didn't think he would when I first started running. I thought I'd be doing bigger, more important work. But when the Lord started asking me to do things like this, I got to looking in the Bible for some answers."

Joe looked at the piles of leaves, Dave's rake, and then at Dave.

"Son," he said, "I don't remember reading anything in the Bible about runners doing yard work."

"Well, Uncle Joe, I don't either," Dave answered. "The runners did do a lot of things we wouldn't consider to be too important. The disciples served dinner to the multitudes. Stephen helped take care of needy widows. Paul gathered up sticks to throw on a fire to keep shipwrecked prisoners warm. And Jesus . . . "

Dave's voice softened, and Joe noticed he spoke with love in his voice and a light in his eyes.

". . . Jesus sat on the edge of the well and talked to a Samaritan woman. He made wine for a wedding reception. He took time to pick up babies and small children and bless them. He went to lunch with Zaccheus. He knelt and washed his disciples' feet. He grilled a fish dinner and then served it to his disciples."

Joe thought Dave had finished talking and was about to walk away when he went on.

"Uncle Joe, do you know what amazes me most about Jesus? When Jesus comes back to earth, he will have all those who watched for him sit down to eat. Luke tells us that Jesus will gird himself and *serve his people!*

"When I think about the King of Kings serving food to sinners he died for . . . how can I expect to be anything but a servant to people? Serving is what running this race is all about!"

Joe walked away without answering and attacked another area of the yard.

A short time later, he went over to Dave and patted him on the shoulder.

120

"I'm proud of you, Son," he said softly.

Then he was gone.

Dave went home tired, but happy. Uncle Joe would probably never know how much his visit and his kind words meant to him.

"Thank you, my God," he prayed softly. "Bless Uncle Joe. He thinks his life is nearly over. Maybe it is. But I pray that he will commit what time he has left to serve you! And Lord, you told us we'd be happy when we serve you by serving people. I just want to tell you . . . I never knew anyone could be as happy as you have made me!"

Dave glanced down at his open Bible.

"He that is greatest among you shall be your servant."

The greatest among you . . .

Dave thought about Gregory, a pope who went down in history as Gregory . . . *the great . . .*

Chapter 28

Gregory the Great
(540 to 604)

*And call no man your father upon the earth: for one is
your Father, which is in heaven. Neither be ye called
masters: for one is your Master, even Christ.*
Matthew 23:9-10

Rome was ravaged by both floods and war. The
floods had claimed its share of victims, homes, and
possessions. The war had taken its toll on husbands,
sons, and fathers.

Then the plague struck the reeling city.

The sickness began innocently enough, with just a
slight sore throat. When the blackness erupted, the end
followed swiftly. Its victims left this world screaming in
agony. Insanity claimed many who escaped the plague,
but were unable to cope with the multiple deaths of loved
ones.

The people of the weary city tried vainly to close their
ears to the continual screams of suffering and wails of
mourning. They turned their heads away from the steady
stream of carts, making their way through the streets to
pick up and dump their cargos of corpses.

The Pope was one of the plague's victims. His office
was left vacant for six months. Church leaders searched
frantically for even one who carried a torch. Their eyes at
last settled on a frail, balding man of fifty, by the name of
Gregory.

Gregory was preaching from Ezekiel when he learned
of their intent. He listened in horror to the messenger.

He could think of only one thing to do. So without
hesitation, he did it. Attempting to conceal his face with
his cloak, he fled through the city to the forest. Finding
the densest spot available, he cowered, hiding among the
trees and brush.

Gregory the Great

The church leaders made their way to the monastery with their pronouncement . . and then frantically formed a search party.

Gregory heard them coming, his heart sinking.

"My God," he prayed frantically. "Don't punish me by making me a pope!"

He was discovered, and dragged, protesting all the way, back into Rome.

It had come to this. He would be forced into the Papal position. How he dreaded it! He looked at the depressed city as he was compelled through its streets.

He sighed deeply. His future was too much to think about. His mind drifted to his past . . .

His family had governed in the senate for farther back than he could remember. Some may have envied the wealth he had inherited by birth, but it meant little to him.

He was only thirty-three years old when he became the mayor of Rome. His responsibilities included the entire economy of the thriving city. He directed its grain supplies, ran its welfare programs, supervised its new constructions, kept the baths and sewers functioning and its riverbanks beautiful.

Then his father died, leaving his vast wealth to him.

He was rich - but only long enough to give his entire inheritance away. He founded seven monastaries for the education of the clergy. He gave away everything else to the poor. He moved into a monastery and cheerfully dined on raw fruits and vegetables.

While others slept their nights away, he chose to spend his praying. He filled his days cheerfuly doing the jobs that others shunned.

Now . . . now he was the Pope.

Sighing, he contemplated his awesome task. He knew of only way to begin. For there was no way to accomplish anything without God's helping hand.

He walked through the streets ceaselessly for three days, praying and singing hymns.

Gregory looked around with despair.

"Surely the end of the world is at hand," he groaned.

"Everywhere," he later wrote, "we see tribulation, everywhere we hear lamentation. The cities are destroyed, the castles torn down, the fields laid waste, the land made desolate. Villages are empty, few inhabitants remain in the cities, and even these poor remnants of humanity are daily cut down. The scourge of celestial justice does not cease, because no repentance takes place under the scourge. We see how some are carried into captivity, others mutilated, others slain. If we love such a world, we love not our joys, but our wounds."

No repentance takes place under the scourge . . .

Finally the plague subsided.

Gregory didn't have much energy. His health was poor, and many days he was unable to rise from his bed.

One of those days, he wrote weakly to a friend, "I have been unable to rise from my bed. I am tormented by the pains of gout. A kind of fire seems to pervade my whole body. To live is pain, and I look forward to death as the only remedy. I am daily dying, but never die!"

He expended what energy he had to labor among a broken people. He had no desire to be great in the world. He desired only to serve his God.

He was enraged at the titles men heaped upon him as the Pope.

"Universal pope!" he fumed. "What an assumption. I want this title revoked. It is a foolish, proud, profane wicked, pestiferous, blasphemous and diabolical usurpation! Anyone who uses it can be compared only with Lucifer! I nor any one else ought to be called anything of the kind. Away with words which inflate pride and wound charity!

"Do you want to call me by a title? I will give you my title. Call me the *servant of the servants of God.*"

He both despised and fought against pride.

"Pride," he wrote in his commentary on the book of Job, "which we have called the root of vices, far from being satisfied with the extinction of one's virtue, raises itself up against all the members of the soul, and as a universal and deadly disease corrupts the whole body."

His thoughts turned to the pompous bishops and clergy who craved the praise of man.

He shuddered, and decided to write a book on what a real pastor should be like.

Dipping his quill, he penned the title:

Pastoral Care

Part of his counsel would extend through the centuries as wise counsel to future shepherds of flocks.

"A spiritual leader should never be so absorbed in external cares as to forget the inner life of the soul, nor neglect external in the care of his inner life. Our Lord continued in prayer on the mountain, but wrought miracles in the cities."

Dave spoke softly, "Lord, I pray for all your runners. Help us to be filled with your love and power during our times in the mountains, alone with you.

"For only then will we be able to return to the people, and give them your love."

His thoughts drifted back to Gregory . . .

How Gregory would have disdained the pompous claims of succeeding popes, fifteen of whom would take not only his name, but arrogantly embrace the titles he had spurned.

Centuries later, Pope Innocent III made a claim that Gregory would have dismissed as conceited arrogance: "I, as pope, am the judge of the world," he declared, "set in the midst of God and man, below God, above man. I am the supreme authority, not only of earth, but over all the souls of men departed to eternity."

Gregory VII echoed his words, then added his own haughty announcement.

"*I* am the mediator between God and man. As such," he proclaimed, "I will judge all and be judged by no one."

He then threatened his critics with excommunication.

They responded with questions. Could a man deprive their souls of the grace essential for their salvation? Was it possible for a mere man, whatever his position, to prevent them from being washed in the blood of the Lamb?

"Yes," the decree from Rome echoed throughout the land. "Not only can we excommunicate *you* from the

church and thus from heaven - we can also excommunicate *angels* if we so desire!"

Many began to examine the scriptures closely. A faint voice began to swell against such unscriptural claims.

Popes looked down with contempt upon those who dared to challenge their supremacy.

"*Scriptural* claims?" they sneered.

"Do you not realize that we have the authority to change and modify the laws of God himself?"

The earth darkened as greedy men, garbed in the cloaks of Christianity, appointed themselves as runners. They held no torch. They brought no light.

Intent on stopping runners who did both, they joined forces and announced new rules for the race and its runners! *They*, not God, would appoint and approve future runners. *They*, not God, would map future courses.

Yes, God's forgiveness and Christ's salvation would still be distributed to the masses - but now with a price attached. What God offered freely, man dared to merchandise. They ran, for an earthly kingdom, not a heavenly. They ran for the gold.

Thomas Aquinas approached Pope Innocent II of the thirteenth century while he was absorbed in counting a huge sum of money.

Smiling at the treasure heaped before him, the Pope said, "See, Thomas, the church can no longer say like Peter, 'Silver and gold have I none' "

Thomas stared at the mass of wealth, then sadly shook his head.

"True," he replied. "But neither can she now say, 'Arise and walk' "

Two or three men jostled for the powerful position of pope at a time, each claiming to succeed Saint Peter. Rivals were often murdered.

Popes proudly wore the title of Chief king of kings. How different from the title Gregory had insisted upon being called . . . simply God's . . .

servant of servants.

Chapter 29

Dave

Be thou faithful unto death, and I will give thee a crown of life.
Revelation 2:10

Dave was running in an area that seemed blacker than usual. It was so dark that his torch only penetrated a small area.

He felt like shouting, "Will somebody here please turn on the lights?"

It had never been this dark in the past. What had changed? Then he remembered. One store had been lit up by the twin torches carried by a beautiful young couple. Perhaps they'd sold the store and moved. It was a rough area.

He groped his way to the store.

They were both inside. Neither carried a torch. They greeted him coldly, shielding their eyes from his light.

"What happened?" he asked simply.

They looked embarrassed. Tension filled the awkward silence. Dave calmly waited for one of them to answer.

Finally the husband spoke.

"It got pretty tough carrying a torch here. Business even dropped . . ."

He glanced at his wife for help with his explanation, but she remained silent.

He looked back at Dave, then almost shouted.

"Look, Man, we don't owe you an explanation. It just got too hard, that's all. Runners get a lot of enemies they don't ask for. We don't expect you to understand, but if we had kept holding the torch here, it could have cost us not only our business, but our lives!"

Dave answered softly.

"Do you two have time to talk for a few minutes??

The wife laughed harshly.

"Time? We have time, all right. We lost nearly all the customers we had. We're trying to recover, but business is still slow."

Dave

Dave prayed for wisdom as he leaned on the counter and began talking.

"The purpose of a torchbearer is to light up their area in this black world. If it wasn't a black world, there would be no need for God to turn on some lights.

"Some areas are blacker than others. Down through history, there were some really black times.

"Can you imagine how it must have been for a runner going into a country or city that didn't have even a flicker of light? Only the bravest ran, and many of them were savagely murdered by those who preferred darkness.

"Let me tell you about just a few of the thousands of courageous runners who faced darkness, demons and death.

"One of the boldest was *Boniface* . . . "

Chapter 30

Boniface
(AD 675 to 754)

A man was famous according as he had lifted up axes upon the thick trees.
Psalm 74:5

Boniface stood beneath the enormous oak tree, looking up at its branches that were bigger than most tree trunks. It was a splendid creation of God. Under different circumstances, he would admire its beauty. He sighed and glanced at the silent crowd surrounding him. Someone had convinced them that this tree was sacred to Thor, their so-called thunder god, so now they bowed before it, prayed to it, sacrificed to it and worshipped it. He would never understand why men worshipped the creation rather than the Creator.

Well, he had better get on with his job, for it was certain he wasn't going to convert this crowd of pagans to Christianity as long as they idolized a tree.

He could feel the awe and fear of the heathen as he picked up his axe. He knew they expected Thor to thunder with vengence from the heavens and strike him dead before his axe could smite their sacred tree.

Boniface had no fear of their nonexistent god. He lifted his axe and sent it crashing against the oak. His mission gave him strength as he continued to chop. Wood flew as he cut deeply into the monstrous trunk. After hours of labor, the final blow was at last struck, and the tree crashed to the ground. The Hessians stood transfixed, awe-struck by this bold Englishman who had come to this west-central part of Germany and had dared to destroy their idol. But what bothered them most was that Boniface was still very much alive. Where was Thor? Was he not their mighty god of war who defended all their other gods with his enchanted hammer? How could he stand by and do nothing against this mere man who had defied his deity?

Boniface

Bonifice had come to Germany for just one purpose - to introduce men and women to the living God, and to persuade them to worship him, through His Son, Jesus Christ. If he had to chop down a tree to accomplish his goal, then so be it. He would do anything possible to reach men for Christ.

Hadn't God told His prophet Jeremiah to "root out, pull down, destroy, throw down, build, and plant?" Sometimes things like this old oak tree had to be destroyed, and only then could the building and the planting begin.

Now that the destroying was done, he would build a church on this very site, and he would use this very oak to begin construction.

The Hessians left the scene, grumbling with disappointment in their impotent god. By the time Bonifice left to find some heathen in another part of Germany, thousands were worshipping the living God in their new church.

For thirty-nine years, this fearless missionary ran through Germany, demolishing pagan temples, preaching Christ, building churches on the ruins of idolatrous structures, and baptizing over one hundred-thousand converts.

At the age of seventy-five, he was still running. With his age came physical infirmities. He had tried to slow his pace, but as long as there were Germans worshipping idols rather than Christ, Bonifice could not rest.

He ran to the region of The Netherlands and Germany, considered by many to be the most dangerous mission field on earth. There he won thousands of Frisians to Christ. Their pagan leaders were incensed. He and fifty-two companions were on their way to confirm a group of them. As he approached his designated meeting place, he looked up to see, not his new Christian brothers and sisters, but a raging crowd of savages advancing menacingly toward him.

"My race is finished," he thought, as he waited calmly for his death. He looked with love upon the fifty-two companions who accompanied him.

Boniface

Bonifice had courageously withstood every enemy who opposed his Lord, and now he would boldly confront death, the last enemy to be destroyed.

As the howling mob came nearer, he turned calmly toward his friends.

"They are coming to bring us our crown of life! Let us wait for them here."

Chapter 31

Dave

They that sow in tears shall reap in joy. He that goeth forth and weepeth, bearing precious seed, shall doubtless come again with rejoicing, bringing his sheaves with him.
Psalm 126:5-6

Dave paused.

Ron spoke.

"He was brave, all right. But Dave, I think I could keep going if I saw results like he did. You said he won over one-hundred thousand people to the Lord!"

He paused and glanced at his wife. She was looking down.

"Ann and I haven't seen one person turn to Christ - oh, unless we count a couple children and one old homeless lady who repented a few weeks before she died. We ran faithfully for seven months! It gets discouraging!"

Dave smiled.

"I'm sure Jesus will count the children and lady. He is no respecter of persons. I think I'll tell you about a runner named Anskar. He's known as the *Apostle of the North.* With that title, we would assume he had tremendous results like Bonifice.

"Instead I think he experienced some of the same discouragements you face. There was one major difference. *Anskar held on to his torch . . . "*

Chapter 32

Anskar
(801 TO 865)

Be not weary in well doing; for in due season we shall reap, if we faint not.
Galatians 6:9

The *Apostle of the North.*

Anskar sighed deeply   He was now sixty-five, tired, and yes . . . deeply disappointed. He knew his run was nearly done.

What an awesome task God had given him. All the heathen of northern Europe was his mission field.

He had begun his race with such high hopes. Born in France, he began his education at five years of age in the monastery founded centuries before by Columba.

His life had been one of constant troubles and trials.

He was twenty-six years old when he had carried the torch into Denmark. Three years of exhausting efforts had followed. He still felt the heartache and pain, as he and his message were both expelled from the country. Denmark was content with its darkness.

He had turned toward Sweden then.

Sweden.

What a challenge! The gospel had never been preached there. The country was black with idolatry and paganism. Satanic practices filled the land. Some Swedes worshiped a dead king. Others worshiped tribal gods, and still others, the sun and the moon. Charms were carried as protection from sickness and misfortunes. Both animals and humans were sacrificed to Odin, their demonic god.

Before he even arrived, pirates attacked his ship and sailed away with all his possessions. He held nothing but his torch when he landed on Sweden's shores.

King Bjorn and his people had never seen a torchbearer, for none had ever run in Sweden. Anskar was the first.

Oh, the king had been cordial. The people had listened to his message. Many responded eagerly and converted with joy to Christianity.

"I was so thrilled with their response," Anskar thought.

It hadn't taken long to realize they were just temporary converts, described by Jesus.

"And these are they which are sown on stony ground; who, when they have heard the word, immediately receive it with gladness."

Then they had come to the same end as the seed on the stony ground. Jesus had predicted the outcome of both.

"They have no root in themselves, and so endure but for a time. Afterward, when affliction or persecution arises for the word's sake, immediately they are offended."

They'd been offended all right. They had apparently received Christ so he would help them win their many wars.

As long as they won their battles, they were faithful Christians. When they were defeated, they rebelled against Christ and returned to their pagan gods.

Their fickleness led Anskar to spend long days and nights praying and fasting.

He spent his days preaching the Word.

"Prayer and fasting are vital to the ministry," he thought, "but never to the expense of useful activity." He had faithfully done both.

He had left Sweden then. He'd become an archbishop when he was thirty-three. The new city of Hamburg, Germany became his base.

Just about the time the work he had begun in Denmark was revived, the Vikings stormed into Hamburg and set the entire city on fire. His headquarters were reduced to ashes in the inferno.

He became the bishop of Bremen.

He returned to Sweden in 853 and 854.

He rejoiced as the king turned to the Lord. Perhaps this time . . .

He and other missionaries preached with power and liberty. Powerful pagan priests were stirred up by the presence of Christ. They plotted a rebellion that would overthrow the kingdom so they could expel Anskar and the gospel from their land.

After thwarting their evil plot, he returned to Bremen.

Rumors about the apostle of the north had spread quickly. He scoffed when they credited him with great miracles.

"The greatest miracle in my life," he responded, "would be if God ever made a thoroughly pious man out of me!"

He was so disappointed.

"I spent my life trying to win Sweden and Denmark to Christ," he thought. "Now both have returned to their pagan practices."

Anskar crossed his finish line, never having seen the fruit of his labors. He did not know that the light he had taken to the black lands yet burned . . .

Chapter 33

Dave

He which converteth the sinner from the error of his way shall save a soul from death, and shall hide a multitude of sins.
James 5:20

Ann spoke for the first time since Dave had entered their store.

"He *had* accomplished something then?"

Dave's eyes met hers squarely.

"There has never been a runner who did not accomplish something. And Anskar was no exception. Even though he died without seeing a harvest, he left behind a flicker here, an ember there. And fire will do one of two things. It will either go out or spread."

Ron and Ann both glanced guiltily at their empty hands.

"Before I go on, I want to tell you about another runner who was almost too discouraged to go on. Have either of you heard of Mr. Kimball?"

Ron and Ann both shook their heads.

"Well, I would tell you all about him, but I don't know much. I don't know where he was born or where he died. I don't know what he did for a living. All I know is that he was a very discouraged Sunday School teacher in Boston. He saw no results. He could have easily laid down his torch and simply given up. And that's what he nearly did. But if he had, the entire world would have been much blacker today."

"The *world?* What did this Mr. Kimball do?"

"He told an eighteen year old shoe clerk named Dwight about Jesus. Then they prayed together, and the clerk received Jesus into his heart. Mr. Kimball was no doubt happy that the clerk had turned to Christ for salvation. But the young man didn't hold much promise. He was only four years old when his father died, leaving his mother with nine children to raise, all under the age of thirteen. His entire schooling was about the equivalent of a fifth-grade education today. Mr. Kimball probably felt about the same way you do. He saw no results - just one young shoe clerk.

"He didn't know that Dwight L. Moody would look up at his Savior, then at his pain-filled world, and cry, *The world has yet to see what God can do with a man fully consecrated to him. By God's help, I am to be that man.'"*

Dave smiled. "Mr. Kimball's insignificant shoe clerk ran more than one million miles and preached about Jesus Christ to more than one hundred million people.

"Moody's course took him to England in 1879, where Frederick B. Meyer, a pastor of a small church, was set ablaze.

"F. B. Meyer carried the torch to an American college campus, where a student by the name of J. Wilbur Chapman was born again. Chapman later hired a young man by the name of Billy to do evangelistic work, as an extension of the YMCA.

"Billy Sunday was an orphan who worked as an undertaker's assistant before he entered professional baseball. He gave up running the bases to run the race . . . and a million people found Christ as their Savior.

"He was running through Charlotte, North Carolina, when a group of men were set aflame. They invited a runner named Mordecai Hamm to Charlotte to preach in their city after Billy left.

"During Hamm's meeting, a young man joined the race. His name is Billy Graham."

He smiled. "I think you've both heard of him."

"And it all started with one discouraged runner who was about to lay down his torch," Ann said thoughtfully.

"Think about it, Ron and Ann," Dave continued. "God sent FIRE from heaven to light the torches of his one-hundred twenty praying disciples gathered in an upper room - and started his church. The reformation of the church began as Martin Luther taught a few students at Wittenberg. John Wesley found Christ at a back alley prayer meeting at Aldersgate. Dwight L. Spurgeon joined the race in a tiny chapel.

"I think that settles the question of giving up in despair when you don't see results. Now let's talk about running through dangerous areas."

Ron glanced at the door.

"I don't see any customers breaking down the door in their rush to get in," he laughed. "You might as well keep talking."

"Then let's start with Adalbert . . ."

Chapter 34

Adalbert
(997)

Be thou faithful unto death, and I will give thee a crown of life.
Revelation 2:10

"**I**s there no end to my troubles?" cried Adalbert, a Bohemian. He sighed bitterly, glancing at his still flickering torch.

He had done everything he had known how to do to bring his people to holiness. But still they stubbornly refused to conform to God's Word. There was tension in the country, tension in the church. Was there anyone who did not hold a bitter grudge of hatred? He could not stand to work among such a people! His own torch had died down to embers.

He was wasting his time and energy.

"I will resign my position as bishop of Prague," he decided. "My work from now on will be to convert the infidels."

He turned to the heathen Prussians on the shores of the Baltic. They listened to the message of the gospel with joy. Many turned to Christ with their hearts . . . and their lives!

Pagan priests eyed Adalbert with murder in their hearts. As their followers turned to Christ they turned away from them. They could no longer control them with their dark superstitions. He would have to be stopped . . . and quickly. They joined to plot his murder.

With a cry of rage, they fell upon him. Moments later, Adalbert crossed his finish line. The devil had used his ministers to pierce his body with darts.

Their fury spent, they looked up.

And their faces darkened.

Adalbert had left runners behind, faithfully carrying their torches throughout the land.

Would the earth never be rid of them?

Chapter 35

Dave

Fear not them which kill the body, but are not able to kill the soul; but rather fear him which is able to destroy both soul and body in hell.
Matthew 10:28

Dave paused and looked at the two faces staring at him in horror.

They both started to talk at once, but Dave silenced them by lifting his hand.

"Please wait before you say anything. This has never been an easy race. Jesus warned us of its dangers. He said, 'The kingdom of heaven suffers violence, and the violent take it by force.'

"Paul told us to endure hardness, as a good soldier of Jesus Christ. We are in a war between Christ and Satan, good and evil, light and darkness. The battle is fierce. And yes, many runners have died on the battle field.

"Even as we talk, runners are rotting in prisons. Some are being tortured. Others are facing their murderers. Over ten-thousand Christians have been killed every year since 1950, due to clashes with anti-Christian mobs, infuriated relatives, state-organized death squads, and so on. Dave Barrett of the *World Evangelization Research Center* tells us that martyrdoms are increasing. In 1900, an estimated 35,000 laid down their lives for the Lord, and in 1990 there were 260,000! Barrett goes on to say, *'All the long-term underlying factors which produce martyrdoms seem to be gradually increasing in our day.'*

"Yes, Aldabert died a horrible death. Has there ever been a war without casualties?

"He left us an example, not only in living, but in dying for Christ. So many left us an example in courage.

"Runners like
> *Alphage . . .*
>> *Gerard . . .*
>>> *Stanislaus . . ."*

Chapter 36

Alphage
(Died in 1012)

The good shepherd giveth his life for the sheep. But he that is an hireling, and not the shepherd, whose own the sheep are not, seeth the wolf coming, and leaveth the sheep, and fleeth.
John 10:11-12

Alphage.

His name brought a gentle smile to the faces of young and old alike.

They loved him - simply because he loved them.

There weren't many men like Alphage.

He could have chosen them as his servants. He was born into a wealthy family and was far better educated than most. He chose instead to serve them as their beloved pastor.

He was archbishop of Canterbury when the Danes invaded England.

News of the attack reached the city. Cities and villages were ravaged, their inhabitants slaughtered.

A messenger reached Canterbury just ahead of the invaders. The city's leaders would have just enough time to escape with their lives.

Snatching their prized possessions, they began to flee the city.

"Hurry!" they called to Alphage.

"I am not leaving. My people need whatever help and encouragement I can give them."

The fleeing men were horrified.

"Don't be a fool, Alphage! You will be killed!"

But his eyes were already fixed on the people he loved.

The city's leaders had barely escaped when the Danes poured into the city, killing and plundering.

Alphage hurried from his home. Everywhere there were victims, some already dead, others writhing in pain.

Men, women, children, the aged, the babies - the Danes had mercy on none.

The city was thick with smoke. Flames leaped to the skies and piercing screams added to the chaos. Alphage gazed at the carnage. Then he turned toward the savage soldiers. Their curses and shouts filled the air. They were laughing as they killed - clearly enjoying the slaughter.

He walked steadily toward them.

They paused to stare. Who was this who dared to approach them? Did he have no fear?

"Save the people!" he pleaded. "Do what you will with me, but save the people! Please. Spend your rage on me."

Seizing him roughly, they laughed sadistically.

They tied his hands together and marched him to his church.

"Watch," they mocked, as they set it afire.

The flames spread quickly. Monks ran from the building to escape the inferno. Alphage cringed as they were cruelly massacred.

"Save the people?" the soldiers sneered.

"We will save your precious people. One out of ten!"

Then brutally and systematically, they killed nine of every ten.

By day's end, seven-thousand, two-hundred and thirty-six people lay dead.

All that remained were four monks, eight-hundred laymen . . . and Alphage..

He lay bound in a dungeon. They found pleasure in tormenting him for several months.

"Give us money," they demanded. He had no money to give. He had long ago distributed it to the people he loved.

Finally they dragged what was left of him to Greenwich for a mock trial.

"Oh, my friends," he implored. "Forsake your idolatry! Embrace Christ! Let him cleanse you from your sins!"

One soldier did.

The Danes were incensed. Would they never silence this voice? Would nothing they did extinguish his dreaded light?

Alphage

They dragged him outside the city and beat his tortured body unmercifully.

Then they beheaded him.

Alphage had given himself first to Christ, then to Christ's people.

How Satan despised such a runner!

How he hated *every* runner!

The race had lasted ten centuries. Still he had devised no torture, no mockery, no method to stop it. He had used ridicule, making the runners a laughingstock before the people. He had used pain, torturing their riddled bodies. He had isolated them in dungeons. He had finally killed them in frustration, only to have them forever out of his reach.

And still valiant runners carried the torch.

Darkness raged, but was no match for their light.

Light was always the victor, even in death.

Chapter 37

Gerard
(Died in 1045)

*So also is the resurrection of the dead. It is sown in
dishonour; it is raised in glory: it is sown in weakness; it
is raised in power.*
I Corinthians 15:42-43

Gerard knew the dangers of the race.

He had loved Christ as a small child. He loved him
still. Nothing the world had to offer attracted him. He
was destined to run.

He read of his Lord's race with a longing in his heart.
He wanted to travel from Veneci to the holy land and
trace his beloved Master's footsteps.

Finally he left Italy to fulfil his dream. Detouring into
Hungary, he met Stephen, the king. A friendship formed
between the two men.

"Stay," Stephen pleaded.

Gerard became the bishop of Chonad.

Stephen's kingdom was overthrown. Violent rivals
fought for the throne. Kings came and went. Finally
Andrew was offered the crown . . but with one condition.

Andrew was eager to meet the condition, whatever it
was. It turned out to be an easy one.

He simply had to abolish Christianity from Hungary.

"Done," agreed Andrew.

Gerard heard the news   He quickly called four
bishops.

"We will go and try to talk to him," he said.

"My God," he prayed as he made his way to the king.
"Use me to persuade King Andrew to stop this violence
against your people!"

He was about to cross the Danube River, when he was
halted by a party of soldiers.

Sneering, they hurled stones at him.

They lifted his bleeding body and beat him unmercifully.

Gerard

Finally they speared him with their lances.

The soldiers grinned, gazing with pleasure at their grisly accomplishment.

"We have finally rid the world of these hateful runners," they bragged.

But the torch would be picked up and carried by other courageous runners, undaunted by persecution, unmoved by the persecutors.

Chapter 38

Stanislaus
(Died in 1079)

Arise, shine; for thy light is come, and the glory of the Lord is risen upon thee. For, behold, the darkness shall cover the earth, and gross darkness the people; but the Lord shall arise upon thee, and his glory shall be seen upon thee.
Isaiah 60:1-2

King Bolislaus shouted furiously at his soldiers, "Kill Stanislaus! I want him dead!"

A malevolent smile curled his lips. How dare Stanislaus warn him that God would judge his crimes if he didn't repent? Was he not the king of Poland? He confessed his sins to no one.

How he hated these insolent torchbearers. He waited impatiently for the news of his death.

The soldiers looked forward to their bloody task. They found the bishop just out of town, all alone in the St. Michael chapel.

He greeted them warmly. They in turn stared at their prey.

Their prey . . .

Gentle, loving Stanislaus.

He had helped so many of them. He had gently taught their children, given liberally to the poor, helped the elderly, nursed the sick, strengthened the weak. He spent his life helping and giving.

The soldiers glanced at his torch, then back at him. They turned as a group and marched back to their king.

He was anxiously waiting to hear the gruesome details of their mission.

He listened in shock as they announced, "We refuse to kill such a man."

His rage turned him purple before their eyes. He stormed violently at them, cursing. Snatching a dagger from the nearest soldier, he ran furiously to the chapel.

146

Stanislaus

Stanislaus was at the altar, kneeling before his King.

Hatred boiled within the king. If no one else would stop this runner, he would! Running to the altar, he plunged the dagger viciously into his heart.

The Psalmist's decree rang out against this pitiful king, even as Stanislaus was crowned with victory in the heavens.

"The kings of the earth set themselves, and the rulers take counsel together, against the Lord, and against his anointed, saying, Let us break their bands asunder, and cast away their cords from us.

He that sitteth in the heavens shall laugh: the Lord shall have them in derision."

Stanislaus was home safe.

His fallen torch would be picked up. All hell had been loosed against Christ and his runners. But all of the forces of earth and hell combined were unable to crush the race.

Yes, some were hurled violently across their finish line, but they were not left there.

Angels gathered them gently in their arms and carried them into the courts of heaven, where a cheering crowd and a loving King welcomed them.

Heaven . . . there they were forever out of reach of depraved men and vile demons.

Satan's vicious hatred accomplished nothing.

For always . . . *without fail* . . . there were more runners that would pick up the fallen torch and begin to run with the despised light.

Satan was finding it impossible to stop this race for it was directed by God Himself.

How he hated the words spoken to him and his diabolical warriors by Tertullian:

"The oftener we are mown down by you, the more in number we grow. The blood of Christians is seed."

Seed.

There was always another crop of Christians springing up from the blood-soaked ground.

The darkness grew black as midnight as the devil dressed his ministers in the robes of Christianity itself.

But still the dreaded light continued to conquer.

In the eleventh century, the torch was carried by Berengarius. He and his followers, the Berengarians, refused to pollute or dilute the message of the gospel. They ignored the counterfeit runners with their empty torches. They just continued to run, fervently, fearlessly, faithfully.

They were followed by Henry of Toulouse and his Henericians. Discarding the bondage of man-made traditions, they held aloft the Scriptures.

"This is the Word given by God," they proclaimed. "Jesus Christ, and Jesus alone, is the Way, the Life, the Truth."

Light banished darkness wherever a runner was found.

It was the twelfth century now . . . and still the race continued.

Ah, yes, the light sometimes grew dim.

But the fire never went out.

For God was in the heavens, conducting his race.

Chapter 39

Dave

*Ye shall be hated of all men for my name's sake: but
he that endureth to the end shall be saved.*
Matthew 10:22

Ron reached out and took Ann's hand.

"Dave," Ron began. "Ann and I have some praying and
confessing to do. The Lord put us in this race, and we
can't just walk away from it when it gets tough. Many of
the runners you told us about didn't even have a
partner."

He smiled at Ann and squeezed her hand gently.

"At least we have one another, Babe."

She nodded as Ron added, "I think I speak for both of
us. We're in this race, for better or worse, for richer or
poorer - right now it seems we're experiencing the poorer
part - and we're going to keep running, no matter what."

He looked at Ann. "Even if it means the death of one
or both of us. I don't mean to be dramatic, but in this
neighborhood, you never know."

Ann nodded again. "I feel the same way."

"Dave," Ron asked. "Are you in a hurry to get
someplace, or do you want to go in the back room and
pray with us?"

About an hour later, Dave left their store.

Ron and Ann stood at the door, their arms around
each other, a smile lighting their faces.

Their torches cast a warm glow over their
neighborhood.

* * * * * * *

Dave was on his way home. He was running past the
park when he noticed Tom with his gang of boys. As soon
as they saw him, obscene filth and curses polluted the
air.

Tom turned toward them savagely with a curse. There
was sudden quiet.

Dave

Dave simply ignored them. He wasn't gaining much headway with Tom. However, it was encouraging that Tom had gone from initiating the harassment to putting a stop to it.

He had shared his food with Tom earlier that morning. That was all he shared. As usual, Tom had eaten the food in sullen silence. Dave spent the time reading his New Testament. He had looked up once and caught Tom staring at him, but he'd scowled and looked quickly away.

He was still thinking about Tom when he turned onto his street. He noticed Uncle Joe's car parked in his driveway and he ran to invite him into his house. The car was empty. Uncle Joe couldn't have gone in the house. It was locked.

He glanced over at Arnolds' yard. He wasn't anywhere in sight. He looked both ways on the street. Then he saw him standing in the window of the Arnolds' house, motioning to him.

Joe opened their door before Dave could knock, his finger to his lips.

"I'll be over soon, Dave, if you're going to be home," he whispered.

"Uncle Joe," Dave whispered back. "What are you doing here?"

"I came over to sit with Ed. He's in a lot of pain, and his wife needed some sleep. Go on now. I'll be over shortly."

"Wait!"

But Uncle Joe closed the door.

By the time he knocked at Dave's door, Dave had the coffee perking.

Dave asked several questions at once.

"How did you know Mr. Arnold was in pain and his wife was exhausted? Were you there to work on their yard? How did you even get in their house?"

Uncle Joe took his time drinking his coffee before answering.

"I just knocked on the door to tell Mrs. Arnold that I was there to work on her yard for my nephew."

"Uncle Joe! She doesn't even know that I work on her yard!"

Uncle Joe smiled.

Dave

"That's what you think. She told me how many hours you have spent there, how hard you work, how much trash you have hauled away. I think she may have calculated the number of leaves you have raked up. She also told me about the prayer you prayed for her husband.

"That's when I said I wasn't much good at praying but I would pray for him too if she liked. She invited me in. He was moaning and restless, but when I finished praying, he was quiet. When I opened my eyes, he was looking straight at me.

"She said, real quiet like, 'I can't believe it.' I looked at her. She looked all done in. So I told her to go and get some rest and I'd sit with him. She wasn't going to do it, but then I told her I was too old for all this yard work you had me doing. I told her that it would be a whole lot easier for me to sit with her husband, and leave the heavy work to you. So . . . she went and took a nap while I sat with Ed."

"How do you know his name is Ed?"

Uncle Joe looked at him strangely. "What do you mean, how do I know? I asked him his name and he told me!"

"You mean he talks?"

"Well, of course he talks! Do you think people lose their voice when they get old?"

"No . . . I mean . . . well . . . he didn't tell me his name."

"I'm sure he didn't. And I'm just as sure you never asked him."

Dave changed the subject.

"How long were you there, Uncle Joe?"

Joe looked at his watch, then quickly stood up.

"Much too long! Most of the day, in fact! I've got to get home!"

"Wait! Just one more thing. Did he stay quieted down after you prayed?"

Joe was already out the door but turned to answer.

"No. He got restless several times."

His uncle had the car running and was ready to leave when Dave asked the next question.

"Did you pray again when he got restless?"

Dave

"You ask too many questions, Son. But if you must know, I read him this."

He patted the New Testament in his shirt pocket.

Dave saw his uncle's car in the Arnolds' driveway often after that day.

He saw other things too . . .

Their drapes were open much of the time now.

More than once, Mrs. Arnold was on the porch rocking in her chair while Uncle Joe sat inside with her husband.

Then there was the beautiful day that Dave ran home early to do some work on their yard. He stopped and stared. Two rockers were going. Between them was a rollaway cot. A shriveled figure lay on it. Dave walked slowly toward the porch, almost hating to interrupt the trio.

His uncle grinned at him. Mrs. Arnold nodded. And Mr. Arnold . . . he didn't even look like the same man. Oh, his body was still shriveled.

But a radiant smile lit his face.

And Jesus looked out from his eyes.

Dave looked from him to Uncle Joe.

Joe was caught off guard, and hoped he had turned his head before Dave saw the tears trickling down his face.

He brushed them roughly away with his sleeve and looked back at Dave. But Dave wasn't looking at his face at all - he was staring at his hand.

For Uncle Joe was finally carrying his torch.

Chapter 40

Dave

Labour not for the meat which perisheth, but for that
meat which endureth unto everlasting life.
John 6:27

"**D**ave! Dave! Please wait for me!"

Dave stopped running and turned around. A young man came running toward him. As he came closer, Dave noticed his expensive jogging suit and tennis shoes. His dark, wavy hair was styled perfectly. He wiped the sweat from his forehead with a monogrammed handkerchief as he reached out to shake Dave's hand. He looked straight into Dave's eyes, and a friendly grin warmed his handsome face.

"Dave, my name is Jim, and I've come to run with you. I was listening as you spoke to the young people at the park the other night. What you said about life and its purpose made a lot of sense to me. I decided I too would follow this Jesus. Please let me run with you!"

Dave liked this young man. He saw in his eyes a sincere desire to follow Christ.

"I would love to have you run with me, Jim!" he answered warmly.

They ran well together. Jim added his vibrant testimony to those they witnessed to. He was as thrilled as Dave was when people responded to the age-old gospel message. But at about 6:00 that evening, Jim said, "Dave, I've got to leave you. I have an appointment at seven that I can't miss. I'll meet you in the morning at ten."

Dave hid his surprise and agreed to meet Jim the following morning.

He was standing at the designated place a little before ten the next morning, when a young woman approached him.

"Are you Dave?" she asked.

"Yes."

Dave

"I am Jim's secretary. He sent me to tell you that he won't be able to run today. A business meeting was called that he can't miss. He asked that you be here this evening at seven."

Dave agreed, without hesitation. He knew Jim had great potential as a runner, and he was willing to adapt his schedule to meet him.

Jim was there early. He met Dave eagerly, anxious to run again.

"Where are we going, Dave? I'm ready to talk about my Lord to anyone who will listen!"

Dave began telling him his plans for the evening, when Jim interrupted.

"Wait, Dave! I can only run for an hour! I have an appointment with a client at 8:30! I've been trying to get a meeting with him for several months. His business will be a big break for me!"

Dave looked into Jim's friendly eyes, and then seemed to look straight into his heart.

"Dave!" Jim cried. "I have to be there!"

"Jim, I want to meet you tomorrow morning at the coffee shop at eight. Please . . . I want you there. You go on to your appointment now.   Don't come with me tonight. We will just get started, and you will have to excuse yourself to leave. I'll see you tomorrow."

Dave stood watching as Jim walked away.

The next morning, Jim was already at a table when Dave entered the coffee shop. He jumped up eagerly when he saw Dave and pumped his hand.

"Dave!" he said, excitement in his voice. "Last night was a turning point in my business! And I was able to witness too! After the man agreed to transfer his business to my firm, I shook his hand and said, 'God bless you, Sir!'"

Dave sat down, and replied, "Sit back down, Jim. I want to tell you about two young men who remind me of you. They wanted to run for Christ too. The first one lived while Jesus was walking the earth. Let me tell you what happened on the day he had a face to face encounter with Jesus Christ . . .

Shouts of "Jesus is here!" reverberated throughout the city.

A woman rushed out of her house and approached a teenage boy.

"Jesus? This Jesus who heals lepers and raises the dead?"

"Yes! Look! He has his twelve with him. The people push and shove just to get close! A mother who ran home to get her baby said that he was blessing children today!"

"Jesus!" a young man breathed.

Without a word to his friends, he began to run down the road. As he got closer, his pace slowed, for many people came from all directions. He made his way through the crowd persistently. He had heard so much about him. He had to talk to him! Finally he made it through the press to Jesus. As he stood staring at him, Jesus suddenly turned and looked fully into his face, his eyes seeming to pierce into his very soul. He radiated light! The young man hadn't planned to bow before him, but somehow he found himself on his knees. He was in awe and barely able to ask the question that had always kept him from having peace of mind and enjoying life to its fullest.

"Good Master," he said, "What good thing shall I do, that I may have eternal life?"

Jesus talked to him for a few minutes. Then he spoke the words that would rob him of peace of mind until his dying day.

"One thing you lack. Go your way! Sell whatever you have, and give to the poor. Then you shall have treasure in heaven! Then come, take up the cross, and follow me!"

The young man could not meet the penetrating eyes of Jesus, for they seemed to light the one dark area of his heart and expose it before everyone. He would give anything to follow this Jesus. Anything . . . but his wealth. It was his security! He had worked so long and so hard for it! Why, of all things, had Jesus demanded this of him? He slowly stood to his feet, turned around, and walked away, his heart nearly overwhelmed with grief. He turned once to look back and saw Jesus still looking at him, an expression of tender love on his face. He didn't look back again.

Jim looked down. His brow was furrowed; his expression troubled. Dave continued.
"Jim, let me tell you now about Waldo . . .

Chapter 41

Waldo

(Ran in the 1100s to about 1217)

*The law of thy mouth is better unto me than
thousands of gold and silver.*
Psalm 119:72

It started out to be just another ordinary day in 1174. Waldo had kept appointments with both wholesalers and retailers. It was business as usual. He loved his active life here in Lyons, France. It was a thriving community, and he had a good working relationship with nearly every store and business in town. Lately, he had been received by the leaders of the city. He hadn't planned to become part of the inner political circle here, but he welcomed the new respect he was given and the influence he was beginning to have among the people.

Then that evening, Jesus came. He spoke quietly to Waldo.

"One thing you lack. Go your way! Sell whatever you have, and give to the poor. Then you shall have treasure in heaven! Then come, take up the cross, and follow me!"

Waldo's heart leaped. Jesus was asking him to give up his earthly wealth and influence to walk with him? There was not even a question or a moment's hesitation in his mind. His possessions would never mean anything to him again! He had come face to face with the priceless Pearl! When Waldo looked into his face, he knew beyond all doubt that he had found the treasure he had been searching for. What did business and politics and money mean, compared to Jesus? Waldo knew in his heart all the earth had to offer would never satisfy him. If he turned and walked away from Jesus, his life would never have meaning again.

He then saw the torch Jesus held. Waldo had learned in business that when opportunity came, it was not wise to hesitate. Life would not be worth living without Jesus.

He reached out for the torch. The expression on Jesus' face brought tears to his eyes. He thought it was alight before! Now his brilliant smile literally filled the entire room with joy!

Waldo smiled back and looked at the torch that he now held in his hand. When he looked back to Jesus, he could no longer see him. But he was here. *He was here!* Never again would he be alone! What a small price to pay! His worldly goods were nothing compared to the awesome presence of Christ!

The flaming torch was still in his hand. He couldn't wait until people got up to begin their day. He decided to go wake up the town! He had a lot of work to do!

He ran throughout the city, giving away everything he owned. He marvelled at how the poor rejoiced as he gave them his possessions. Didn't they know that these material things would never bring the peace and joy they sought? He longed to have this day over, so he could offer everyone the real treasure. He ran into his business and greeted his faithful employees.

"Draw up deeds," he shouted happily. "I'm giving you my business! I have met Jesus!"

When the day was over, Waldo had nothing. His Master would now have to provide for him. He was happier than he had ever been in his entire life. In fact, he couldn't quit smiling. What an uproar he had caused in Lyons! He knew that his relatives and friends were convinced he was crazy, even though they had been careful not to express their opinions to him. They didn't want him to change his mind about giving away his wealth until they owned a piece of it!

He had given some of his money to a printing company, commissioning it to translate several books of the Bible from Latin to French Provencal. He wanted plenty of Bibles on hand to give away!

He opened his Bible now to his favorite passage. He had read these words of Jesus many times before, but tonight he could almost see Jesus sitting on the mountain, enjoying the view, and then turning to smile at his disciples and teaching them his ways.

"Blessed are the poor in spirit . . . "

Waldo

Waldo was richly blessed!

"Let your light so shine before men . . . "
He glanced at his torch.

"Give to him that asks you, and from him that would borrow of you, turn not away."
Waldo smiled. He planned to spend the rest of his life giving to those in need.

"Where your treasure is, there will your heart be also."
His treasure was Jesus now. He would seek nothing or no one else.

"Take no thought for your life, what you shall eat, or what you shall drink; nor yet for your body, what you shall put on."
Waldo knew that everyone who had joined this race had been provided for. Why should he worry? His Lord would take care of him! He was a runner now!

The following day, Waldo ran through Lyons. One friend approached him warily.
"Waldo! What has happened to you? The things I heard . . .they're not true, are they?"
Waldo's face lit with a smile.
"I have decided to live by the words of the Gospel. I am going to live the Sermon on the Mount and the Commandments of Jesus Christ! I will live for my Lord in poverty. For the first time in my life, I will have absolutely no concern for tomorrow!"
A crowd gathered around them, and Waldo told them of his encounter with Christ, mixing with his testimony the Scriptures that meant so much to him.
When he saw the hunger in their eyes, he said, "Won't you repent of your sins, and turn to Jesus Christ, and be saved?"
While some bowed in prayer, repenting of their sins and receiving Jesus as their Lord and Savior, one man broke away from the group and rushed to report Waldo to the Archbishop.

"Waldo is in the streets, preaching the gospel in public!"

"He'll get over this," the Archbishop replied. "I've heard that he has been carried away by his excitement."

Waldo continued to walk the streets, talking, sharing, preaching.

"This has to be stopped," the Archbishop finally decided.

He sent for Waldo.

"I am warning you to stop your preaching! You have no right to speak of Jesus to the people. You are not ordained by the Church to speak the Word!"

But even as he was speaking, Waldo was looking not upon him, but upon the face of his Lord. He smiled, and then lowered his eyes to face his accuser.

"It is better to obey God, rather than man," he answered simply. Then he returned to the streets to proclaim the gospel to men, women and children.

Waldo did not intend to oppose the Church. He did not plan to found another sect. Nor did he wish to build himself a name or gain a following. He had no new revelations to share. He merely wanted to live as Jesus told his followers to live. He continued to run.

Again he was called before the Archbishop.

"Do you still not understand that only the clergy has the right to preach? I have told you that the Church alone can give a man authority to preach, and you have been given no such power!"

Waldo met his eyes steadily. His voice was polite but firm, as he replied, "I preach the Gospel, not because the Church has commissioned me, but because Christ has commissioned me."

The Archbishop seemed to undergo a transformation right before Waldo's eyes. Rage and raw hatred contorted his features.

He spoke in a low voice, through clenched teeth.

"Then get out of my city! And don't *ever* enter Lyons again! You are excommunicated from the Church! You and your followers are nothing but heretics!"

Years later, a police report was found among the church documents in Carcassone, France. Perhaps the voice of one of Waldo's enemies will most clearly portray his life.

> Waldo was a rich man but, abandoning all his wealth, he determined to observe a life of poverty and evangelical perfection, as the Apostles. He arranged for the Gospels and some other books of the Bible to be translated in common speech. Infatuated with himself, he presumes to preach the Gospel in the streets, where he made many disciples, and involving them, both men and women, has sent them out, in turn, to preach.
>
> These people, ignorant and illiterate, went about through the towns, entering houses and even churches, spreading many errors round about. The Archbishop of Lyons had forbidden such presumption, but they by no means wished to obey him, cloaking their madness by saying that they must obey God rather than men, since God had commanded the Apostles to preach the Gospel to every creature.
>
> Because of this disobedience and their undertaking a task which did not pertain to them, they were excommunicated and expelled from their country.

So light spread throughout the land. Many runners, banished from France, settled in the Alps of Italy. They chose to live their lives as the one who led them to Christ, simply living Christ's sermon given to his disciples on the mountain.

As the world hated Jesus and his disciples, neither will it endure anyone who follows their example. Many *"Waldensians"* were cruelly massacred. But in spite of massive extermination campaigns to rid the earth of those who followed Waldo's example of following Christ, the chain of souls born into the kingdom of God through his ministry has survived for over 800 years.

Chapter 42

Dave

How long halt ye between two opinions? if the Lord be God, follow him.
I Kings 18:21

Jim was silent for several moments after Dave finished. He still looked down, not wanting to meet Dave's eyes.

"Jim," Dave said softly. "You need to make a decision. Our Lord told us clearly that we would not be able to serve God and mammon. Mammon is the wealth of this world. But mammon is even more than that, Jim. It's the personification of money. It's a god of this world with seducing and enticing power, compelling people to give their entire lives to it, rather than to Christ.

"The first young man chose to serve Mammon. He made the wrong choice, Jim. All the lands and riches that he accumulated in his lifetime are now either buried under mountains of rubble or owned by someone else.

"Waldo forsook Mammon, took the torch and ran for Christ. His treasures are still accumulating today. He is rich for eternity.

"Jim, you alone can make the decision whom you will follow. Christ demands one thing of his torch-bearers. He requires each one of them to love and follow him, with all their heart, with all their soul, with all their mind, and with all their strength."

Dave stood up and laid his hand on Jim's shoulder. "I'll pray for you, Jim. You would make a great runner."

"Thanks, Dave," Jim mumbled, but remained sitting with his head bowed as Dave left to resume his run.

"Oh, God," Dave breathed, "may Jim see through the deceptive outer splendor of Mammon to its inner rottenness. May he one day say like Paul, 'I have suffered the loss of all things and do count them but dung, that I may win Christ!'"

* * * * * * *

Dave

The campus lay in darkness. Dave noticed only one glow of light to the right.

He had planned to bring Jim along. As usual, he was alone.

He knocked on the dorm door, wondering which one of Phil's friends would answer.

He was shocked to see that it was Ray, the one who sneered more than the others the night he had visited Phil.

He was more shocked by the cold reception.

He extended his hand and said, "Phil called and said you wanted me to come talk with you."

Ray ignored his hand and shrugged.

"I wouldn't put it exactly like that. I made a few comments after you left. Phil told me to shut up about you and your torch. This morning I said something that set him off. He stormed out the door and told me you would be here to talk to me tonight. I was going to leave but couldn't think of anyplace to go that interested me."

Dave sighed. He didn't know whether to stay or leave.

"What kind of comments were you making?"

"Oh, nothing to get all riled up about. All I said this morning is that at least Dave has something to live for."

He shrugged and made a half-hearted attempt to smile. Dave thought he looked better with his perpetual sneer.

Dave decided to stay.

"Do you want me to talk, Ray? Or do you want to question me?"

"Neither, really. But since you're here, I do have one question. It's bad enough for an Olympic champion who has everything going for him to run around waving a torch. But that old book you're carrying - that's too much."

Dave looked at his Bible, then at Ray.

"What is your honest opinion about this old book?"

"I told you before. It's an antique. It's irrelevant to life. It's meaningless to me. So what's your opinion of it?"

"It's the Word of God."

"Oh, come on, Dave! Do you believe God sent the book from heaven on the wings of an angel?"

"I realize my belief that God anointed men to write a message to his creation brands me as a fool in your mind. I also realize I wouldn't be sitting here with you if you had all the answers to life. You're still searching for truth. You're right about one thing. I have found life worth living. And I found the answers in the pages of this book."

Ray laughed. "You're a fool."

Dave smiled. "Yes . . . one of many. If you don't mind, I'll name a few."

"Go ahead. Rattle off your list of old ladies, prissy girls and feeble-minded men."

Dave ignored his comment as he removed a paper from the back of his Bible.

"I'll read these quotes so they will be accurate.

George Washington said,

It is impossible to rightly govern the world without God and the Bible.

John Quincy Adams agreed with him. He said,

So great is my veneration of the Bible, that the earlier my children begin to read it the more confident will be my hope that they will prove useful citizens of their country and respectable members of society.

"A friend of Andrew Jackson asked for his opinion of the Bible. He answered,

That book, Sir, is the rock on which our republic rests.

"Was Abraham Lincoln a fool? Hear his words.

I believe the Bible is the best gift God has ever given to man. All the good from the Savior of the world is communicated to us through this book.

"Horace Greeley recommended the Bible, saying,

It is impossible to mentally or socially enslave a Bible-reading people. The principles of the Bible are the groundwork of human freedom.

"Woodrow Wilson asked the audience he was addressing to make a commitment to read the Bible every day.

I ask every man and woman in this audience that from this day on they will realize that part of the destiny of America lies in their daily perusal of this great book.

"Douglas MacArthur ended every day by reading the Bible. Listen to his words:

Believe me, Sir, never a night goes by, be I ever so tired, but I read the Word of God before I go to bed.

"Herbert Hoover joins the others in his praise of the book:

The whole of the inspiration of our civilization springs from the teachings of Christ and the lessons of the Prophets. To read the Bible for these fundamentals is a necessity of American life.

Benjamin Franklin adds his counsel:

Young man, my advice to you is that you cultivate an acquaintance with, and a firm belief in, the Holy Scriptures.

"Next in the lineup of old women, prissy girls and feeble-minded men are the founders of Yale, Princeton and Harvard.

"Yale College was granted a new charter in 1745. There was nothing peculiar about reading the Bible then. Included in its regulations were these words:

If any scholar shall deny the Holy Scriptures or any part of them to be the Word of God, or be guilty of heresy or any error directly tending to subvert the fundamentals of Christianity, and continuing obstinate therein after the first and second admonition, he shall be expelled.

All scholars shall live religious, godly, and blameless lives according to the rules of God's Word, diligently reading the Holy Scriptures, the fountain of light and truth . . .

That the president, or in his absence one of the tutors, shall constantly pray in the college hall every morning and evening, and shall read a chapter or suitable portion of the Holy Scriptures . . .

"Princeton's first president, John Witherspoon, said:

Cursed be all learning that is contrary to the cross of Christ.

Cursed be all learning that is not coincident with the cross of Christ.

Cursed be all learning that is not subservient to the cross of Christ.

"Harvard University clarified its main educational priority in its Rules and Precepts adopted in 1646:

(1) Every one shall consider the main end of his life and studies to know God and Jesus Christ which is eternal life.

(2) Seeing the Lord giveth wisdom, every one shall seriously by prayer in secret seek wisdom of him.

(3) Every one shall so exercise himself in reading the Scriptures twice a day that they be ready to give an account of their proficiency therein, both in theoretical observations of languages and logic, and in practical and spiritual truths."

Dave replaced the paper and looked straight at Ray.

"Isn't it amazing in the light of that lineup that America has forbidden the Bible to be read in its schools?"

He paused reflectively.

"Ray, only governments that wish to enslave its people despise this book. Confiscation of the Bible was one of the first things on the Communist agenda to enslave a people. It's rather frightening to me that America's Supreme Court has declared it illegal for a teacher to even place one on his desk!"

Dave tapped his Bible with his forefinger.

"It may surprise you to know that in past centuries men and women alike were not only excommunicated, but strangled, imprisoned and burned at the stake . . . not by the government, but by the church . . . simply for translating and distributing the Bible! Tell me . . . why this hatred and fear for what you refer to as just 'another old book?'

"Let me introduce you to a brilliant scholar who held his doctorate from Oxford University. John Wyclif was hated so intensely by his enemies that they referred to him as the child of the devil . . . "

Chapter 43

John Wyclif
(About 1334-1384)

And the Lord answered me, and said, Write the vision, and make it plain upon tables, that he may run that readeth it.
Habakkuk 2:2

The light of the word of God did not shine on the path of the masses of England in that day. The only Word they could know was that chosen by their priests to give to them.

Out of this gripping darkness stepped a tall thin scholar, clothed in a long black gown and a girdle about his body. He had a full, flowing beard, and his eyes were clear and penetrating. His appearance was one of lofty earnestness, dignity and character. And John Wyclif carried a torch.

People gasped as he emerged from the shadows. For Oxford University was Europe's most outstanding university in the 14th Century, and John Wyclif, having studied for sixteen years to obtain his Doctorate of Divinity, was its leading theologian and philosopher.

Born in 1330, this Catholic priest had one consuming goal. He loved his Christ, and he had become acquainted with him through the Scriptures. He wanted everyone to be able to feast on the Word of God!

He wrote, "The Bible is necessary for all men, not for priests alone. It alone is the supreme law that is to rule Church, State, and Christian life, without human traditions and statutes."

His purpose was met with the fury of the church!

"Heresy!" was the outcry.

John ignored the threats and sat down at his desk. He opened his Latin Bible, a hand written copy of a thousand year old translation. There were no verse numbers. He faced his awesome task with anticipation.

John Wyclif

Dipping his pen into ink, he began to write the first Bible in the English language.

Waiting outside were men, their own torches burning, ready to take the Word of God throughout the countryside. They were committed to their task, preparing to spend their life living and dressing simply, preaching wherever there was even one to hear them. John kept at his work diligently, pausing only long enough to distribute to these itinerant preachers portions of the Word.

The leaders of the Church were stunned.

A Catholic chronicler, Henry Knighton, began to fight John viciously with his pen and ink.

"Christ gave his gospel to the clergy and the learned doctors of the Church so that they might give it to the laity and to weaker persons, according to the message of the season and personal need. But this Master John Wyclif translated the Gospel from Latin into the English, making it the property of the masses and common to all and more open to the laity, and even to women who were able to read! The pearl of the Gospel is thrown before swine and trodden underfoot . . . What used to be the highest gift of the clergy and the learned members of the Church has become common to the laity!"

The light of God's Word had begun to spread, and no man and no church could quench the fire.

People received the Bible hungrily, devouring the Word of God. John Wyclif was summoned to London to answer the charges of heresy. Pope Gregory XI denounced him.

He was expelled from his teaching position at Oxford University.

He kept writing.

Along with his translation of the Bible, he wrote that the Head of the Church was Christ, not man. He stressed the need for renewed spiritual life through the teachings of Christ. He preached that each individual needed a direct relationship to God through Jesus Christ.

He clashed with the church, declaring that every Christian had the right to know the Bible. He longed for the day that every Christian would understand that Christ alone is the way of salvation.

Pope Gregory XI described him as "a deadly pest who must be plucked up by the roots, who hath gone to such a pitch of detestable folly, that he feareth not to teach, and publicly preach, or rather to vomit out of the filthy dungeon of his breast false conclusions!"

Wyclif, ignoring the avalanche of accusations raging against him, wrote a tract in English for his followers to distribute.

A Short Rule of Life

First, when you are fully awake, think upon the goodness of your God . . .

Second, think on the great sufferings and willing death that Christ suffered for mankind.

Third, think how God has saved you from death and other mischief. And for this goodness and mercy, thank God with all your heart. Pray him to give you grace to spend in that day, and evermore, all the powers of your soul (as mind, understanding, reason, and will) and all the powers of your body (as strength, beauty, and your five senses) in his service and worship, and in nothing against his commandments, but in ready performance of his works of mercy, and to give good example of holy life, both in word and deed, to all men about you.

Be well occupied, and no idle time, for the danger of temptation.

Besides this, do right and equity to all men, your superiors, equals, and subjects, or servants; and stir all to love truth, mercy, true peace, and charity; and help all people to be in harmony with one another.

Most of all, fear God and his wrath; love God and his law, and his worship: and ask not principally for worldly reward, but maintain a virtuous life.

At the end of the day, think about how you have offended God, and amend it while you may. And think how graciously God has saved you; not for your desert, but for his own mercy and goodness. And pray for grace that you may dwell and end in his true and holy service, and real love, and according to your skill, to teach others to do the same.

"Preaching," Wyclif explained to his followers, "is to spread God's Scriptures!"

When people of his parish came to this priest, he counselled, "It is not confession to man but to God, who is the true Priest of souls, that is the great need of sinful man. Private confession and the whole system of medieval confession was not ordered by Christ and was not used by the Apostles, for of the three thousand who were turned to Christ's Law on the Day of Pentecost, not one of them was confessed to a priest! It is God who is the forgiver!"

People gathered from all walks of life to receive the Word from this torchbearer.

"What of our faith?" one cried out of the crowd gathered to hear him preach.

Wyclif turned to him. "Trust wholly in Christ; rely altogether on his sufferings; beware of seeking to be justified in any other way than by His righteousness. Faith in our Lord Jesus Christ is sufficient for salvation."

Wyclif crossed his finish line at home in bed on New Year's Eve. He had completed his task. He laid his torch down joyfully, knowing that its light was spreading throughout his country, lighting both huts and mansions.

While John Wyclif rested from his labors with the Lord he loved and served, his enemies had no rest. The Archbishop of Canterbury fumed: "That pestilent and most wretched John Wyclif, of damnable memory, a child of the old devil, and himself a child or pupil of Antichrist, who, while he lived, walking in the vanity of his mind . . . crowned his wickedness by translating the Scriptures into the mother tongue!"

His hatred for John Wyclif consumed him. Everywhere the Word of God was being read and preached! Doctrines taught by the church but not found in the Scriptures were no longer passively accepted.

He summoned a council meeting of clergymen, and in 1408 this decree was published:

John Wyclif

"We decree and ordain that no one shall in future translate on his authority any text of Scripture into the English tongue or into any other tongue, by way of book, booklet, or treatise. Nor shall any man read, in public or in private, this kind of book, booklet, or treatise, now recently composed in the time of the said John Wyclif under penalty of the greater excommunication."

Hatred against his memory intensified as men, both rich and poor, discovered in the Bible that they too could be runners who carried the torch for Christ! Light was being turned on everywhere, exposing the greed and lust for power of corrupt leaders.

"John Wyclif must be condemned as a heretic!" demanded those who vainly attempted to put out the embers from his torch.

Thirty-one years after John Wyclif died, he was condemned as a heretic at the Council of Constance on 260 different counts.

"Burn his writings!" came the order. "Exhume his bones! Cast them out of consecrated ground!"

His body was dug up and banished to ground unsanctified by the Church.

But still his enemies were not satisfied.

Thirteen years later, nearly half a century after John Wycliffe's death, the Pope gave the command to dig up his remains the second time, burn them, and scatter the ashes into the little river *Swift*.

Men rushed to carry out his order. But the burning of his body did nothing to extinguish the light his torch had brought to the world.

The historian, Fuller, contemplated John Wycliffe's life and death, thinking about the waters carrying Wycliffe's ashes throughout the world. Then he smiled, as he thought about the Word of God now bringing light throughout a dark world. Another one of heaven's great runners had finished a great race. He wrote:

"They burnt his bones to ashes and cast them into the Swift, a neighboring brook running hard by. Thus the brook hath conveyed his ashes into Avon; Avon into Severn; Severn into the narrow seas; and they into the main ocean. And thus the ashes of Wyclif are the emblem of his doctrine which now is dispersed the world over."

The fires that destroyed John Wycliffe's body were unable to destroy his writings. For those who hungered to hear God's Word were running with them, dispersing them throughout the land. Some would find their way into Prague, Czechoslovakia, where they would burn their way into the heart of another John, a priest who would become a heroic runner in this unceasing race.

Chapter 44

Dave

Many pastors have destroyed my vineyard, they have trodden my portion under foot, they have made my pleasant portion a desolate wilderness. For the pastors are become brutish, and have not sought the Lord.
Jeremiah 12:10 and 10:21

Ray shrugged. "I don't understand. I thought it was the church that pushed the Bible on the rest of the world. Now you're telling me that the church outlawed it."

Dave prayed silently for wisdom to explain.

"Ray, there is *the* church . . . . and then there is *a* church. Wyclif was part of the true church, founded by Christ himself. He loved and taught the Scriptures - and he carried a torch.

"Then there is another church. A government can exist to serve its people or to enslave its people. A church can also either serve or enslave its people. Do you remember Horace Greely's words? *He said:*

'It is impossible to mentally or socially enslave a Bible-reading people. The principles of the Bible are the groundwork of human freedom.' "

Dave opened his Bible. Jesus said:

If you continue in my word, then are you my disciples indeed; and you shall know the truth, and the truth shall make you free.

He looked at Ray.

"Now do you see, Ray, why the government or the church that desires to enslave its people despises the Bible?

"When a government or church begins to attack the Bible and writes laws against it, it has marked itself as an institution whose ultimate desire is to totally dominate its people. Any man who dares to go among the people of that church or nation with the Bible will be marked for destruction.

173

"Thank God for brave men who were willing to incur the wrath of tyrannical leaders. They blazed a path of freedom for future runners.

"John Hus was one who gave the ultimate sacrifice at the hands of cruel and sadistic men . . . "

Chapter 45

John Hus
(1372 to 1415)

Princes have persecuted me without a cause: but my heart standeth in awe of thy word.
Psalm 119:161

John Hus looked across the multitude and felt pity for them. They wouldn't have much longer to wait for the sport of seeing his body consumed by fire, for wood and straw were even now being piled around his feet and his legs.

Today was his forty-third birthday. Events of his life flashed before him.

He was born in 1369 in a village in *Bohemia. His parents were not wealthy, but they were determined he would be well educated. Teachers and professors in both the private school he attended and the University of Prague were impressed by their brilliant young scholar. He received his Bachelor of Divinity degree and became the pastor of the Bethlehem Chapel and the dean and rector of the prestigious University of Prague. It was then that his life had begun to change - for it was then that he began reading Scriptures and messages distributed by Wyclif. And they began to burn their way into his soul.

He saw sin as God saw it, in all its raw ugliness. He looked within his heart and recoiled in horror, for it fit Jeremiah's description, *"The heart is deceitful above all things, and desperately wicked."*

"God," he cried. "I am a sinner in need of a Savior!" And God lifted his sins from him and clothed him in the righteousness of His only begotten Son.

His congregation, faculty, and students gasped as they saw their pastor and dean running toward them, lighting both the church and the campus with his presence. He preached with authority, his message now the life-changing, sin-cleansing Gospel of Jesus Christ.

175

The truth of Psalm 119:9 had become reality in the life of John Hus: *"Wherewithal shall a young man cleanse his way? by taking heed thereto according to thy word."*

The Archbishop of Prague stared at this new runner. "How dare Hus bring the Scriptures and Wycliffe's heresy into my jurisdiction?" he raged. "He must be silenced! Send out a decree! Suppress by any means possible the further spreading of Wycliffe's writings!"

Students and faculty alike reacted to the decree in outrage. They called a meeting to decide what to do.

"We will not give up the Scriptures," they decided. "We will instead increase our efforts to circulate them!"

"For who is the one," they reasoned, "who would dare confiscate the letters written by a king to his queen? The Bible is a letter written by the Lord God, the KING of Kings, to His bride! How dare man confiscate God's letter to His beloved?"

Hus joined their cry, informing the Archbishop, "You are putting unlawful bonds upon the Word of God!"

The Archbishop responded in fury.

"Wycliffe's writings and Scripture translations are condemned," he declared. "I want all his writings delivered to me. Anyone who refuses to deliver any copies in their possession will henceforth be forbidden to preach in any church!"

John refused to give up his Scriptures and Wycliffe's messages.

"Why do you insist on reading the writings of Wyclif, the heretic?" he was asked by the infuriated Archbishop.

John Hus answered calmly, "I am attracted by his writings, in which he expends every effort to conduct all men back to the law of Christ, and especially the clergy, inviting them to let go pomp and dominion of the world, and to live, like the apostles, according to the law of Christ. I am attracted by the love he has for the law of Christ, maintaining its truth and holding that in no point can it prove to be false."

"Then you will no longer preach at Bethlehem Chapel - or anywhere," came the reply.

John remembered the apostles facing authorities of their day, fourteen hundred years earlier. They too had been commanded to quit preaching the Gospel of Jesus

John Hus

Christ. Their stand gave John courage, for they had answered their accusers, "Whether it be right in the sight of God to hearken unto you more than unto God, you judge. For we cannot but speak the things which we have seen and heard."

John Hus would follow their example.

When he was excommunicated from the church, he moved to the village of his birth where he continued to run - preaching, writing, distributing the Gospel message. For what man can stop the race God Himself had established? And what runner, commissioned by God, dare take orders from mere men?

He was watched constantly by his enemies. They called a meeting of the General Council in 1414, and summoned John to Constance, Germany.

His friends, concerned for his safety, pleaded with the Emperor on his behalf, "John Hus needs a letter from you, assuring him of his safety. He will not be allowed to return home without it."

The Emperor called for his scribe and dictated,

> "Receive the honorable man, Master John Hus, whom we have taken under our protection and safeguard, and under that of the Empire. When he arrives among you, receive him kindly and treat him favorably. Let him freely and securely pass, sojourn, stop, and return."

John's friends were elated and ran to give him the Emperor's letter. John read it, then looked at the friends surrounding him. He appreciated their efforts, but the letter he held in his heart was the only one that truly assured his safety. For it was written by the King of Kings and Lord of Lords, and read, *"I will never leave you nor forsake you. Lo, I am with you alway, even unto the end of the world."*

John knew in his heart he would not return from Germany, but would die there for his Lord. No earthly Emperor could see him safely through the portals of death, but Jesus would. He alone gave him comfort.

As he made his way to Germany, he was amazed to see the streets and roads lined with people, honoring him, praying for him.

"I thought I had been an outcast," he told his fellow travelers. "But I now see my worst friends are in Bohemia."

His adversaries had reached Constance before him, and were already at work, poisoning the minds of those who would judge him.

Guards were stationed to await his arrival. As they watched the road, they saw in the distance a runner approaching, his torch shining brightly. They arrested him as soon as he reached them. He offered no resistance, but his companions cried, "Look at this letter from the Emperor! This man is not to be arrested!"

The guards looked at one another, confused by two conflicting orders.

"We will lock him in a palace chamber," they decided. "Then we will show this letter to the proper authorities."

They took it to the Pope. He scarcely glanced at it before dismissing it with a wave of his hand. "I am not bound to the pledge of the Emperor," he scoffed.

John was taken before the Council, where he spoke fearlessly. The members of the Council jeered loudly, drowning out the message they hated. John ignored their derision and calmly continued proclaiming the Word of God, not regarding the fact that it was branding him a heretic in their eyes.

"Union with Jesus Christ is the essential condition of membership in His church," he proclaimed. "For Christ alone is the Head of the church."

"Heresy," the mockers screamed.

"The Scriptures are our only source of truth," he replied with composure.

"Oh!" answered one Council member. "So you will obey the apostolic commands?"

"I surely will," John agreed.

Then he looked his accusers in the eye unflinchingly and added, "Understand me, Gentlemen! I term the doctrine of Christ's apostles the only true apostolic commands! So far as the commands of the Pope of Rome agree with that doctrine and those commands, I am willing to obey them gladly; but when I see the contrary, I shall not obey, even if you place before me fire to consume my body."

"Take him to the dungeon," the men yelled.

He was grabbed and dragged to a foul dungeon. The guards opened the door and threw him in, closing it quickly to escape the awful stench. They left John there for days. John was only forty-six years of age, but no man could retain his health in such rancid living conditions.

His body deteriorated rapidly. It wasn't long before his imminent death was reported by the guards to their superiors.

"Move him to a better cell," they ordered. "He needs to be kept alive for his execution."

Shortly afterward, his trial began. The Council had met earlier to plot their strategy.

"We must prevent Hus from speaking, for he will continue to quote Scripture," they declared.

For this was to be Hus's trial, not their own, and God's Word somehow condemned them, rather than him. They had to reach a verdict swiftly and condemn Hus to death. They must force him to be silent.

They dressed John in priestly garments and a chalice was given to him to hold. He was brought into the room and seated before the Council.

A bishop thrust documents into his hands.

"These are your teachings," he was told. "We will read them aloud. Then you will be given the opportunity to retract them or approve them."

John listened in shock as the Articles were read. Heresy had been filtered in with the Scriptural teachings. He was given no opportunity to differentiate between the false and the true.

He tried to interject a few sentences at intervals during the reading but was sharply reproved.

When the reading was completed, his judges looked upon him sternly. "Retract or acknowledge these Articles!" he was commanded.

John did not dare to denounce the Articles, as some were the truths of the Scriptures. Neither did he dare agree with them, as many of the Articles were outright lies.

He lifted his head to face his accusers.

"I refuse to denounce the Articles," he stated.

"Then you are condemned to die," came the verdict.

John fell to his knees when he heard his sentence and prayed, "Lord Jesus Christ! Pardon all my enemies, I pray, for the sake of Your great mercy. You know that they have falsely accused me, brought forward false witnesses, and concocted false articles against me. Pardon them for the sake of your infinite mercy."

The Council grew even angrier as John prayed. They looked on this man they were unable to dominate and his torch they were unable to extinguish.

"Strip him of his priestly garments!" they screamed. "Remove the chalice from his cursed hand!"

As a bishop grabbed the chalice from his hand, he spoke to John furiously, "We take from thee, accursed Judas, the cup of salvation."

John replied fervently, "I trust in God, my Almighty Father. He will not take from me the cup of his salvation, and I have a steadfast hope that I shall yet today drink it in his kingdom."

The council was enraged. How could they humiliate this man?

They called for paper, painted devils on it, fashioned it into a miter, and then inscribed on it, **"A Ringleader Of Heretics."**

John smiled as they placed it upon his head. He turned toward the laughing Council, but their sneers died abruptly as he said, "My Lord Jesus Christ, for my sake, did wear a crown of thorns; why should not I then, for His sake, again wear this light crown, be it ever so ignominious? Truly I will do it, and that willingly."

The bishop was infuriated. The time he had longed for was at hand. He snarled, "Now we commit thy soul unto the devil."

"But I," John answered, his eyes lifted toward heaven, "do commend into Thy hands, O Lord Jesus Christ, my spirit which Thou hast redeemed."

He had been dragged mercilessly to the stake and secured to it with a rusty chain. Even then he had smiled. "My Lord Jesus Christ was bound with a harder chain than this for my sake," he said, "and why then should I be ashamed of this rusty one?"

The time had come for John Hus to cross his finish line. His race was nearly finished. He had blazed a trail for others to follow in life. He must now blaze a trail that future runners could follow in death.

His thoughts returned to the present. The wood and straw were piled up to his neck now.

If he had known his life would end like this, would he change the way he had lived, alter the message he had preached? No, he would live as he had lived, preach as he had preached, run as he had run, carry the torch regardless of whom it offended.

He turned his attention to the man standing before him.

"Abjure!" he was demanding of him. "Abandon your beliefs!"

"No," John answered, without hesitation. "What I taught with my lips, I now seal with my blood."

The wood and straw were set aflame, and a hush settled over the crowd. They listened intently to the crackling of the fire. What was this they heard? Their minds could scarcely comprehend what their ears were hearing. For John Hus was loudly and cheerfully singing a hymn.

Would this heretic never be silenced?

Finally the singing stopped as the fire of his torch mingled with the flames that consumed his body.

His enemies looked upon the pile of ashes, and they couldn't stand the sight of anything that remained of this runner.

"Gather his ashes together!" they commanded. "Cast them into the River Rhine!"

They left then, but somehow they did not feel the victory they had anticipated. Yes, the earth was rid of one more torch-bearer. But would the joyful hymn he had sung as fire consumed his body ever quit echoing in their minds?

Chapter 46

Dave

*I send unto you prophets, and wise men, and scribes:
and some of them ye shall kill and crucify; and some of
them shall ye scourge in your synagogues, and persecute
them from city to city.*
Matthew 23:34

Dave glanced at Ray - and looked again. He had decided his sneer was permanent, but now it was replaced with anger.

Ray spoke with a controlled voice that seethed with fury.

"How dare the church treat its own runner that way?"

"I told you, Ray. There is a church whose only desire is to enslave its people. God's true people are here only to serve."

Dave paused, then said, "Perhaps you will understand better if I tell you about a mighty preacher by the name of Girolamo Savonarola. The church leaders could think of only one way to stop his scathing sermons. For stop him they must. His finger pointed straight at their corruption."

Chapter 47

Girolamo Savonarola
(1452 to 1498)

And when they had left their gods there, David gave a commandment, and they were burned with fire.
I Chronicles 14:12

The visitor in Florence, Italy walked toward the sound of singing. He didn't know what was going on, but he aimed to find out. Ever since his arrival, people were rushing about. Many carried clothing and furniture. Was this whole city moving?

He found the mob at the main square, placing their things at the foot of a giant wooden pyramid. It was a happy crowd, alternately talking and singing.

He pushed through them for a closer look at the piles heaped around the pyramid. There were cards, carved gaming tables, a few books, dresses, wigs, paintings, jewelry, and many pornographic pictures.

He stepped back just as a song ended.

Young men torched the straw - and it exploded. He discovered later it was laced with gunpowder. The mob cheered as the structure and their possessions burned.

"What is going on here?" he asked the man next to him.

"We are *Burning our Vanities*," he replied, looking at him closely. "You must not be from here. We have these often since Savonarola became the Prior of St. Mark's."

The stranger smiled.

So this was the work of Savonarola.

The friars had never heard such a scorching sermon.

"Repent! If Italy does not repent, terrible catastrophes will befall us! God *will* pour out his wrath upon this sinful and wicked country!

"We are governed by tyrants who heap abuse on the poor.

"People have replaced the worship of God with humanistic paganism! It has corrupted our manners, our art, our poetry . . . and yes, even our religion!

"The Roman Court is vile! Its only concern is its power and wealth. The gold and silver hoarded by the church should be sold to feed the poor!

"And the *Pope!* His private life is *scandalous!*"

A shock rippled through the congregation of friars. It was common knowledge that Pope Alexander VI was corrupt. It was obvious to everyone that he cared nothing about spiritual matters. He sought only the world, with its pleasures and fortunes. Pope Alexander didn't even attempt to hide his enormous wealth or all the children he had fathered.

One scandal would scarcely be over before another one would begin. News of his depravity had rocked the church at first. Now the people scarcely noticed.

Yet . . . how dare Savonarola denounce *the Pope?*

Had he gone too far this time? His words would surely reach Rome. The Pope would be enraged. Had Savonarola forgotten the Unam Sanctum of 1302 - *Every human being is subject to the Pontiff of Rome?* Did Savonarola not know the meaning of the three tiered crown . . . the lower tier signifying his rule over departed souls in hell, the middle tier signifying his rule over all souls on earth, and the top tier showing he also ruled over all the souls in heaven?

Savonarola was unimpressed.

"The church desperately needs reforming," he continued to preach fearlessly.

He paused in his sermon to talk to God.

"My Lord," he cried. "As a child I have not been able to suffer the blind wickedness of the peoples of Italy! Our only hope is for you to intervene. Chastise us with your scourge!"

He remained silent a moment, then looked at the friars and prophesied.

"The church will be scourged.

"Following its scourging, the church will be renewed."

The Pope issued him a brief, forbidding him to preach. Ignoring it, he taught the books of Ruth, Micah and Ezekiel.

He further incurred the wrath of the church by selling much of its property. He sent friars out to distribute the proceeds to the poor.

"The friars under Savonarola are so different than they used to be," the people remarked. "They are living like holy men. They are truly servants of God!"

Government officials discussed ways to stop his preaching. They gathered the rabble and incited sacrilegious riots against him. Absorbed in his Bible study and prayer, he paid no attention to them.

He began a series of sermons from Exodus, preparing his congregation for his own exit from the world.

His departure came swiftly. He was seized like a common criminal. A commission of his worst enemies was appointed to examine him by savage torture. As blood poured from his wounds, he remembered the offer he had spurned.

The church had decided to stop his rebukes by promoting him to a cardinal.

"We will give you the red hat," they bribed.

"A red hat?" he had scoffed. "I want a hat of blood."

He had one now. He would not exchange it for all that the world or a corrupt church had to offer.

Unable to find sufficient evidence to brand him a heretic, they falsified records to charge him with crimes.

They hanged his broken and bruised body, then burned his remains. Dumping his ashes in the river, they heaved a sigh of relief.

Savonarola's detestable sermons would be heard no more.

But future generations would have reason to remember his prophecy.

"The church will be scourged.

"Following its scourging, the church will be renewed."

Chapter 48

Dave

They kept not the covenant of God, and refused to walk in his law. The nation that will not serve thee shall perish; yea, those nations shall be utterly wasted.

Psalm 78:10
Isaiah 60:12

"**A**nother Bible thumper put to death."

Dave was angry at Ray's flippant comment, but remained silent.

Ray glanced at the Bible Dave held.

"It must be a pretty powerful book," he observed.

"This is the only book in America that has been declared illegal in the schools by the federal government. A teacher breaks the law by reading it to students or even referring to its wisdom when counselling. It has been removed from all school libraries. Portions of it have been torn from our school walls. Ray, doesn't that tell you something?"

Ray nodded grimly, then answered.

"Two things, as a matter of fact. One, as I said, it must be a pretty powerful book. Two, the United States government is in the beginning stages of enslaving its people."

Dave nodded, for the first time thinking maybe he was getting somewhere with Ray.

"This country didn't start out this way. The Confederation of the United Colonies of New England met in Boston in 1643 to adopt a resolution. It states, in part:

Whereas we all came into these parts of America with one and the same end and aim, namely, to advance the kingdom of our Lord Jesus Christ and to enjoy the liberties of the Gospel in purity with peace . . .

William Penn, the overseer of the founding of Pennsylvania said,

If we will not be governed by God, we must be governed by tyrants.

Dave

Dave leaned forward. "Ray, have you been to a middle school or high school recently?"

"No."

"I have. An armed security guard walked the grounds. Another one stood by the main entrance. A police car patrolled the parking lots. Their presence indicated violence brewing inside. Students armed with weapons are common today, and teachers and students alike fear assaults, rapes, thefts and murder.

"Martin Luther made a statement about universities that applies to our present grade schools. He said:

I am afraid that the universities will prove to be the great gates to Hell, unless they diligently labor to explain the Holy Scriptures and to engrave them upon the hearts of youth. I advise no one to place his child where the Scriptures do not reign paramount. Every institution where men are not unceasingly occupied with the Word of God must become corrupt!

Ray leaned forward. "I've never paid any attention to all this Bible ban. Where did it all begin?"

"It began with the Board of Education of Union Free School District Number 9 of Hyde Park, New York."

"What did they do?"

"They asked that the schools in their district begin their day by having the students repeat a prayer every morning. Someone complained and the courts declared the prayer illegal."

"It must have been a very biased prayer!"

Dave smiled. "Biased? This was the prayer. You judge.

Almighty God, we acknowledge our dependence upon Thee, and we beg Thy blessings upon us, our parents, our teachers, and our country."

"That's it?"

"That's it."

"Seems general enough to me," Ray mused.

"The United States Supreme Court upheld the decision in 1962 with a vote of six to one. That decision became the precedent that banned both prayer and Bible reading from America's schools.

"Let me ask you a question, Ray. How far do you think America will go in banning this book? How far will it go to prevent not only schools, but parents from teaching its truths to their children? Will parents be imprisoned . . . tortured . . . even killed?"

"That's absurd!"

"Is it, Ray?

"Let's take a look at
    another time
        another nation
            a pushing crowd
                and a horrible scene . . ."

Chapter 49

William Tyndale
(About 1494 to 1536)

They are of those that rebel against the light; they
know not the ways thereof, nor abide in the paths thereof.
Job 25:13

*T*he crowd shifted, shoving one another in their
eagerness to watch a woman and six men set aflame.

"What is their crime?" a stranger asked the man
standing beside him.

He turned and stared. "Don't you know? They have
taught their children the Lord's Prayer, the Ten
Commandments and the Apostles' Creed - in the English
language!"

"That is a crime that deserves death?" the stranger
asked.

"It surely is a crime to translate the Bible into the
English language - and well it should be!" the man
answered firmly, turning back to view the twisting,
blistering bodies.

It was just seven years later, in 1526, that William
Tyndale stood in a small room, fascinated by the
marvelous invention of Johannes Gutenberg. It was a
tremendous printing machine, accomplishing in moments
what took scribes years to do! Ever since William had
first seen one, he had devoted his life to the dream that
today had finally become a reality.

He thought about his past few years, as he stood
watching the first printed English New Testaments roll
through the press.

He remembered vividly his frustration at Oxford and
Cambridge Universities.

It had all begun the day he had listened in horror to a
clergyman. He could scarcely believe the statements he
was making. They were in direct opposition to the

Scriptures! And finally, he could stand listening to his lies no longer.

"Why do you teach these things?" William asked. "Do you not realize that what you are saying is in direct opposition to the Bible?"

The clergyman had looked at him with a look of utter bewilderment.

"What do you mean?" he asked.

As William showed him passages of God's Word, he realized from the confusion on the man's face that he was totally ignorant himself to Scriptural truths.

Other renowned clergymen joined their conversation.

"What do these things matter?" one asked William.

"What do they matter?" William declared vehemently. "Our authority for our faith is based solely upon the Word of God!"

"*Our* authority comes solely from the church!" the clergymen replied.

They walked away from him, shaking their heads.

William knew the world would remain in darkness without the light of the Scriptures to guide man's path. The clergymen who were sent out from the universities to teach men the ways of God were themselves ignorant to God's truths. What hope was there for the common people? They had no Bibles and never would have them! They could never know the truths of the blessed Scriptures! There were scattered portions of Scripture that John Wyclif had translated and had men faithfully smuggle to the people. But William dreamed of the day when the English Bible would be available to every man.

God had commended the Jews of Berea, because they searched the Scriptures daily to see if Paul preached the truth! Congregations did not have that privilege today - for the church had declared it illegal to translate the Bible into English! All men had to rely upon were the sermons of men, who neither knew nor respected the Bible themselves!

"The universities have ordained that no man shall look on the Scripture until he be nozzled in heathen learning for eight or nine years, and armed with so many false principles and is clean shut out of the understanding of the Scripture," William declared to his fellow clergymen.

William Tyndale

They remained unconcerned and could see no reason for his distress.

William's heart was deeply troubled.

"My God!" he cried. "People need to be able to read your Word!"

God came to him and William knew immediately why he had come. A torch was in his outstretched hand. William also realized that if he took the extended torch, he was signing the warrant for his own death.

He neither hesitated, nor did his hand waver, as it closed around the torch. His world needed a runner, and he was honored to be called to the race!

The very next day, he boldly declared his intention to the clergyman he had argued with.

"If God spare my life, before many years pass, I will cause a boy that drives the plow shall know more of the Scripture than you do!"

"The fellow is demented," the man muttered, as he hurriedly walked away from the light cast from William's torch.

William Tyndale did not waste time worrying about the opinions of men. He spent his time faithfully laboring over the one task God had appointed to him. Verse by verse, he translated the Scriptures into the English language.

He was mocked.

"Who are you to translate the Scriptures? Will they be the words of Tyndale when you finish with them?"

"I call God to record against the day we shall appear before our Lord Jesus, that I never altered one syllable of God's Word against my conscience, nor would to this day, if all that is in earth, whether it be honor, pleasure, or riches, might be given me," William Tyndale replied.

And he toiled on.

And now . . . now the first copies of the New Testament were rolling from the press. The common man would at last be able to have a Bible to read. Those seeking God and longing to know his ways would no longer be dependent upon blind leaders to lead them to truth.

Bishops raged as their congregations began reading the Scriptures. Doctrines that were contrary to the Bible were now being rejected by the common people! The authority of the church was being undermined by the Word itself!

"Stop Tyndale!" William Warham, the archbishop of Canterbury, roared.

Men plotted to destroy the press.

A lad left their company and ran to William, who even then labored over the printer.

"Mr. Tyndale! Mr. Tyndale! They're coming to destroy your printer and your New Testaments!"

William hastily grabbed the unfinished copies that had just been printed, and fled, escaping just in time.

The archbishop was infuriated.

"Buy every single New Testament you can find and bring them all to me!" he yelled, while dumping money into the hands of his men.

They dashed away to search for New Testaments to buy. People, including William himself, offered them their copies at vastly inflated prices. While they rushed back to Warham to burn them, William lifted his hands in praise to God.

"God! I have prayed for money to finance a better and bigger second edition! But who would have dreamed that you would cause the Archbishop himself to pay for it!"

Catholic priests preached furiously against Tyndale's illegal English Bible. Copies that could be found were confiscated and ceremoniously burned at St. Paul's Cathedral.

There was only one way to stop the work. Tyndale himself must be stopped. But where was he? Several English agents were sent throughout Europe to search for him. William Tyndale knew he was a hunted man, and he barely escaped capture time and again, slipping in and out of areas and houses.

Henry Phillips arrived in Antwerp. He worked his way into the hearts and lives of many of William's friends. They didn't realize that his sole mission was to deliver William to the authorities. He desperately needed the money William's arrest would bring him, and he didn't care how long it took to fulfil his ambition.

Henry was dining at the home of a friend one evening, when William Tyndale was announced. Henry tried to subdue his excitement. He at last met his prey face to face. During the dinner, Henry turned all of his charm upon William. Before long, William, who was kind to everyone, became Henry's close friend.

As they were going to lunch one day, William and Henry walked together down a narrow, twisting alley, darkened by overhanging buildings on each side. Henry suddenly shoved William roughly ahead of him. William, startled by the action of his friend, looked back at him just in time to see his finger pointing him out to two men who were waiting in the shadows. Almost before he realized what was taking place, William was grabbed and quickly bound with ropes.

He had always known it would come to this. This was part of running the race. But the shock of being betrayed by his friend was almost too much for him to bear.

He was carried to a state prison just six miles north of Brussels. William looked at the castle looming ahead of him with its moat, seven towers, three drawbridges and massive walls. He knew he would never escape this place.

"My God," he breathed. "I will continue to serve you . . . *even here!*"

He was thrown into a foul-smelling, damp dungeon. William stared at the dripping walls and the rats that would be his cell mates for the next nearly two years.

The cell was both wet and cold. William shivered through the days and long nights. It didn't take long for his health to fail, but he spent every bit of the strength he had to work for his Lord. Dim light penetrated the gloomy prison only a few hours a day. During the time he was able to see, William continued writing and trans-lating the blessed Scriptures. He would gladly rot in a cell and give his life to proclaim the Word of God!

The day came that he was dragged to trial. He listened as the charges against him were read.

"First, you have maintained that faith alone justifies!"

"Second, you have maintained that to believe in the forgiveness of sins and to embrace the mercy offered in the gospel, are enough for man's salvation."

And the list went on and on . . .

The Bible, for which he was being condemned, came to comfort him now.

> If you suffer for righteousness' sake, happy are you: and be not afraid of their terror, neither be troubled. If you be reproached for the name of Christ, happy are you; for the spirit of glory and of God rests upon you. On their part he is evil spoken of, but on your part he is glorified! If any man suffer as a Christian, let him not be ashamed; but let him glorify God on this behalf!

He looked squarely at his accusers, even as he lifted his torch higher. His body was weak, ravaged by sickness, clothed in foul rags, the stench of the prison clinging to him. He was a man condemned by men, an object of ridicule. But he had no shame, and he would leave this wretched world, glorifying his Lord.

"Heretic!" he was branded. That accusation by the Catholic church sealed his sentence.

He submitted quietly, as he was taken away and dressed in priestly robes. He was then taken to the town square. He glanced at the high platform where a great assembly of prominent doctors and dignitaries proudly sat in all their pomp and splendor.

A huge crowd had gathered to watch the degrading ceremony. His thoughts drifted to the words penned by Paul who had so bravely run in his day:

> We are made a spectacle to the world! We are made as the filth of the world, and are the offscouring of all things!

Paul was in heaven now, and it was up to William to be the spectacle today. Branded a heretic, he would now go through the formalities of being cast from the church.

His thoughts were interrupted by an arrogant voice.

"Kneel!" he was commanded.

He was struck to his knees, and the ritual of scraping his hands with a knife began.

William Tyndale

"You have now lost the benefits of the anointing oil with which you were consecrated to the priesthood," man's voice intoned.

William glanced at his torch, still shining brightly in the darkness. He knew his anointing had not been given to him by man and could never be taken away from him by man.

He was jerked to his feet and was ceremoniously stripped of his priest's robes.

He submitted calmly, for he knew man could never strip him of the fine, clean, white linen that Christ had clothed him with. What did earthly robes matter, compared to the blessed robes of righteousness?

Man's ritual was finally over, and man no longer considered William Tyndale a priest.

But what a comfort to know that Jesus, by his own blood, had made him not only a priest, but a king unto God! Was man so foolish that he thought any threat could persuade him to forsake that holy office?

William was handed over to the attorney for punishment. The attorney sent him back to his cold dungeon for two more months.

It was an early morning in October of 1536 that William was again led from the prison to the town square.

So this was the day he would cross his finish line! He was ready!

A vast crowd of onlookers was already gathered around a circle of stakes to celebrate his final disgrace. Men, women, and children, some with a devilish glee in their eyes, parted as he was led through the circle to the large pillar of wood in the form of a cross.

He glanced at the chain hanging from the top and noticed the noose threaded through a hole.

The attorney walked over to him.

"You are to be given one final chance to recant."

William looked at him steadily then lifted his head toward the God he loved and served and prayed one last prayer.

"Lord," he cried, "Open the king of England's eyes."

Two soldiers bound his feet cruelly to the stake. Another fastened the iron chain around his neck and placed the noose at his throat. Piles of wood were heaped around him.

They stepped back, and the executioner came forward. He yanked the noose down, and within seconds, William was strangled. The torch fell from his hand even as the attorney set the wood aflame. The spectators watched as the fire raged. Even as the body of William Tyndale burned, the spirit of the victorious runner was being ushered into the courts of heaven, where angels were assembled to cheer his triumphant entrance into the celestial arena.

Chapter 50

Dave

*So shall my word be that goeth forth out of my mouth:
it shall not return unto me void, but it shall accomplish
that which I please, and it shall prosper in the thing
whereto I sent it.*
Isaiah 55:11

"**S**o, was his prayer answered?" Ray asked, a cynical expression on his face.

"What prayer are you referring to, Ray?"

"Tyndale's! His last prayer. He asked God to open the king of England's eyes."

"Yes, as a matter of fact it was. Less than one year later, King Henry gave his official approval for the distribution of an English Bible. He didn't realize nearly seventy percent of it was Tyndale's translation! King Henry proclaimed, 'If there be no heresies in it, let it be spread abroad among all the people!'"

Ray's cynical expression faded.

Dave looked at him.

No sneer.

No anger.

No cynicism.

Ray was even beginning to look interested in the conversation.

"So Wyclif, Hus, Tyndale . . . they all accomplished what they set out to do."

Ray seemed to be thinking aloud, so Dave kept quiet. Finally Ray broke the silence with a question.

"What do you think will happen in the United States, Dave?"

"What do *you* think will happen here, Ray?"

He shrugged. "I'm not sure. Churches that are more concerned about their power over people than . . than . . "

"God," Dave inserted.

" . . . Okay, we'll call him God. As I was saying, power-hungry churches will probably just sort of put the Bible on a back shelf.

197

"Possibly the courts will ban the Bible in more places. The work place, perhaps. Maybe the public library. Who knows how far they'll take this thing. Before it's finished, the Bible and prayer and God himself may be banned from America!"

"They could try, Ray, but it will never work."

"Why? It worked in the schools."

"No, Ray, it didn't. The courts may as well enact a law against oxygen or declare it illegal for the sun to shine. No court can keep a teacher or a student from praying. I've prayed to God several times since I've been here with you. Nothing you could have done or said would have been able to stop me. As long as I live, I can pray. Laws can forbid prayer and ban the Bible, but God's people will still pray.

"As far as banning the Bible, it is hidden safely in the hearts of God's people. No search party can find it and no nation can destroy it. All they can do is kill God's people."

Ray interrupted with a snort. "I'd say that's enough!"

"Not really. Christians don't shun death. They're out of reach of Satan then."

"Satan? This is too much! You believe there's a devil?"

"Let me quote you part of the Massachusetts School Law, written in 1647:

It being one chief project of that old deluder Satan to keep men from the knowledge of the Scriptures, as in former times by keeping them in an unknown tongue . . .

"But let's not get on the subject of Satan right now. Let me illustrate the statement I made about the Bible being hidden in the hearts of God's people with a true story.

"A few years ago before the war, a humble villager in Eastern Poland was given a Bible by Michael Billester, a peddler of religious books. The villager read it and was converted to Christ. He passed the book on to others. Two hundred more became believers.

"When the peddler returned to the town in the summer of 1940, the group gathered to worship and listen to him preach.

"Michael said, 'Instead of giving the usual testimonies, I wonder if each of you could recite a verse of Scripture.'

"A man stood and asked, 'Perhaps we have misunderstood. Did you want us to recite just a verse - or a chapter?'

"Billester replied, 'Do you mean to say there are people here who can recite entire chapters of the Bible?'

"The man asked, 'Do you mean entire chapters - or books?'

"Billester soon learned that the villagers had memorized whole books of the Bible. Thirteen of them knew Matthew and Luke and half of Genesis. One could quote the entire book of Psalms. Together the two-hundred Christians could quote the complete Bible. The worn-out book had been passed from family to family and carried to their Sunday gatherings. Its words were barely legible."

Ray picked up the Bible and flipped through its pages reflectively. Giving it back to Dave, he commented, "That's a lot to memorize."

"Ray, Christians throughout the whole world have portions of this book memorized. There was one monk who could quote nearly all of the New Testament and much of the Old. He caused a reformation that literally shook the foundations of the church. Believe me, the church desperately needed shaking! Savonarola's prophecy was about to come true . . . "

Chapter 51

Martin Luther
(1483 TO 1546)

See, I have this day set thee over the nations and over the kingdoms, to root out, and to pull down, and to destroy, and to throw down, to build, and to plant.
Jeremiah 1:10

The people gaped at the dark figure emerging from the shadows.

He was clothed in the garb of a monk. His deep-set eyes and brows were dark black.

His eyes . . .

One who tried to look into them remarked, "They sparkle and burn like stars so that I can hardly bear looking at them."

Anger radiated from him.

Even the flames in his torch seemed to rage and leap in anger.

"Yes. I am angry!" he cried. "I was born to war with fanatics and devils! I must root out the stumps and trunks, hew away the thorns and briar, fill in the puddles! I am the rough woodsman, who must pioneer and hew a path!"

"I was born to war with fanatics and devils . . ." he repeated. And his finger pointed straight at Tetzel.

"How dare this fraud travel around selling sin?" he raged.

Luther's parishioners joined the mad rush to Tetzel when he came near Luther's parish in Wittenberg, Germany. They returned excitedly, waving their documents. They could now indulge in sin and God wouldn't punish them. Did they not have a written guarantee, backed by the Pope himself? The rich among them purchased not only indulgences for themselves but bought releases from purgatory for their deceased loved ones.

The carnival-like procession began with a parade. Bells pealed and banners flew. With the papal decree displayed on a pillow of gold and scarlet and the stacks of printed letters of indulgence nearby, Tetzel began his disgusting performance. He painted a vivid picture of deceased parents whose wails of pain could only be stilled when their children gave liberal offerings.

A huge sign was propped in front of Tetzel's money box.

> As soon as the coin in the coffer rings,
> The troubled soul from Purgatory springs.

"Just deposit your twenty silver coins here," his assistants called to the swarming crowds. They were kept busy hauling money.

Half of the money was rushed to Rome to finish building St. Peter's Basilica. The other half went toward paying an enormous debt at Fugger's banking house. For Albert of Mainz had borrowed heavily to buy his office of Archbishop from the Pope.

If Luther hadn't discovered the Bible in the library, he would have blended into the blackness along with the rest. Before he began to study the Scriptures, he, like Tetzel, was a monk without a torch.

He had settled into the life of a monk easily enough, wearing the robes and beret of a doctor of theology. But his relationship with God . . . he simply had none. He had done everything possible to become righteous. He remained celibate. He renounced his family and his possessions. He trudged eight-hundred miles to say masses at Rome. He fasted, he confessed every sin he could imagine, he abased himself, he lay prostrate before the altar, he did penance, he studied, he sang, he labored, he faithfully taught theology to his students at the university in Wittenberg . . . and he prayed.

It was when he tried to pray that he came face to face with the bitter truth. No matter what he did or how he lived, Luther knew - and Luther knew that God knew - that he was a vile sinner.

He dreaded prayer. Who was he to approach a holy God? Guilt hounded his every waking moment and prevented his sleeping ones. Others may be able to fool themselves, but he couldn't. Hopelessness nearly overwhelmed him. He was miserable.

Then he had discovered the Bible.

Day after day, month after month, for ten years, Martin devoured its pages.

When he lay on his cot at night, he still pondered the words.

For therein is the righteousness of God revealed . . .

The just shall live by faith . . .

Live by *faith?* Faith in *what?* Faith in *whom?*

He read about others who strived for righteousness but remained in the depths of sin.

For they being ignorant of God's righteousness, and going about to establish their own righteousness . . .

"I try so hard to be righteous," he groaned. Sighing bitterly, he read on.

. . . have not submitted themselves unto the righteousness of God. For CHRIST is the end of the law for righteousness to every one that believeth.

For therein is the righteousness of God revealed . . . The just shall live by faith.

"That's all then?" he thought. "Is salvation simply . . . faith in the finished work of Jesus Christ for *my* soul?"

"Yes," the Scripture declared.

"Yes," his heart responded.

"Yes!" he finally shouted.

"At this," he later recorded, "I felt myself to have been born again, and to have entered through open gates into paradise itself!"

He penned his personal testimony in a victorious second verse to *A Mighty Fortress Is Our God.*

Did we in our own strength confide,
Our striving would be losing,
Were not the right Man on our side,
The Man of God's own choosing.
Dost ask who that may be?
Christ Jesus! It is He!

His joy and relief had to overflow. He wanted the world to know - especially the poor - that the wondrous gift of salvation was *free!* For the poor could not afford the perverted gospel offered by the church.

The church . . .

How it had corrupted the simple truth of the Scriptures.

Trusting people filled the coffers of a church growing rich by peddling redemption.

Luther snorted.

How could a church claiming Peter as its head promote such blasphemy?

Did they never read Peter's words? "You know that you were *not* redeemed with corruptible things, as silver and gold . . . but with the precious blood of Christ!"

Luther's rage kept him from sleep. How could the church stoop to such a bogus fund-raising scheme? The more Martin thought about it, the angrier he became.

Peter's prophecy had surely come true in his generation: "Through covetousness shall they with feigned words make merchandise of you."

His fury could not be silenced.

He had to speak.

Dipping his pen, he began to write. He would fight with his pen and post his beliefs on the door of Castle Church. When people gathered there to read the daily news and announcements, they could read his views along with it. Perhaps no one would notice, but he would feel better. *Number 1. . .*

When our Lord and Master Jesus Christ said, "Repent," He willed the entire life of believers to be one of repentance.

He attacked the church viciously for its sale of indulgences.

If the Pope knew the sharp practices of the indulgence purveyors, he would prefer to have St. Peter's collapse in ruins rather than build it with the skin and flesh and bones of his sheep.

He sighed. Obviously the Pope was fully aware of the scheme. He had authorized the indulgences.

If for the sake of money the Pope can free suffering souls from purgatory, why not for the sake of love empty out purgatory altogether?

The list grew. And still he wrote. *Number sixty-two . .*

The true treasure of the church is the most holy gospel of the glory and the grace of God.

He was nearing the end now.

Being a Christian involves embracing the cross and entering heaven through tribulation.

He would surely have his share of tribulation if anyone read this edict! Finally he dropped his pen and leaned back in his chair. It was finished. It had taken ninety-five theses to bare his soul.

He glanced at the calendar. October 31, 1517 - as good a day as any to begin his war against heresy.

A few passers-by glanced his way as he nailed his theses to the university chapel.

It took just four weeks for all hell to erupt. Someone translated his theses into German and rushed it to John Gruenenberg, the printer. Copies were distributed among the people. Groups of illiterate crowded around readers as they stood on the streets reading the theses aloud.

The sound of the hammer, pounding his theses to the church door, echoed throughout Europe!

The Archbishop of Mainz forwarded the documents to Rome with his urgent request: "This man must be stopped!"

"Impeach Luther!" screamed the Dominicans.

Slowly but surely the dreaded word *Heretic* was attached to his name.

"Drag him to Rome in chains!" some advised.

His days and weeks became a hectic flurry of meetings, interrogations and trials.

He was denounced by one crowd, and hailed as a hero by another.

"Burn Luther's books!" was the decree. His writings and his effigy lit up Rome in a mighty bonfire.

"Recant!" Rome commanded.

"Reform!" he thundered back.

A jagged streak of lightening had scared him into the ministry. Now he himself became a lightening bolt, part of the mighty storm that shook the church.

Man insisted he denounce his beliefs, but he was bound by the Word of God to cling to them. Other leaders and laymen joined him in his protest against unscriptural practices. A new word began to be heard in the land to describe them . . . *Protestants*.

He had to be stopped. The Pope issued a decree, giving him sixty days to recant or be excommunicated. On the sixtieth-first day, Luther tossed the decree into the fire.

He was forced into hiding, a hunted outlaw. Wanted posters were scattered throughout the land. Would his life end at just thirty-three years old?

Well-meaning friends faked a kidnapping and smuggled him to a remote castle. He shed his monk's garb and let his hair and beard grow long to conceal his face.

He spent his days working at a furious pace. He wrote fourteen works and translated the entire New Testament from Greek to German in just eleven weeks. How he loved the Scriptures! He could quote most of the New Testament and large sections of the Old by memory. But he was so restless. He dubbed the isolated castle *Land of the Birds*, for they were his only companions. He endured the loneliness and frustration for nearly a year. He could stand no more. Had he been called to run with the torch or cower in a castle?

He ran back to his church. If Rome wanted him, let them come to Wittenberg where he was under state protection and get him. Until then he planned to preach. He announced his typical weekly teaching schedule to his congregation.

Sunday at 5 a.m.:	Pauline Epistles
Sunday at 9 a.m.:	The Gospels
Sunday Afternoon:	The Catechism
Monday:	The Catechism
Tuesday:	The Catechism
Wednesday:	The Gospel of Matthew
Thursday:	The Epistles
Friday:	The Epistles
Saturday:	The Gospel of John

He taught, preached, sang, strummed his lute and played his flute.

He turned his entire congregation into his choir, further enraging his enemies. Did he not know that only the clergy was allowed to sing?

He shed his monk's garb with finality.

His rebellion against the church was complete when he married Katherina, a feisty, redheaded, twenty-six year old ex-nun. He was forty-two.

Actually he shocked even himself. "There's a lot to get used to in the first year of marriage," he wrote. "One wakes up in the morning and finds a pair of pigtails on the pillow that were not there before."

Katie took some getting used to. "If I should ever marry again," he told a friend, "I would hew myself an obedient wife out of stone."

Six noisy children soon filled his house. He and Katie adopted four more.

There were times he longed for silence. He locked himself in his study for three days, but Katie simply removed the door off the hinges.

He invited needy students to move in with them, along with the homeless, the sick and the dying. His home was open to scholars, exiled clerics, and visiting dignitaries. He refused to concern himself with the problem of financing the growing household. He simply left it all to God and Katie.

So Katie cared for the orchard, the fish pond and the barnyard. She harvested the fruit and caught the fish and slaughtered the pigs. There were usually about twenty-five or thirty people gathered around her table to eat.

Martin gave away what money he had. "God divided the hand into fingers so that money would slip through," he explained.

"Do you love her, Martin?" he was asked by his friends.

"Of course! A Christian is supposed to love his neighbor, and since his wife is his nearest neighbor, she should be his deepest love."

Then he laughed. "In domestic affairs, I defer to Katie. Otherwise, I am led by the Holy Ghost."

Katie paused in her work long enough to notice her husband was unsuccessfully battling a deep discouragement. He was constantly bombarded with betrayals and misunderstandings of friends, vicious rumors, hatred of enemies, endless debates, excommunication by the church and threats of death. Besides enduring poor health, he was branded a heathen, a wild boar and the devil incarnate. The load slowed his run to a crawl. Katie stared. His eyes had lost their glow. His torch hung at his side.

He finally became too depressed to walk, much less run.

His concerned friends gathered around to encourage him, but left in defeat.

So Katie took manners into her own hands.

He heard her wails the moment he entered the house. He followed the noise and found her dressed in mourning clothes. She was too lost in grief to even notice him.

"Who died, Katie?" he cried. "Who died?"

She finally quieted enough to answer him between her wrenching sobs.

"Oh, Martin! God is dead! I can't bear it, for all his work is overthrown."

His face flushed angrily.

"That is utter blasphemy, Katherina!" he raged.

Her sobs ceased abruptly.

"Well, Martin," she said sternly, "you have been going around acting as if God is dead, as if God is no longer here to keep us. So I thought I ought to put on mourning to keep you company in your great bereavement."

Her words, as usual, hit their mark.

He straightened his shoulders and picked up his torch.

He was unmoved by the threats of a representative from the pope.

"Do you not understand how much power the Pope has?" he warned menacingly. "Don't you realize that the day will come when your supporters will all desert you? Tell me, Martin, where will you be then?"

Martin grinned.

"Then, as now, in the hands of Almighty God," he replied.

Enemies surrounded him. Their opposition to his message only stirred him to run faster.

"God has used my enemies to compel me to raise my voice even more insistently," he claimed. "I must speak, shout, shriek, and write till they have had enough!"

"What is Martin Luther *really* like?" someone asked one of Martin's close friends.

"Go see for yourself," came the quick reply. "Martin Luther hides nothing from anyone. His life is an open book, and he speaks freely to everyone about himself."

He laughed and added, "And if you want to know what he thinks of somebody else, ask him that as well. He will give you his honest opinion and hold back nothing!"

Luther was at work in his study when one of his students burst in with good news.

"Your followers are calling themselves *Lutherans!*"

Luther's black eyes bored into the messenger.

"Lutherans?" he thundered. "What is *Luther?* The teaching is not mine. Nor was I crucified for anyone. How did I, poor stinking bag of maggots that I am, come to the point where people call the children of Christ by my evil name?"

He ran at a furious pace. He preached 4,000 sermons and penned over 60,000 pages. Both his preaching and his writing kept his enemies stirred up.

"Couldn't you try to keep from offending people?" his friends asked.

"What good does the edge of the sword do if it does not cut?" he scoffed.

He was forty-seven when he went on strike against his own congregation.

"I refuse to preach to you!" he announced. "You remain godless. It annoys me to keep preaching to you!"

When the shocked congregation mended their ways, he returned to his pulpit.

His barber and lifelong friend, Peter, asked him simply, "How should I pray, Martin?"

Martin Luther responded with a pamphlet.

A Simple Way to Pray

It is a good thing to let prayer be the first business of the morning and the last at night. Guard yourself carefully against those false, deluding ideas which tell you, "Wait a little while. I will pray in an hour; first I must attend to this or that." Such thoughts get you away from prayer into other affairs which so hold your attention and involve you that nothing comes of prayer for that day.

Do not leave your prayer without having said or thought, "Very well, God has heard my prayer; this I know as a certainty and a truth." That is what Amen means!

It is of great importance that the heart be made ready and eager for prayer. What else is it but tempting God when your mouth babbles and the mind wanders to other thoughts?

A good and attentive barber keeps his thoughts, attention, and eyes on the razor and hair and does not forget how far he has gotten with his shaving or cutting. If he wants to engage in too much conversation or let his mind wander or look somewhere else, he is likely to cut his customer's mouth, nose, or even his throat. How much more does prayer call for concentration and singleness of heart!

Hopefully his barber took his advice.

Someone innocently referred to his doctrine in his presence - and faced his wrath head-on.

"It is not *my* doctrine," he cried, his voice rising and his eyes snapping. "Dear Lord God, it was not spun out of my head, nor grown in my garden. Nor did it flow out of my spring, nor was it born of me. It is God's gift, not a human discovery!"

He summed up his race in the third verse of his most famous hymn, *A Mighty Fortress Is Our God.*

> And though this world with devils filled
> Should threaten to undo us.
> We will not fear, for God has willed
> His truth to triumph through us!

He had just turned sixty-two when he left Wittenberg for Mansfeld. Suffering in the winter's cold, he was violently ill by the time he reached Eisleben. He knew his race was nearly finished. He spent his remaining few days settling a dispute, preaching four sermons, ordaining two pastors, founding a school, writing letters to his beloved and worried Katie, and jotting down notes for another treatise.

Even as his voice faded in death, he crossed his finish line quoting John 3:16:

FOR GOD SO LOVED THE WORLD
 that he gave his only begotten Son
  that whosoever believeth in him
   should not perish
    but have everlasting life.

Chapter 52

Dave

I will run the way of thy commandments, when thou shalt enlarge my heart.
Psalm 119:32

Ray leaned back in his chair smiling.

"No wonder churches and governments don't particularly like the Bible. When they're corrupt, that old book causes them quite a few problems."

"It causes a corrupt person quite a few problems too," Dave answered.

Ray quit smiling abruptly.

"What exactly do you mean?"

Dave stood to his feet and was prepared to leave. At the door he turned and handed Ray his Bible.

"Take it."

Ray stepped back. "I'm not taking your Bible!"

"I want you to have it. I have another one at home. Please."

Reluctantly Ray took the Bible and turned around to toss it nonchalantly on his bed. When he turned back, Dave was gone.

He was left alone . . . with God and whatever message he had for him in his awesome book.

* * * * * * *

People of nearly every description crowded the street. Women dressed in fine silk and jewels rubbed shoulders with stooped and tattered women who carried all their worldly possessions in bags. Leftover hippies moved among the crowd. Young men with shaved heads bulldozed through the crowd. Their muscled, tattooed arms jostled disoriented wanderers with flowing beards and drug-glazed eyes. Brief cases carried by impeccably groomed young men and women bumped against emaciated legs barely clad with torn jeans.

Dave

A group of this mixture of humanity waited for a bus at the corner. Standing near them was a young man with a clipboard and a pen, taking a survey. Most swept on past, ignoring him. Some who had nothing better to do while waiting for their bus answered his questions.

Dave had no plans to stop - but then he caught the last words of the question.

". . . . . . . heaven when you die?"

Dave edged closer to hear. He was talking now to a woman whose attire advertised her trade. Layers of makeup failed to conceal her years of sin, but she answered haughtily.

"Of course I am going to heaven! I was saved as a child!"

With a look of disgust, she turned her back on him.

He spoke to a young man with rippling muscles whose head was shaved. Dave had to admire the man's nerve. Who could tell how this one would respond?

"Do you believe you will go to heaven when you die?"

Foul curses filled the air, followed with, "If anybody goes, I will. I'm as good a Christian as anybody that goes to church!"

Dave shuddered as he listened to the same answer, over and over again. They were all planning to be welcomed into heaven . . . drunks, prostitutes, blasphemers, drug addicts and business people alike.

Dave waited until the bus came and the young man took a break. When he got closer to speak to him, he noticed he was no more than eighteen or nineteen years old.

"It's your turn now," Dave said. "I have a question for you."

"Go ahead," the boy answered, grinning.

"Why are you taking this survey?"

The young man looked into Dave's eyes and he recognized a fellow runner.

"Let's have a cup of coffee together, and I'll tell you about it," he answered, pointing to a nearby restaurant.

When they were seated, he said, "My name is Dan. I've been out here for over two hours today. The answer is always the same. Everyone plans on making heaven their

Dave

home. I guess they think living in *'Christian America'* gives them a ticket.

"I felt the same way they did. Then I met Jesus Christ and invited him into my heart and life. He not only saved me from my sins, he delivered me. I am no longer in the drug scene. Christ turned my life from darkness to light, from sin to righteousness, from death to life.

"I wanted to tell everyone about Jesus. I started with my family and friends."

He shook his head slowly.

"I discovered pretty quickly that they couldn't understand what the big deal was. According to them, they had been Christians all their lives. Of course, he was never mentioned in our home except when his name was used to curse someone. I never saw anyone talk to him in prayer. No one read his book or lived by his commandments. If any of them had met him, Jesus obviously hadn't made a big enough impact on them to change their way of living one bit. It was the same thing with my friends.

"So I got curious. Was it just my family and my crowd that professed Christianity while ignoring Christ?

"I decided to find out. What better place could there be than here in this city? I can meet all kinds right here! This is my third day here. And the answer is always the same. A lot of people don't bother to answer me, but the ones who do assure me in no uncertain terms that they are on their way to heaven. I've even asked, 'Are you born again?' They all assure me they are.

"It's pretty discouraging to realize that all these people have no fear of judgment for their sins and no desire for cleansing from their sins. Some are really insulted when I ask them if they know Jesus Christ, the Son of God. Sure they know him! They celebrate Christmas, don't they? Now tell me . . . what did you say your name was?"

Dave grinned.

"I didn't have a chance to say. But go on. What you are saying is very interesting. And I'm Dave."

"I know you are a runner, Dave. So can you tell me something? What have these people heard in church? How can they think they are Christians without Christ?"

Dave thought a minute before answering slowly.

213

"Many you have questioned have probably never attended church. I'm sure that some were raised in church from their childhood, and possibly some still attend regularly.

"This isn't a problem unique in our society. Christianity has always had its share of both professors and possessors. Dan, have you ever heard about a young man by the name of Auguste Francke?"

"I haven't heard of hardly anyone yet. I just met Jesus three weeks ago!"

"Then let me tell you about him. He was raised in church. In fact, his life revolved around church services. If you had interviewed him today, he would have assured you that he was on his way to heaven.

"Then came the day that the very foundations of his faith were shaken. It was not until Auguste realized he was an atheist that he came face to face with Jesus Christ, the God he had professed but had never met . . ."

Chapter 53

Auguste Hermann Francke
(1663 to 1727)

*Ye cannot be partakers of the Lord's table, and
of the table of devils.*
I Corinthians 10:21

"**T**his is written that you may believe that Jesus is
the Christ, the Son of God, and that believing, you may
have life in his name.
"This is written that you may believe . . . "

Auguste Francke tried to shut the verse from his mind.
Why, with all the verses in the Bible, did it have to be this
verse that kept crowding its way again and again into his
head, interrupting his thoughts and even keeping him
from sleep?

Auguste quit his restless pacing and sat down, his
head in his hands.

". . . that you may believe that Jesus is the Christ,
the Son of God . . . "

"Well, I *don't* believe Jesus is the Son of God. I don't
believe there even *is* a God. So how can I believe in a Son
who supposedly saves souls? In fact, I don't believe I
even have a soul to be saved!"

There. He had admitted it.

"I guess this makes me an atheist," he mumbled.
What would his church friends think if they knew that he
was an atheist? Everyone in the *Church of St. John*
thought he was a believer. In fact, he thought so himself
until he was asked to preach a sermon on Sunday.

He groaned as he remembered his response. He was
just twenty-four years old. He knew he could not only
preach a suitable sermon, but could undoubtedly preach
a much better sermon than most preachers he had heard.

215

He surely would *look* better than most of them, he had thought with a smile, trying to decide which of his elegant suits to wear.

He decided to favor the congregation with an eloquent speech that would keep them praising him for weeks.

"And I shall also attempt to build up the listeners with my sermon," he decided as an afterthought.

That was when that verse had taken over his waking thoughts. The more he pondered the text, the more troubled he had become.

Now it had all come to this. All the doubts he had pushed aside for years had suddenly demanded his attention.

Thinking of himself as an atheist seemed strange. His family and most of his friends attended church so he had made church a big part of his life too. Being a member of the church had never affected his life in the world. In fact, he had always thought it gave him an even better image. He remembered praying now and then that God would improve him so he would be respected by everyone who had the opportunity to meet him. It hadn't taken much to act religious while he was with the church crowd. When his other friends were around, he joined in their sin with reckless enthusiasm.

Now that he thought about it, he realized he had tried to grasp heaven with one hand and earth with the other.

Well, if he was going to give up one, he supposed it must be heaven since he realized now it didn't exist. He certainly would never give up the world. He loved the world and its pleasures and the world in turn loved him.

But what should he do about this wretched sermon? The Sunday he was to preach would be here all too soon. Should he back out of his commitment? What would people think? What explanation could he give? He certainly could not tell his church friends that he didn't believe there was a God!

What should he do?

Almost without thinking, Auguste got on his knees. Looking up to the heavens and seeing no one, Auguste said, "God, if indeed you are a true God, save me from this miserable state of unbelief!"

The God he had denied both heard and instantly answered his simple prayer. God literally filled the heart and life of Auguste with a glory he would never be able to describe. Joy and peace and an unshakable assurance that vanished all his doubts nearly overwhelmed him!

"My God!" he cried. "You are *real!* You are full of mercy and grace and love! You have given Jesus, your only begotten Son to save my soul! I love You! I will serve you all the days of my life! You are not only my God - you are my beloved Father!"

Auguste laughed and cried. He felt as if a stream of unspeakable, glorious joy was running through his entire being. How could he even describe the peace that flooded his soul?

"Never again will I distrust you, my Father," he prayed, for I have met you personally. I would give up my blood without fear for such a God as you!"

Finally, rising from his knees, he went to bed and tried to sleep. But how could anyone this happy sleep?

"My God," he breathed. "You are the living God! You are my new Father, through your Son, Christ Jesus! I honor You! I adore You! Thank you for revealing yourself to me! I love you so much!"

Auguste closed his eyes for a few moments, trying to sleep, but then began praising God again.

"My Father," he whispered. "I can't sleep! I feel as if I have spent my entire life in a deep sleep! Everything I have experienced up to now has only been a dream! I have just now been awakened! I feel as if I have been dead and am just now alive!"

Auguste leaped out of bed and again began praising God.

"You angels in heaven," he shouted. "Praise the name of the Lord with me! Praise the Lord who has shown me such mercy!"

After a wonderful time of praise and worship to his new found God, Auguste again went to bed and tried to sleep. He remembered the words penned by Martin Luther - words that for the first time in his life made sense to him.

Faith is a living, moving trust in God's grace, so certain that one would die for it a thousand times. And such trust and knowledge in divine grace makes one joyous, bold and delighting in God and all creatures; this the Lord God does in faith!

Faith is a divine word in us that changes us and gives us new birth from God and makes us completely other men in our hearts, minds, thoughts and all our powers and brings the Holy Spirit with it."

"I understand now what Luther was saying," Auguste thought, "for I have experienced this wondrous faith for myself."

Sleep never did come. Auguste spent the entire night worshiping Christ.

The next morning, Auguste, with tears of joy streaming down his face, told his friends that he had met God. Some laughed and cried with him. Others just stared, wondering, nervously backing away from the brilliant light of his testimony that exposed their own unbelief.

The world stared at Auguste even as Auguste stared back at the alien world he had been so comfortable in just yesterday.

"I am a new person in Christ," Auguste realized. "I care nothing for promotion, honor or visibility in this world. I no longer desire riches and worldly pomp. And where is my idol of education? Why, faith the size of a mustard seed counts for more than a hundred sacks full of learning! All the knowledge learned from the wisest of men is as dirt beside the super-abundant knowledge of Jesus Christ, my Lord!"

He had a sermon to preach now! His life would be meaningless if he did not dedicate all his strength and days to tell everyone he met about God and his beloved Son.

"Why wasn't I told by the teachers and pastors of my church that I must be born again?" he wondered. "Could it be that some of them are as I was? How many have no faith, no new birth, no Savior? How many of them have no joy, no peace, no life, *no message?*"

His experience with Christ drove him to his knees and led him to the pulpit and moved him to found an educational community to train pastors and teachers for the ministry.

"You spiritual leaders must go into your communities with a burning message born of your own experience," he counselled them.

"For only when we preach this marvelous new birth," he continued, "will we see a life changed, a church revived, a nation reformed, and a world evangelized."

Chapter 54

Dave

Ye that love the Lord, hate evil. Light is sown for the
righteous.
Psalm 97:10 & 11

". . . a life changed
a church revived
a nation reformed
a world evangelized.

And it all begins with a life changed."

Dave and Dan sat thinking for a moment, then Dave
spoke again.

"Dan, people who meet Jesus Christ and receive him
as their Lord *change.* Jesus and John were both still in
the womb when their mothers met. John leaped even
there by just being in the presence of Christ!

"Wise men knelt at his crib, fishers of fish became
fishers of men, lepers were cleansed, and Mary Magdalene was delivered of seven devils. Lazarus floated from
his tomb, Legion published his testimony in ten cities,
Zacchaeus gave away half his riches and Paul became a
leader of the church he had despised.

"The two on the road to Emmaus looked at one
another and said, "Didn't our heart burn within us while
he talked with us?"

Dave shook his head.

"Dan, when Francke met Christ personally, he became
a new man. But the people you questioned today claim
to know him, and yet their lives have not been affected in
the least."

Dan shrugged.

"That is exactly what bothers me. So how do you
suggest we introduce people to someone they already
claim to know?"

Dave looked around at the people in the restaurant.
He heard a man at the counter make a suggestive remark

to a waitress. She responded with a laugh and a lewd remark of her own. He heard the Lord's name mentioned by a businessman at the table next to his, but he realized it was spoken as a curse.

He thought of Christ's words to John about a group he would one day spit from his mouth.

You say you have need of nothing. But don't you know that you are wretched, and miserable, and poor, and blind, and naked?

He turned to Dan.

"Dan, some of these people may realize they don't have Jesus in their lives when they face a crisis they can't handle and desperately need his help.

"Others may have a friend or relative who will meet Jesus and be transformed. The change in that one's life may cause them to question their own salvation.

"But I'm afraid most people won't realize they are lost until they stand before him in judgment. It will be too late for them then. He said many would travel the broad road to destruction."

He stood and extended his hand to Dan.

"Dan, you've made me realize more than ever that we torchbearers have a big job to do. I am going to take Jesus to as many as I can, while I can."

He smiled.

"Don't be discouraged, Friend. There are still men, women, and children today who have met Jesus and whose lives will never be the same. I am one of them."

Chapter 55

Dave

*My heart panteth, my strength faileth me: as for the
light of mine eyes, it also is gone from me.*
Psalm 38:10

Dave ran wearily, neither knowing nor caring which
direction he took.

He no longer derived joy from the race. The excitement was gone. Days lengthened into weeks, and he ran
on mechanically.

"How long have I been running like this?" he wondered
to himself.

It didn't really matter. He ran simply because he had
answered the call of God and was committed to the race.
He would continue to run until he died.

But the thrill of running was gone.

He looked ahead, knowing the sneers of the scoffers
would never end, and wondered how he could keep going.

He thought he saw a gleam of light in the distance.
But then it vanished. He was approaching another hill,
and his pace slowed.

He finally reached the top and paused to rest. He was
tired so much of the time lately. He looked ahead. Yes,
there was a light. Another torch bearer was running
toward him. There was no leap of joy at the thought of
the meeting. Dave remembered the days when he would
have run forward in anticipation, thrilled with the
thought of sweet fellowship with another runner.

Today his pace slowed to a walk.

"Dave! Dave!"

The shout grew louder as the runner grew closer.
Dave didn't recognize him, but apparently they had met
somewhere in the past.

Finally their paths crossed at the bottom of the hill.
The runner pumped Dave's hand enthusiastically. Dave
worked at being polite.

Dave

After awkward attempts at conversation, the runner grew silent, looking through the eyes of Dave and into his very soul. Then he looked at Dave's torch. And back again. Dave looked away.

"Dave."

Dave's eyes met the runner's. He saw love and compassion. And there was something else. Was it concern?

"Dave, how long have you been running like this? The light you carried was brilliant, and you were an inspiration to all of us. But look at your torch now, Dave. There are just a few sparks left, and they are about to go out. What has happened to you?"

Dave couldn't answer. He lowered his torch and stared at it. The runner was right. Only a few embers remained. How long had he been carrying it this way?

The runner led Dave to the side of the road.

"Dave, sit here with me for awhile. You have encouraged so many of us by your stories of valiant runners who ran before us. Let me remind you of the way Count Zinzendorf found renewed power and vigor during his race when he grew weary."

Dave simply nodded, and the runner began his story.

Chapter 56

Count Zinzendorf
(1700 to 1760)

Is not this the fast that I have chosen? Is it not to deal thy bread to the hungry, and that thou bring the poor that are cast out to thy house? Then shall thy light break forth as the morning!
Isaiah 58:6-8

"Count Zinzendorf is the beast of the book of Revelation!

"Count Zinzendorf is the beast of the book of Revelation!

"Count Zinzendorf is the beast of the book of Revelation!"

The angry cry shattered the peace as it echoed throughout the lush estate at Berthelsdorf.

When the dreadful words were carried to Count Zinzendorf, he silently bowed his head and walked to his study and shut the door. He sat quietly for the next few hours, reflecting about his life.

He recalled the life changing commitment he had made when he was just twenty years old, while on a tour of France. He would never forget standing in the art museum at Dusseldorf, gazing at the painting by Domenico Fetis, Ecce Homo - *Behold, the Man.* He could not take his eyes away from the portrait of Jesus. He stared at the wounds caused by the thorns that crowned the head of the King of Kings. His eyes drifted to the inscription.

I have done this for you; what have you done for me?

He stared until the question was no longer simply engraved below the painting but reverberated throughout his entire being, piercing his heart. He realized his Savior was using this painting to personally ask him the question: "I have done this for you; what have you done for me?"

He knew the living Christ required his answer.

He trembled as he gazed at the picture. He still remembered the prayer he had prayed when only four years old.

Dear Savior, do Thou be mine and I will be Thine!

Finally he answered the Lord. "I have loved you for a long time. But I have never actually done a single thing for You. From now on, I will do whatever you lead me to do."

And Christ placed a torch in the hand of Count Zinzendorf.

Just a few months later, he purchased his grandmother's huge estate at Berthelsdorf in southeastern Saxony.

It was there that his work began.

He smiled as he remembered the day he had greeted the stranger at the door of his manor. His eyes had been immediately drawn to his burning torch.

"I am Christian David," the runner announced himself.

Christian wasted no time but boldly stated his mission.

"I have come to ask for your help. Christians are being severely oppressed and persecuted. They are fleeing for their lives from Beohemia, Moravia, Germany, and beyond! Many are in desperate need of a place such as this for a refuge!"

Count Zinzendorf smiled. "My Lord has my life," he told Christian David, "and along with my life, all my possessions."

Ten Moravians came with Christian David just a few days later. When they first arrived, they scarcely looked at their new home for their thoughts were filled with their escape. But the next day, they gazed at their new home in wonder. There were evergreen woods on two sides of the rising ground. On the other sides were beautiful, well-tended gardens. Just a short distance away, lofty hills dominated the spectacular view.

Someone softly broke the silence.

"Let us call this beautiful refuge *Herrnhut.*"

Herrnhut. The word could be translated two ways: *"Under the Lord's watch"* or *"On the watch for the Lord."*

Yes, this land would be called *Herrnhut.*

Christian David returned again and again, leading Christians who had left all their possessions behind them, stealing them across borders by night, placing them safely in Herrnhut.

And Christian did his work well. By 1726, there was a community of three-hundred people living in two hundred houses on the Count's estate. Count Zinzendorf, along with twelve elected elders, served as the town council. There was the home for *Single Brethren* and another for *Single Sisters.* A boarding house for children had been built, and there was now an academy, the print shop, an apothecary. The Christians had been industrious, anxious to work. There were the woolen mills. Linen was woven and sold. The potters toiled, along with the carpenters, farmers, bakers, and cooks.

Count Zinzendorf sighed. He had not once regretted his decision to turn his estate into a haven for Christians. He had committed his life and his wealth to serving Christ by serving His oppressed people.

But along with the beautiful people of God had come the wolves, always seeking the tender lamb, the weakened sheep.

Even now a wolf was stalking the community, howling that Count Zinzendorf was the beast referred to in the book of Revelation!

"My Lord," Count Zinzendorf groaned aloud. "Show me what to do!"

And instantly he knew.

"We must move out of our new manor," he told his wife and children. We will make our home in the orphanage."

They lived in the midst of the community, and the Count spent hours each day going from house to house, reading the Scriptures and counselling the believers in the ways of the Lord.

Count Zinzendorf

Still the peace that Count Zinzendorf longed for was shattered by constant division, bitter grudges, accusations and strife. He grew so weary of it.

Again he knelt before his Lord.

"Lord, I long to see this place a haven of rest and peace and love!

"And my Lord, where is your power among this people? My heart yearns for You to move among us!"

Again the answer came from his Lord.

He was just twenty-seven years of age when he called twenty-four couples together.

"We must pray," he told them.

"And we must pray *without ceasing.*"

It was on August 27, 1727, that twenty-four men and twenty-four women began praying one hour each day.

Day after day, night after night, they prayed. Herrnhut literally became God's house of prayer.

There was not a moment that prayer was not ascending from that community of believers to the throne room of God.

God in turn descended upon Herrnhut.

The Count's vision of peace and power at last became a reality. His fatigue was replaced with renewed vigor. Love and sweet fellowship replaced bickering and dissension.

Power swept through the community of believers and began to spread across its boundaries.

The prayers continued. Unending. Unceasing.

Others joined in the prayer watch.

At Herrnhut and abroad, on land and at sea, history's longest prayer meeting continued.

Revival began in the hearts of the prayer warriors themselves.

After just six months of this hourly intercession, Count Zinzendorf challenged the Christians to march across Greenland, Turkey, Lapland, South Africa, England, Wales and Ireland, and to preach the gospel to the Indians of North America and the black slaves of the West Indies.

Three-hundred missionaries, their torches blazing, ran from Herrnhut, intent on bringing the Gospel of Jesus Christ to the neglected people of the world.

They left running, undaunted by confinements in dank prisons, shipwrecks, plagues, poverty and constant death threats.

Still the prayers continued to ascend to God.

John Wesley visited Herrnhut one day in 1738 and wrote of his visit:

"I would gladly have spent my life here; but my Master calls me to labor in another part of his vineyard. I was constrained to take my leave of this happy place; O, when shall this Christianity cover the earth, as the 'waters cover the sea?'"

The prayer meeting began in 1727 by Count Zinzendorf and, carried on by dedicated prayer warriors, continued nonstop until 1827. One-hundred years of unceasing prayer ascended to the heavens!

The *Great Awakening* swept across England and America during those years, birthing hundreds of thousands of souls into the Kingdom of God.

All because of one runner who kept praying . . .

Chapter 57

Dave

For if they fall, the one will lift up his fellow.
Ecclesiastes 4:10

The runner paused, looked at Dave, and then gently continued.

"Dave, Count Zinzendorf found he could run - but not without the power of God. The believers at Herrnhut, to be under the Lord's watch, found they had to also be on the watch for the Lord.

"Dave, how long have you been trying to run in your own power and strength? How long have you been so busy running that you have neglected to spend time with your Lord?"

Dave sank to his knees, tears steaming down his face.

"My God," he cried. "Make me a man of prayer! Your people today need to dwell together in unity and love and peace! And your church is in dire need of your power!

"Lord, I need to be filled with your power and your love! Let me be one of your servants who will tap in to your vast supply of power daily, and may I never again be guilty of running in my own strength.

"For my strength is weakness.

"My wisdom is foolishness.

"May I never get so involved in this race that I run in circles, carrying a worthless torch, its fire gone out.

"Refill me, my Lord Jesus, with the Spirit of the living God."

Dave felt the hand of the runner briefly on his shoulder and knew their prayers were merging.

Hours later, Dave looked up. The runner was gone.

Dave looked at his torch. Fire blazed from it, casting a glow over the entire area.

"My God," he breathed, his face glowing in the light of his torch. "Lead me daily in the direction you want me to go. And help me never again - *ever* - to run a single day without first coming to you for power, to have my torch refilled with the fire of the Holy Spirit!"

Strength coursed through his being, filling him with anticipation for what lay ahead. Eagerly he began to run, his voice shouting and singing praises to the Master whom he loved with his entire being.

His torch cast a glow over a vast area. He looked ahead with pleasure, his spirit soaring with new vitality.

"Lord Jesus," he breathed. "I love you! I want you to know that there is nothing I would rather be doing than running for you! And Lord . . . there is no one I would rather run with than you.

"Thank you, thank you, for refilling me with

your love,
your power,
your awesome Presence."

Chapter 58

Dave

He that taketh not his cross, and followeth after me, is not worthy of me.
Matthew 10:38

The old man's pace had slowed. Pain filled his eyes as he limped along. His hair was snow white and deep furrows lined his face. But still he ran.

Dave greeted him warmly, but he made no response. Dave was running on by, when something about the man made him pause.

"Sir, could we talk for a few moments?" Dave asked.

The man looked at the young runner sharply. Then with a curt nod, they made their way together to a nearby park.

The gentleman sighed deeply as he sat down. He bent and removed his shoes from his swollen and gnarled feet.

"How beautiful are the feet of them that preach the gospel of peace, and bring glad tidings of good things," Dave quoted softly.

The man gave no indication that he had heard.

Leaning back against the bench, he closed his eyes.

Dave sat quietly. A deep voice suddenly penetrated the silence.

"They are not the same today."

Dave waited for him to continue, but when there were no further comments, he asked, "Who, Sir?"

"The young ones. The new ones. They come to the mission field expecting, always expecting."

Dave finally spoke into the lengthening pause.

"Expecting what, Sir?"

The eyes snapped open and seemed to stare right into Dave's soul.

Dave saw something more in those eyes now. He had noticed the pain, the weariness earlier. But now shining through them was a clear and discerning mind. The man sat erect then and spoke sharply.

"Young man, don't be one of them. Don't run this race for what you can get out of it. Run, expecting only to give all that you have to give, even if it means your life.

"The young runners expect too much today. They want riches, fame, the applause of men, comfort, ease. They expect a harvest even before they have tilled the land and sown the seed! They are coming overseas in the name of Christ for an adventure, a thrill!

"When will they quit saying, 'What can I get,' and say instead, 'Ah, my Lord! What can I give?' "

The man leaned back again. Dave's heart ached for this weary man whose flame still soared from his torch, but whose arm was nearly too exhausted to lift it.

A few minutes passed.

Dave thought the man was sleeping, so he just sat quietly, breathing a prayer for him.

Again he spoke.

"I wish every young runner could have been at the ordination service of my friend. It was at this service that I entered the race. It was back in 1920. Dr. John Lake was the speaker. Young Man, as long as I live I will never forget his challenge to us that night . . .

"How I wish every beginning runner could hear it!"

The eyes pierced into Dave's.

"Young Man, you are one who will."

The Message Given By
Dr. John G. Lake
(1920)

The thirteenth chapter of Acts tells the story of the ordination and sending forth of the apostle Paul, his ordination to the apostleship. Paul never writes of himself as an apostle until the thirteenth chapter of Acts. He had been an evangelist and teacher for thirteen years when the thirteenth chapter of Acts was written, and that ordination took place. Men who have a real call are not afraid of apprenticeships.

There is a growing up in experience in the ministry. When Paul started out in the ministry, he was definitely called of God and was assured of God through Ananias that it would not be an easy service, but a terrific one, for God said to Ananias:

"Arise, and go into the street which is called Straight, and enquire in the house of Judas for one called Saul of Tarsus: for, behold, he prayeth . . . He is a chosen vessel unto me, to bear my name before the Gentiles, and kings, and the children of Israel: For I will shew him how great things he must suffer for my name's sake."

He was not going to live in a holy ecstasy, wear a beautiful halo, have a heavenly time and ride in a limousine. He was going to have a drastic time, a desperate struggle, a terrific experience. And no man in Biblical history ever had more dreadful things to endure than the Apostle Paul. He gives a list in his letter to the Corinthians of the things that he had then endured.

Of the Jews five times received I forty stripes save one. Thrice was I beaten with rods, once was I stoned, thrice I suffered shipwreck, a night and a day I have been in the deep; in journeyings often, in perils of waters, in perils of robbers, in perils by mine own countrymen, in perils by the heathen, in perils in the city, in perils in the wilderness, in perils in the sea, in perils among false brethren;

In weariness and painfulness, in watchings often, in hunger and thirst, in fastings often, in cold and nakedness. II Corinthians 11:24-27

They stripped him of his clothing, and the executioner lashed him with an awful scourge until he fell unconscious, bleeding and broken. They doused him with a bucket of salt water to keep the maggots off, and threw him in a cell to recover. That was the price of apostleship. That was the price of the call of God and His service. But God said, "He shall bear my name before the gentiles and kings and the children of Israel." He qualified as God's messenger.

Beloved, we have lost that character of consecration. God is trying to restore it in our day. He has not been able to make much progress along that line with the average preacher. "Mrs. So-and-so said such-and-such, and I am just not going to stand for it." That is the other kind of preacher with another kind of call: not the heaven call, not the death call if necessary - not the kind the apostle Paul had.

Do you want to know why God poured out His Spirit in South Africa like He did nowhere else in the world? There was a reason. This example will illustrate. We had one hundred and twenty five men out on the field at one time. We were a very young institution; we were not known in the world. South Africa is 7,000 miles away from any European country. It is 10,000 miles by way of England to the United States. Our finances got so low under the awful assault we were compelled to endure, that there came a time I could not even mail to these workers at the end of the month a $10 bill. It got so I could not send them $2! The situation was desperate. What was I to do? Under these circumstances, I did not want to take the responsibility of leaving men and their families on the frontier without real knowledge of what the conditions were.

Some of us at headquarters sold our clothes, sold certain pieces of furniture out of the house, sold anything we could sell, to bring these 125 workers off the field for a conference.

One night in the progress of the conference, I was invited by a committee to leave the room for a minute or two. The conference wanted to have a word by themselves. So I stepped out to a restaurant, drank a cup of coffee, and came back. When I returned, I found they had rearranged the chairs in an oval with a little table at one end, and on the table was the bread and wine. Old Father Vander Wall, speaking for the company, said, "Brother Lake, during your absence we have made our decision. We want you to serve the Lord's Supper. We are going back to the fields if we have to walk back. We are going back if we starve. We are going back if our wives die. We are going back if our children die. We are going back if we die ourselves. We have but one request. If we die, we want you to come and bury us."

The next year I buried twelve men and sixteen wives and children, and there was not one of the twelve in my judgment that might not have lived if they had had the things a man should have when ill. Friends, when you want to find out why the power of God came down from heaven in South Africa like it never came down before since the days of the apostles, there is your answer.

Jesus Christ put the spirit of martyrdom in the ministry. Jesus Christ Himself instituted His ministry with a pledge unto death. When He was with the disciples on the last night He took the cup, "When he had drunk saying." Beloved, the saying was the significant thing. It was Jesus Christ's pledge to the twelve who stood with him, "This cup is the New Testament in my blood." Then He said, "Drink ye all of it."

Friends, those who were there and drank to that pledge of Jesus Christ entered into the same covenant and purpose that He did. That is what all pledges mean. Men have pledged themselves in the wine cup from time immemorial. Generals have pledged their armies unto death. It has been a custom in the race. Jesus Christ sanctified it to the church forever, bless God.

"My blood is the New Testament, Drink ye all of it!" Let us become one in our hearts. Let us become one in our purpose to die for the world. Your blood and mine together. "My blood in the New Testament." It is my demand from you. It is your high privilege.

Dear Friends, there is not an authentic history that can tell us whether any one of the apostles died a natural death. We know that at least nine of them were martyrs, possibly all. Peter died on a cross; James was beheaded; for Thomas they did not even wait to make a cross. They nailed him to an olive tree. John was sentenced to be executed at Ephesus by putting him in a caldron of boiling oil. God delivered him, and his executioners refused to repeat the operation, so he was banished to the Isle of Patmos. John thought so little about it that he does not even tell of the incident. He says, "I was in the Isle of Patmos for the word of God, and for the testimony of Jesus Christ." That was explanation enough. He had committed himself to Jesus Christ for life or death.

Friends, the group of missionaries that followed me went without food, went without clothes, and once when one of my preachers was sunstruck and had wandered away, I tracked him by the blood marks of his feet. Another time I was hunting for one of my missionaries, a young Englishman, 22 years of age. He had come from a line of Church of England preachers for five hundred years. When I arrived at the native village, the old native chief said, "He is not here. He went away over the mountains, and you know mister, he is a white man and he has not learned to walk barefooted." (But he was barefooted.)

That is the kind of consecration that established Pentecost in South Africa. That is the reason we have a hundred thousand native Christians in South Africa. That is the reason we have 1,250 native preachers. That is the reason we have 350 churches in South Africa. That is the reason that today we are the most rapidly growing church in South Africa.

I am not persuading you, dear friends, by holding out a hope that the way is going to be easy. I am calling on you in the name of Jesus Christ, you dear ones who expect to be ordained to the gospel of Jesus Christ tonight, take the route that Jesus took, the route that the apostles took, the route that the early church took, the victory route, whether by life or by death. Historians declare "the blood of the martyrs was the seed of the church." Beloved, that is what the difficulty is in our day - we have so very little seed. The church needs more martyr blood.

If I were pledging men and women to the Gospel of the Son of God, as I am endeavoring to do tonight, it would not be to have a nice church and harmonious surroundings and a sweet do-nothing time. I would invite them to be ready to die. That was the spirit of early Methodism. John Wesley established a heroic call. He demanded from every preacher to be "ready to pray, ready to preach, ready to die." That is always the spirit of Christianity. When there is any other spirit coming into the church, it is not the spirit of Christianity. It is a foreign spirit. It is a sissified substitute.

I lived on corn meal mush many a period with my family, as I preached to thousands of people, and we did not growl. When my missionaries were on the field existing on corn meal mush, I could not eat pie. My heart was joined to them. That is the reason we never had splits in our work in South Africa. That is one country where Pentecost never has split. The split business began to develop years afterward, when pumpkin pie eating missionaries began to infest the country. Men who are ready to die for the Son of God do not split. They do not holler the first time they get a stomach ache. *Uncle Bud* Robinson tells a story on himself. He had gone to preach in the southern mountains. It was the first time in his life that no one invited him to go home and eat with them. So he slept on the floor, and the next day, and the next night. After five days and five nights had passed, his stomach began to growl terribly for food. Every once in a while, he would stop and say, "Lay down, you brute!" and he went on with his sermon. That is what won. That is what will win every time. That is what we need today.

Our spirit refuses to sacrifice. It refuses to die. It refuses to suffer. That is not the spirit of the Christ or the spirit of the Father. We have forgotten how to suffer or die to win for God. I went to Oregon, twelve miles from the highway, to pray for a woman that was dying. I inquired for a Bible. There was not a Bible in the community, and on the fifth day, an old woman from up in the mountains came down and brought me a Bible.

At Carlton on the Pacific highway, forty miles from Portland, a woman came to our meetings that had lived twenty-five miles back in the hills for twenty-five years, and she said, "Mr. Lake, there has not been a preacher in our community for twenty-five years, not even to bury our dead. There is an old woman who comes to the graves and we invite her to pray." You can find that condition almost anywhere in the back country. When I started to preach the Gospel, I walked twenty miles on Sunday morning to my services, and walked home twenty miles in the night when I got through. I did it for years for Jesus and souls.

In early Methodism, an old local preacher would start Saturday and walk all night and then walk all night Sunday night to get back to his work. It was the common custom. Peter Cartwright preached for sixty dollars per year and baptized ten thousand converts.

Friends, we talk about consecration, and we preach about consecration, but this is the kind of consecration that my heart is asking for tonight. That is the kind of consecration that will get answers from heaven. That is the kind that God will honor. That is the consecration to which I would pledge Pentecost. I would strip Pentecost of its frills and fantangles. Jesus Christ, through the Holy Ghost, calls us tonight, not to any earthly mansion and a ten thousand dollar motor car, but to put our lives - body, soul, and spirit - on the altar of service. All hail! Ye who are ready to die for Christ and this glorious gospel, we salute you. You are brothers with us and with your Lord.

* * * * * * *

The stirring voice ceased. Dave looked at his companion, amazed. He did not even seem like the same man! His eyes were ablaze, and rather than being spent by delivering the message, he was full of vitality and vigor.

"Young Man, what is your name?"

"David."

"Ah. David."

Then, pointing a bony finger straight under Dave's nose, he said, "Are you acquainted with David Brainerd, the young man who labored in your country and literally laid down his life and crawled at times to reach one more soul for Christ?"

Dave shook his head. "I don't know about David, Sir."

"Then listen. And don't forget him. We need Davids today who will run this race to give of themselves, not to get for themselves."

He looked at Dave critically. Then he shook his head slightly.

"I don't know. You may be one. But perhaps you won't even want to be like David when you hear his story."

Chapter 59

David Brainerd
(1718 to 1747)

We ought to lay down our lives for the brethren.
I John 3:16

"**My** God," whispered the dying old man. "There is a dark cloud upon the work of the Gospel!"

He lay silent for a few moments, and then he sighed his last prayer.

"Lord, revive and prosper the work and grant that it may live when I am dead."

"Revive the work, Lord," was the cry of John Eliot's heart.

Known as the Apostle to the Indians, John's work was in Eastern America. He had left his job as a schoolmaster in England to take Jesus to the Indians who lived in the vicinity of Massachusetts Bay of America. He had trudged along countless trails and through dense forests to find their villages. He had struggled with learning their languages. He had faithfully preached to them about Jesus Christ. He had even purchased land and built entire towns for them. With great expectations he had named one town **Noonatomen**, the Indian word for "Rejoicing."

There had been little cause for rejoicing.

Though his labors had been rewarded with many Indians receiving Christ, and he rejoiced to see their transformed lives, still the widespread move of God for which John Eliot had dedicated his entire life had never come.

The torch lay where he dropped it, even as his final prayer ascended to the heavens and made its way to the throne of God.

Nearly twenty years later, a boy was born in Connecticut who would be the answer to John's prayer. His father died when he was eight. Six years later, his mother died.

David Brainerd

In 1743, David Brainerd picked up John Eliot's torch and held it aloft to be lit by the Christ who baptizes with fire. Then David began running as John had before him, through the states of New Jersey, New York, and Pennsylvania, thrilled to be bringing the gospel to the Seneca and Delaware Indians.

It did not take long for David Brainerd to become as discouraged as his predecessor. He had not even been running a year, and he was weary and depressed. David wondered if he would ever have cause to rejoice. He sat dejectedly on a log, his diary in one hand, his other pressing against his throbbing head.

How could he continue to take money from the Scottish Missionary Society who supported his work?

For he was a dismal failure.

He had come with noble hopes and dreams - at first. He had doggedly fought his way through swamps, forests, streams and storms. He had forded the Hudson River, plodded on through drenching rains and walked his nearly dead horse through unfamiliar swampland in the blackness of night. More than once he had wrung out his clothes, and putting them back on his shivering body, struggled forward.

It all had taken a toll on his body. He had always been weak and sickly, but now his head ached constantly. He had a persistent fever and his strength was drained by a wracking cough. How many nights had he tried to sleep on a bundle of straw or a few branches in the dense woods during the cold winter?

But the physical difficulties were not what sunk his spirit into depression. He had expected them when he volunteered for his work.

The one thing he could no longer tolerate was his spiritual failure.

Where were the longed for results? Where were the answers to his hours, days and long nights of prayer?

He loved the Indians, but how desperately they needed the salvation Jesus offered. Could he ever forget the scenes he saw the night he lay hidden on a hilltop? The Indians had carefully arranged their offering of ten deer on the altar of fire. He watched in fascinated horror as they writhed and leaped their frenzied sacred dance, their demonic screams piercing the air. Finally, the satanic ritual completed, they had eaten the flesh of their sacrifice before falling into an exhausted stupor.

How would he ever persuade them to turn to Christ for salvation? For he knew they had no desire to give up their idolatrous practices to worship the white man's God.

Could he blame them?

They had seen firsthand the treachery of the white men, and they believed every white man was a Christian. They had been raided by white thieves, slaughtered by white murderers, given "fire water" by white men who coveted their land. The white man's firewater had made them lash out cruelly at one another, quarreling and killing, the peace in their families and tribes shattered by drunkenness. But even while hating the devastation that came with this drink, they were giving up all they owned to get more of the white man's venom.

Alcohol held them in the white man's power. Alcohol was steadily stripping them, leaving them with no hope, no possessions. They would awake from their drunken stupor and discover that they were deeply in debt to the white traders who supplied the drink. They would then be arrested for their debt, thrown into prison, where they were offered freedom only by signing over all their possessions to the white man. Almost worst of all were the sneers, the never-ending ridicule, as these evil men called Christians stole from them their goods, their lands, their very way of life.

Was it any wonder that David had been unable to persuade even one Indian to listen to Christ's offer of salvation?

How would his feeble efforts ever bear fruit? Of all the despised "pale faces" he had ever met, he was the palest of them all!

Yes, the Indians had allowed him to build his strange little log and turf huts in their villages. Still he knew they watched him warily, believing that soon they would learn what evil motive lay behind his kindness.

In a few villages, he had been invited into their wigwams, but the thick smoke had sent him running back out, coughing fitfully. He sighed. Why couldn't he have been strong and healthy? He was pitifully weak and sickly. Often he was so exhausted by the time he dismounted in their villages, that he could not even stand.

Full of disappointment, he wrote his decision in his diary.

"If at the end of this year there are still no results, I will resign my mission."

Laying back down on the ground, he slept. With the brightness of the morning came a stirring of renewed hope. Prostrate before the Lord, David once again poured out his desires to God in prayer, promising Him he would patiently and even cheerfully suffer all things if only God would bless his labors with converts to Christianity.

When David finished praying, he slowly got to his feet. He was still in his twenties, but his body was so weak that it was a great effort to mount his horse.

"One more thing, Lord," he prayed as he made his way to the closest village. "How am I ever going to learn their languages?"

It had taken thirty-six letters just to write down one tribe's word for *question*. It seemed to him that they could have thought of a simpler word than *kremmogkodonaltootiteavreganumeouash!*

His *kremmogkodonaltootiteavreganumeouash* was how he would ever pronounce, let alone memorize such words! And for every Indian village, there was another dialect to learn!

At the end of the year, David began receiving invitations from several churches.

"David, come be our pastor! You will have a home and will no longer have to work among unreachable people in such deplorable conditions."

David struggled with his decision. What did he have to show for his efforts? All his accomplishments could be counted in a few scattered Indians, mostly women and children, who had received Christ. His health had deteriorated so rapidly that he often thought it would be a great relief just to die. His constant coughing kept him awake night after night.

But burning inside his heart was the dream that if he continued his labors, God would do a mighty work among the Indians.

"My Lord," he prayed. "I am not yet ready to abandon this work. But how desperately I need Your help!"

Prayer had become as natural to David as breathing. He often awoke, realizing that even as he had slept, he had dreamed he was praying!

His most urgent prayer had been that God would send him an interpreter who would travel with him, for he realized that he was incapable of learning the language. He had often used a fifty year old Indian who knew English and most of the Indian dialects. But Tinda was drunk more often than he was sober. And how did David know what he was even saying to the people?

Then came the morning Tinda came to David, greatly distressed.

"I dreamed," he said, "that to be saved I had to climb a huge mountain. I tried over and over and over to reach the top. Finally I gave up, knowing it was impossible to climb. I was lost with no hope to be saved. Then I heard a voice calling to me and saying, 'There is hope! There is hope!' And I knew that you are the one to show me the way to be saved."

Tears ran down David's face as he knelt with Tinda, his new brother in Christ! Tinda added *Moses* to his name on the day of his baptism. And Moses Tinda Tautamy became a faithful interpreter, touched by the anointing of God.

No longer did David have to worry about Tinda being drunk. Moses was as excited about preaching as David was now, and he interpreted David's messages with power and zeal.

David never knew exactly when it all happened. But suddenly wherever he went, Indians crowded around him, asking him to show them how to be saved.

Before he could even dismount from his horse in the villages, they would come running from every direction, crowding around his horse, all talking at once. Tinda's face would light up, and he would say, "David! They all want you to tell them about Jesus!"

The magicians, called *pow-wows,* were enraged. More than once they dressed in their skins, put their knives in their belts and brandishing their spears, danced before David and his converts in a frenzied fury, shaking their rattles, trying to scare them into renouncing Christ.

Something was wrong. David and the Christians were not dying from the poison of their spells. These followers of Jesus were immune from their curses. The pow-wows shook their rattles harder, cut themselves deeper, screamed louder to the devils they served.

But their spells were ineffective. Many of them came humbly before David, offering to him their worthless rattles and charms.

David gave them to his Indian brothers in Christ, who burned them while the medicine men knelt and invited Jesus to become their personal Savior and Lord.

One beautiful June Sunday afternoon, David and Moses began to preach about the agonizing death Jesus had endured because He loved the Indians so much. Sitting in front of them, eagerly listening to their every word, were three to four thousand Indians, tears streaming down the faces of even the most hardened warriors. When David asked how many wanted to receive Jesus into their hearts, hundreds immediately responded!

From that day on, David got no rest. When he came out of his hut in the mornings, Indians were waiting outside, eager to learn more about Jesus.

One morning he saw a group of Indians, all sobbing bitterly.

"What do you want Jesus to do for you?" he asked them quietly.

They answered simply, "We want Him to wipe our hearts quite clean!"

David himself could scarcely believe the scene before him. Tribes came from far and wide, children, men and women. As David preached, nearly all who listened wept over the state of their souls. One young Indian woman lay prostrate before God for hours, praying over and over, *"Guttummaukalummeh wechaumeh kmeleh Nolah!"* David was told that she was crying out to Christ, "Have mercy on me, and help me to give You my heart!"

White men came to see "this babbler" who was ruining their liquor business among the Indians. When they heard his preaching, they openly sneered at the idea of Redskins becoming Christians. Some disturbed the meeting, but other scoffers found themselves on their knees being saved!

Families and entire villages were transformed! Where there had been fighting and drunkenness and idolatry, there were now love and peace.

One day a young man ran to David.

"David," he said excitedly. "There is a tribe that has settled not too far from here! They have never heard about Jesus!"

"Call the Christians together," David instructed.

When they stood before him, he said, "I need to go to them. I ask that you pray with me that this tribe will listen to the gospel and receive Christ."

David had a victorious meeting, and when he returned to the village, he learned that everyone in the village had spent the entire night in prayer!

Prayer became a way of life for whole villages. One woman told David the day she was water baptized, "I am so thankful for the kind Christians in Scotland who sent you to us! My heart loves these good people so much," she said, "that I can scarcely help praying for them all night."

"Never," David wrote later, "have I seen such a display of Christian love among any people."

David often would go to sleep while listening to the Indians singing hymns until after midnight.

David's health was giving out completely. He had worked among the Indians for just less than three years and had travelled by foot or on horseback over three-thousand miles during that time. His body was ravaged by tuberculosis. He knew he did not have long to live and welcomed his impending death, even though he was not yet thirty years of age. Only one question plagued him. Who would continue his work among his beloved Indians?

Then John, David's brother, came to visit him. His heart was broken when he saw the state of David's health.

David Brainerd

"David," John promised. "You may die in peace. I will carry on your work among the Indians."

David gazed at his beloved brother. Seeing the torch in his hand, he knew God had answered yet another prayer.

David spent his last days in the home of Jonathan Edwards, the preacher who brought thousands to their knees with his acclaimed sermon, *"Sinners in the Hands of An Angry God."*

"David," Jonathan said one day. "Thank you for letting me read your diary. It needs to be read by all men. It has been a great encouragement to me and will be to others. Please allow me to publish it."

David was horrified at the thought of people reading his diary. He had recorded his innermost prayers, his private confessions, his daily struggles. The pages he wrote were for God's eyes alone. He wanted no glory, no praise, no honor for his name.

But he reluctantly consented with the prayer that someone, somewhere would be encouraged by his life.

Jonathan Edwards counted it a great privilege to have David in his home for his nineteen final weeks. He wrote, "I and my family were richly blessed by David's dying behavior, hearing his dying speeches, receiving his dying counsels, and benefiting by his dying prayers."

David Brainerd died as he lived, breathing a prayer with his last breath on October 9, 1747.

Chapter 60

Dave

*Take, my brethren, the prophets, who have spoken in
the name of the Lord, for an example of suffering
affliction, and of patience.*
James 5:10

"Well?"

Dave was brought abruptly back to the present and
the old man sitting next to him.

"Sir?"

"Well, are you willing to go through the things David
Brainerd went through?"

"Yes, Sir."

The old man was still unsure.

"Jonathan Edwards published his diary," he went on.

Dave realized he was referring to David Brainerd.

"There was a young man in England who literally
poured over that dairy, receiving strength from its pages.
After reading it, he advised every minister he met, 'Let
every preacher of the Gospel read carefully the life of
David Brainerd!'

"Do you know who that young man was?" the old man
asked, his black eyes boring into Dave's.

Dave reluctantly admitted he didn't.

The old man shook his head disgustedly.

"That young man was John Wesley, a runner who
changed his world as he ran with his torch. Men and
devils alike joined forces to stop him, but he just kept
running."

He snorted.

"I would tell you about his life, but young people today
need to study for themselves."

He grew silent as he stared into Dave's eyes.

Dave knew the conversation was ended.

As far as the old man was concerned, it was time for
Dave to get up and get running.

Chapter 61

Dave

*It is not the will of your Father which is in heaven that
one of these little ones should perish.*
Matthew 18:14

Dave was deep in thought as he ran toward his house and nearly ran into Joe's car parked in his driveway. Joe was just crossing the street, heading for the Arnold's house.

"Uncle Joe! What are you doing out so early?"

"Ed had a bad night. I just stopped by to pray with him. What are you doing out so early?"

"I go to the park every morning to eat my breakfast."

"Well, I'll stop by in a bit and we'll talk if you're still home when I finish here."

Dave answered with a quick nod and returned to his uneasy thoughts.

Where was Tom?

This was the first day that he hadn't come to eat since Dave had started buying food for him. Dave knew it was probably foolish to worry, but he couldn't shake off his concern that something was wrong.

He was just leaving his house to return to the park when Uncle Joe walked up the driveway.

"Uncle Joe, why don't you come along with me to the park? We'll talk on the way."

Joe nodded and Dave started out the drive.

"Wait!" he called. You mean . . . walk?"

"Yes, walk!"

"Get in," Joe commanded, motioning to his car. "I never walk when I can ride."

"Ed's sleeping now."

"That's great, Uncle Joe," Dave replied absently, his mind on Tom.

There were several police cars and an ambulance in the roped off park. Dave jumped out of the car and hurried through the bystanders.

"What happened?" he asked a man next to him.

Dave

"Someone said a boy was stabbed. I don't know if he's dead or not."

There were two boys with the policemen. One saw Dave and walked over to him. Dave recognized him as one of Tom's gang. He didn't look so tough today. He looked like a badly frightened small boy.

"It's Tom," he said. "We found him lying on a bench bleeding when we got here this morning."

Dave's stomach lurched.

Tom had been just a few steps from him, possibly dying. And Dave hadn't known he was even there.

The ambulance sped away.

"Follow it, Uncle Joe," Dave said.

"Is he someone you know?" Joe asked, as he tried to keep the ambulance in sight.

"We eat together every morning in the park," Dave answered simply.

Joe parked at the hospital and they hurried into the emergency entrance.

A policeman overheard Dave telling the receptionist that he was there for the stab victim.

"Are you a relative?" he asked.

"No, a friend. How is he?"

"He's still alive. We're trying to identify him. All we've got so far is Tom. What's his last name?"

"I don't know. All I know him by is Tom."

"Well, you're the only one who has shown up. We need to find out who he is and where he lives so we can notify his family."

"I can tell you where he lives, Sir," Dave offered. "His home is the park. He sleeps on one of the benches."

The burly man sighed heavily. "Great. Another one. Is he a runaway? Or doesn't he have parents?"

"I don't know. But I'm going to wait here. If he's able to see someone, I'm available."

The policeman glanced at Dave, then at his torch, then back again. He nodded.

Dave and Joe settled in a waiting room. He wondered about Tom.

If he was a runaway, what had caused a twelve or thirteen year old boy to run away from home? A house filled with violence and abuse? A mother with an endless procession of live-in boyfriends? A home whose only relief came when the dad passed out in a drunken stupor? A kitchen with empty cupboards and refrigerator because all the money for food went to buy crack or cocaine?

Was Tom just one of an endless procession of children whose gnawing physical hunger equaled the craving for love?

Dave's burden for Tom became a heart-wrenching prayer for all such children.

"My Lord, give us godly mothers.

"Give us mothers who will face the hardships of life and yet keep their hand firmly in yours. Give us mothers who will fill their homes with love for their children and their children with love for you."

He remembered reading about the mother in Russia who raised her children during the reign of Communism. Her children were forced to attend the state schools, where atheism was daily drilled into their minds. But she was determined that Satan would not rob her precious children of their faith in God. She faithfully spent six hours every single evening, teaching her children the Word and the ways of God."

"Give us more mothers like that dedicated Russian mother and more women like *Susanna . . . "*

Chapter 62

Susanna and John Wesley
(1669-1742 AND 1703-1791)

*These words, which I command thee this day, shall be
in thine heart: and thou shalt teach them diligently unto
thy children, and shalt talk of them when thou sittest in
thine house, and when thou walkest by the way, and
when thou liest down, and when thou risest up.*
Deuteronomy 6:6-7

Susanna Wesley stood transfixed, staring in horror as her house burned to the ground. She gazed, yet did not even see, as roaring flames devoured all her earthly possessions. Her mind's eye saw only John, her beloved six year old son. He was alone inside the fiery grave.

Her husband, Samuel, had tried again and again to reach him but was driven back by the blaze. Finally, in exhausted defeat, he knelt on the ground and committed John's soul to the Lord.

Susanna still stood frozen in shock, a silent scream repeating her son's name over and over in her mind. She stared at the flames, stupefied, and then her eyes focused on a window.

Could it be John, or was her mind cruelly deceiving her? No! It *was* John! She watched a neighbor run through the scorching heat and pull him from the house just seconds before the burning roof collapsed.

Susanna and Samuel knelt with their eight children and their neighbors, thanking God for sparing the family.

What did it matter that their three-storied, seven room house was reduced to ashes? Their clothes and furniture could be replaced! Their library, purchased over the years at a great sacrifice, would never be restored - but what were books, compared to people?

Susanna stole a look at her son while kneeling on the ground with her husband. His escape was truly a

251

miracle. Silently, she made a promise to God concerning John.

"My Father," she prayed, "I do intend to be more particularly careful of the soul of this child that you have so mercifully provided for! I will endeavor more than ever to instill into his mind the principles of your true religion and virtue! You surely have some great purpose for him!"

When the flames settled to ashes, the family sifted through the remains. All that they found were two bits of charred paper from their library. One was the song, penned by Samuel, *"Behold, the Saviour of Mankind."*

The other was just a fragment of his beloved Bible with only this sentence still legible: *"Sell all thou hast. Take up thy cross, and follow me."*

Samuel, later writing a friend of the fire, added, "All this, thank God, does not sink my wife's spirits."

Susanna was no stranger to hardship. She, the youngest in a family of twenty-five children, bore nineteen children. Only nine lived to adulthood. One child died in his sleep. Susanna, her first daughter, died. Then death claimed her precious twins. Between the four years from 1697 to 1701, five more of her babies died. The carelessness of a maid caused another daughter to be deformed for life. She had nursed several of her children through smallpox. Her first-born son did not speak until he was nearly six years of age. She battled disease, and this was not the first fire that had claimed her earthly possessions.

Days were a constant struggle to provide for her family. There was the time when the full responsibility of her family fell upon her, for her husband was imprisoned because of accumulated debts. Samuel was a minister, but an impractical man, unconcerned about the management of his financial affairs.

She was thankful for her dairy herd during this devastating period of her life, for the cows were her main means of support. Then came the dark morning that she viewed their corpses littering the field. One of Samuel's enemies had slaughtered them all during the night.

Tragedy caused Susanna, a physically frail woman, to cling more tightly to her Savior's hand, to immerse herself more fully in His Word, to spend more hours on her knees in prayer.

Her one purpose was to raise her children in such a way that their souls would be saved from the eternal fires to come. And she was now determined to spend extra hours training her fifteenth child, John, for she knew in her heart that God had destined him for a special work.

Her days were full.

On Sunday evening, Susanna led a special service in her home during her husband's many prolonged absences. It began as a simple service for her children, but then her friends and neighbors asked if they could join her family. Susanna read a sermon, prayed, and talked of Jesus, her Lord and her Friend. At first, only a few people gathered in her kitchen, but soon over two-hundred people filled her house and overflowed into the barn!

After the birth of her ninth child, Susanna set aside two hours each day for her private time with her Lord.

She spent six hours of every day for twenty years teaching her children. She began teaching them when they were still infants, teaching each one obedience to their parents. She taught them to cry softly, to eat and drink whatever was given to them. She did not allow drinking or eating between meals, unless they were ill. The family ate promptly at 6:00 each evening, following family prayers. The children were sent to bed at eight, and were instructed to go to sleep. All who visited Susanna's home were amazed at the large family of quiet, but happy and playful children.

Then there was the spiritual training. She wrote three religious textbooks for their studies.

Having invested so much time and energy in her children, Susanna's heart ached when several of her daughters chose unworthy, but wealthy husbands, eager to leave behind them their life of poverty.

Her faith did not waver when Mary, her crippled daughter, died in childbirth a year after her marriage or when her daughter, Kezia, died at the age of thirty-two.

She lived to see the fulfillment of God's promise, "Let us not be weary in well doing: for in due season we shall reap, if we faint not."

Susanna reaped a bountiful harvest for her labors. John, in whom Susanna had invested so much of her time, lived a life of strict discipline all through his childhood and young years.

Then came the day at age thirty-five that he met Christ. With his new birth, his life was transformed.

The year Samuel died, John and his younger brother, Charles, prepared to leave as missionaries to Georgia to preach to the Indians and the settlers of the New World. John was concerned about leaving his newly-widowed mother, but she assured him he was making the right choice.

"Had I twenty sons," she said cheerfully, "I should rejoice that they were all so employed, though I should never see them again!"

John returned to England heartsick, feeling that his efforts to evangelize had miserably failed. Not one Indian had received Christ through his ministry.

And then John experienced the mighty touch of God that revolutionized his ministry.

He recorded the event in his journal:

"Monday, January 1, 1739, I and my brother Charles were present at our love-feast in Fetter-lane, with about sixty of our brethren. About three in the morning, as we were continuing instant in prayer, the power of God came mightily upon us, insomuch that many cried out for exceeding joy, and many fell to the ground. As soon as we recovered a little from that awe and amazement at the presence of His majesty, we broke out with one voice, "We praise thee, O God, we acknowledge thee to be the Lord!"

After that day, there was a powerful anointing upon John, and wherever he preached, huge crowds gathered to hear him. A mighty conviction of sin smote the hearts of the multitudes.

During the last half of the eighteenth century, he preached and taught every day, making an annual circuit from London to Bristol to Newcastle and back to London, with many side trips along the way.

He and Charles introduced singing of hymns in public worship.

Charles wrote over 6,500 hymns and has been referred to as "the greatest hymn writer of all ages." He penned

"Jesus, Lover of My Soul", "O for a Thousand Tongues to Sing", "Hark, the Herald Angels Sing", "Love Divine, All Love Excelling".

When John returned to England, crowds of over twenty-thousand people lined the hillsides to hear him proclaim the gospel. Countless lives, families, and villages were transformed as people turned to Jesus Christ for salvation.

He ordained men to go into the world and preach. They were called "Methodists."

"Give me a hundred men," John cried, "who fear nothing but sin, and desire nothing but God, and I will shake the world! I care not a straw whether they be clergymen or laymen; and such alone will overthrow the kingdom of Satan and build up the Kingdom of God on earth!"

Theologians around the world looked amazed upon this five foot, three inch, one-hundred twenty-eight pound man who drew the huge crowds. Finally one dared to ask him, "Wesley! How do you attract these crowds?"

John's answer was quick and sure.

"I simply set myself on fire, and the people come to see me burn."

Could any godly mother fail to be pleased with such a son? He described himself as "a man of one book" - the Bible. Yet he wrote over two-hundred books, edited a magazine, compiled dictionaries in four languages, and composed a home medical handbook - all in his own handwriting!

He travelled over 250,000 miles on horseback - the equivalent of riding ten times around the world along its equator!

He preached more than 40,000 powerful sermons!

John, like his mother, was no stranger to adversity. He married a widow at the age of forty-eight, but her greatest pleasure was to torment and annoy her faithful husband. Finally, unable to break him, she deserted him, taking with her some of his prized journals and papers.

John was constantly heckled and jeered. He was riding along a road one day when it occurred to him that three whole days had passed in which he had suffered no persecution! No bricks had been thrown - he had not even been bombarded with an egg!

He immediately stopped his horse with a shout and fell to his knees.

"My Lord," he cried. "Show me my fault! Am I backslidden? Have I sinned?"

A fellow on the other side of the hedge heard his prayer and recognized him.

"I'll fix that Methodist preacher," he said, picking up a brick and throwing it at him.

The brick fell short of its mark, but John, leaping to his feet, joyfully shouted, "Thank God! It's all right! I still have His presence!"

John's ministry transformed not only men's hearts, but the country itself.

One day, as he rode his horse through the countryside, he noticed the drabness of the land and the ugliness of the villages.

"I will bring beauty to England," he thought to himself. From then on, John carried with him flower seeds, and distributing them to housewives, he offered them prizes for the most beautiful gardens. Today the English countryside is one of the most colorful places in the world!

There were other lasting changes.

A British nobleman, passing through a village in Cornwall, England, searched vainly for a drink. In desperation, he finally stopped a villager. "How is it that I cannot get a glass of liquor in this wretched village of yours?" he asked.

The old man, recognizing the rank of the stranger, respectfully removed his cap, bowed, and then replied, "My lord, over a hundred years ago a man named John Wesley came to these parts."

Susanna, in her seventies now, stood beside her son as he preached to the crowd filling the hillside. Her mind travelled back to the six-year old child appearing at the window of the house engulfed in flames and the promise she had made to plant the Word of God firmly in his heart.

Susanna and John Wesley

Could she have spent her life in any more profitable way than this? Yes, trials and hardships had been ever present. But God had sustained her through them all.

"My God," she sighed. "We are of yesterday and know nothing. But Your boundless mind comprehends, at one view, all things, past, present, and future. As you see all things, you understand what is good and proper for each individual - and for me - with relation to both worlds."

Her last words to her loved ones were, "Children, when I am gone, sing a song of praise to God."

And John had faithfully followed in her footsteps.

At eighty-three years of age, he complained that he could no longer read or write more than fifteen hours a day without his eyes hurting. He regretted that he had to limit himself to two sermons a day. He was ashamed to confess that he had an increasing tendency to lie in bed until 5:30 A.M.!

His blueprint for living was:

Do All the Good You Can,
By All the Means You Can
In All the Ways You Can,
In All the Places You Can,
At All the Times You Can,
To All the People You Can,
As long as Ever You Can!

A lady once asked him how he would spend his time if he knew he would die at midnight the following day.

He seemed bewildered at her question, then answered, "Why, Madam, just as I intend to spend it now! I would preach this evening at Gloucester, and again at five tomorrow morning; after that I would ride to Tewkesbury, preach in the afternoon, and meet the societies in the evening. I would then go to Martin's house, who expects to entertain me, talk and pray with the family as usual, retire to my room at 10 o'clock, commend myself to my heavenly Father, lie down to rest, and wake up in Glory!"

What a legacy Susanna and John Wesley have left to not only the Methodists, but
    to every mother
        to every son
            and to every child of the living God!

Preach the Word
Charles Wesley

Shall I, for fear of mortal man,
the Spirit's course in me restrain?
Or, undismayed, in deed and word
Be a true witness to my Lord

Awed by a mortal's frown, shall I
Conceal the Word of God most high?
How then before Thee shall I dare
To stand, or how Thine anger bear

Shall I, to sooth the unholy throng
Soften Thy truths, and smooth my tongue?
To gain earth's guilded toys, or flee
The Cross, endured my Lord, by Thee.

What then is he whose scorn I dread,
Whose wrath or hate makes me afraid?
A man! an heir of death, a slave
To sin! a bubble on the wave!

Yea! let men rage, since Thou wilt spread
Thy shadowing wings about my head;
Since in all pain Thy tender love
Will still my sure refreshment prove.

Give me Thy strength, O God of power;
Then let winds blow or tempests roar;
Thy faithful witness will I be;
'Tis fixed; I can do all through Thee.

Chapter 63

Dave

When he saw him, he had compassion on him, and went to him, and bound up his wounds, pouring in oil and wine.
Luke 10:33-34

Dave's thoughts were interrupted by a tap on his shoulder. He looked up to see a nurse.

"Tom is very restless and frightened. We have him stabilized and are preparing him for surgery. Since you're the only one here, we'd like you to talk to him before we take him in."

Dave followed her to the bed behind the curtain, wondering what Tom's reaction would be when he saw him.

Tom hadn't noticed him, so Dave just stood looking at him for a moment. He looked so vulnerable. Tears were sliding down his colorless face. An IV and blood transfusion dripped into his vein. Two nurses worked to staunch the flow of blood from his side and his chest. Tom turned and saw him and grabbed his arm.

Dave suddenly knew Tom was going to be all right. He was not only going to live, he would one day live for the Lord. He couldn't say how he knew. He just knew.

"Tom," he said. "I'm here to pray for you. I love you. Jesus loves you too. I will stay right here and be in your room when you wake up."

Tom grew still as Dave prayed for him. Dave had to gently remove Tom's hand from his arm when an orderly came to take him to surgery. He kept his panic-filled eyes on Dave until the elevator door closed behind him.

Uncle Joe went home and Dave settled down for a long stay in the surgery waiting room.

About an hour later, the policeman came into the waiting room.

"They said you were still here," he greeted Dave. "We still don't have any idea who this boy belongs to."

He shrugged and added, "We may never know."

He left and Dave was again left alone with his thoughts. A short time later, Joe came in.

"How's the boy, Son?" he asked.

Dave smiled. "He'll be okay, Uncle Joe. What brings you back?"

"I got to wondering about you and the lad. Here, I brought you a sandwich." He handed Dave a bag.

It was late afternoon when a doctor came in the room.

"Are you here for Tom?" he asked Dave.

Dave stood. "Yes. How is he?"

"He'll make it. The knife missed his heart by less than an inch. He's going to be in the hospital for a good while though. He's in recovery now. You can see him in about an hour or so."

Dave was given his room number nearly three hours later. Tom was sleeping and looked even whiter than before. Dave napped but woke up suddenly when Tom grabbed his arm. His grip was weaker this time.

Tom drifted back to sleep, and Dave slipped out quietly to tell his uncle he planned to spend the night.

Tom and Dave were both asleep when a nurse came in with the policeman the next morning.

"Tom!" the nurse said, shaking him gently. "Tom, there is someone here to ask you a few questions."

Tom's eyes filled with fear when he saw the policeman. He closed his eyes and kept them and his mouth firmly shut.

"Just tell me where to find one of your parents, Tom."

"Did you see who assaulted you?"

"What is your last name?"

Finally they left the room and Tom instantly opened his eyes.

"Tom," Dave began, "someone needs to notify your family."

Tom's eyes narrowed.

"Why?" he asked softly. "You're the only one who cares."

He was sleeping when Dave left word at the nurses' station to tell Tom he would return later that afternoon.

He was about to enter the room when he heard voices through the half-opened door. Looking in, he saw Uncle Joe. He was holding Tom's hand. Dave listened in shock to the sentences he kept repeating. "It'll be okay, Son. Dave will take care of you."

Dave quickly backed out.

"I guess I will at that," he thought. "Tom might just as well eat at my table as the park table."

All kinds of objections flooded his mind. He brushed them aside and was smiling when he entered the room. Tom grinned back through the maze of needles and tubes.

They all talked for awhile before a nurse came in. Joe and Dave moved to the hall and Joe said, "It's about like you figured, Son. Tom and I have had a long talk. His mother is spaced out on drugs. Her house is a gathering place for sots and addicts."

He shook his head.

"Believe me, it's no place for kids. Tom left almost six months ago."

"Has Tom been living in the park for half a year?" Dave asked.

"No, he moved and slept wherever he found a place to bed down. He decided to stay at the park when he discovered a hot breakfast was served there every morning."

Dave ignored the remark.

"Who attacked him?"

"A couple of older teens looking for kicks."

"Uncle Joe, Tom has been a wild kid. He doesn't have much going for him. I'm not sure why, but I know he will be in the race someday."

Joe nodded.

"I wouldn't be surprised. He's already praying."

"Praying!"

"Sure. He and I had a prayer meeting this afternoon while you were gone."

"Tom prayed?"

"It sounded like a prayer to me. Oh, it wasn't anything with fancy words, but he was sincere. He confessed a lot of sins. But he only broke down and wept when he told the Lord he was sorry for cussing at you. Then he asked the Lord if he would come into his heart and make a new person out of him. He told the Lord he wanted to be just like you. So when he finished praying, I told him you would take care of him."

Tom continued to improve under Joe's watchful eye. The afternoon came that Dave made his daily run to the hospital room and found it empty. Fighting panic, he went to the nearest nurse.

"Where did they take Tom?"

"He was released."

"Where did he go? He has no home!"

She looked puzzled.

"Why, he went with his uncle, of course. We all referred to the gentleman as Uncle Joe."

Dave dialed Joe's number.

"Where is Tom?" was his greeting.

"Settle down, Davey. He's here with me, of course. I've fixed the spare bedroom for him. As soon as he's feeling better, we're going shopping for some things he needs and we want you to go with us. We'll let you know when we're going."

"Uncle Joe, I thought you wanted me to . . ."

"Tom and I talked. We agreed you had work to do. As for me, I don't have anything but lots of time on my hands. Believe me, we'll be calling on you often enough."

"Uncle Joe, Tom isn't an innocent . . ."

"Well of course he isn't! Neither am I! Quit worrying like an old woman, will you? We're getting along fine. He's in there now teasing his new dog."

"Dog! You hate dogs!"

There was a silence.

Joe finally broke it with a low, "I never cared much for boys either, Dave. But Jesus and Tom have changed all that. We'll be okay. Now go run someplace."

A click and the dial tone followed his words. Dave was left staring at the telephone.

There was no doubt about it. His uncle was surely carrying a torch.

Chapter 64

Dave

Discretion shall preserve thee, understanding shall keep thee: to deliver thee from the strange woman, even from the stranger which flattereth with her words; which forsaketh the guide of her youth, and forgetteth the covenant of her God.
Proverbs 2:11 & 16-17

Dave picked up his journal. He hadn't made an entry in over three months. He skipped all the blank pages and found the current date. He picked up his pen and prepared to write down the events of this day.

But instead of writing, he again leafed through the blank pages. Lost days. Lost weeks. Lost months. What people and events could have filled the pages if he hadn't run in the wrong direction?

He thought about the time he had lost. The moments and hours and weeks all seemed to blur together. He wished he could erase them or just keep them blank like these pages in his journal. But they were part of his life. Turning back to the first blank page, he began to write ....

I was tired. Oh, I had been tired before, but it was different this time. My fatigue was coupled with a gnawing loneliness. Almost daily, I passed husband and wife teams running together, their hands clasped. Each time I glanced their way I was conscious of my solitary run. Finally I was consumed by an intense hunger that would only be satisfied by finding a mate to run with me.

I only ran a few steps after making my decision to find a wife, when I heard someone running behind me. I turned and stared at the beautiful woman approaching me. She was vibrant, literally pulsing

263

with life and laughing as she tried to catch up with me. I slowed my pace and finally stopped. That was my first mistake. Then I made my second.

I ran toward her. Her hair was windblown and she laughed with joy as she tilted her face toward me. All the restlessness of the last few weeks vanished as I took her hands in mine.

How many weeks passed? I don't know. I only know my heart pounded with fear of her answer the night I asked, "Will you run with me?"

"I have come to run with you," she replied, her expression one of love.

My joy was complete. I was captivated by my beloved. I did take time to thank the Lord for sending her to me. I realized that he had sensed my need and had sent me the desire of my heart.

"Thank you, Lord, thank you," I whispered, as I walked hand in hand with the one who would soon be my running mate. "But I will need to quit running, just temporarily, in order to wed my lovely one."

My family and friends were estatic when they met her and learned of our decision. They could fellowship with me while my torch was lowered, its rays no longer blinding them. They helped me prepare for my wedding festivities. I had not known life could be so exhilarating. I delighted in the presence of my beloved, even as I became familiar with her personality and diverse moods. I discovered she could carry sorrow. At those times, I gently wiped away her tears. But nearly always, I found her radiating joy and delight.

One evening, while she was in preparation for the wedding day with friends, I was alone.

Alone?

I asked my Lord where he had gone. I kept calling for him, but I received no reply. I cried loud and long, but my pleading availed nothing.

I finally fell into bed, exhausted with my search, and slept.

It was that night that my Lord came and gave me his Word.

Be not unequally yoked together with unbelievers.

I pondered his message.

"Lord! Do you speak of my Beloved? She is not an unbeliever! She talks about you! She approves of my race! She has promised to carry the torch with me!"

But the heavens were silent, and my Lord was gone again. I tossed and turned the night through but could find no rest for my soul. It was dawn before I finally slept. When I awoke, words of Scripture filled my mind.

Now concerning spiritual gifts, brethren, I would not have you ignorant.

What were these words to me?

I tried to ignore them but the words refused to leave. Over and over again they echoed. Finally I reached for my Bible and searched for the list of spiritual gifts. I read them from the twelfth chapter of I Corinthians, not knowing what it was that I was searching for.

Three words leaped from the page, became flames, and burned their way into my heart. They were included in the list of spiritual gifts.

Discerning of spirits.

I knew this was the gift God meant for me to have.

265

I prayed, "God, I need this gift! I need to be able to distinguish between right and wrong and good and evil. I need to perceive the spirit of man."

Then I _knew_.

I fought the prayer I knew I must pray. I battled long and hard.

Finally I lay prostrate on my face before God and wept and prayed the hardest prayer I have ever prayed: "Please Lord, help me to discern the spirit of my beloved."

I was to pick her up for lunch that same day. The hours dragged until the time came for me to leave. I was frantic.

I rang her doorbell and she came to the door. I looked at her with despair.

Was this my beloved who had enchanted me with her beauty? She was dressed in filthy, tattered garments. I lifted my eyes from her despicable clothing and stared into the eyes that had so often melted their way into my heart. They were unseeing. There was no light in them. Darkness emanated from this wretched and miserable creature. I looked at the hands that I had held so tenderly. They hung at her side. She carried no torch.

Had she changed so much? No. My Lord had given my blinded eyes sight. For the first time I was looking not at her flesh, but at her spirit.

I turned to flee. As I stumbled away from her, she called out, "But Dave! I believe! I will run with you! I believe in your Lord too!"

I turned to face her one last time.

"You believe that there is one God. You do well. The devils also believe, and tremble. But will you know, O vain one, that faith without works is dead?"

I ran from her and as I ran, her foul, blasphemous curses followed me.

"God," I whispered. I thought you had sent me this one. Now I know she was sent by our enemy and I was deceived by her beauty. Lord, if you want me to run with a mate, please send one to me. But until then, I will be content with you. I thought I was lonely before, but I have never known the meaning of loneliness until I called for you and discovered you had left me."

My Lord answered immediately.

"Lo, I am with you alway, even unto the end of the world."

"But Lord, you didn't come when I called!"

"Lo, I am with you alway."

He had not left me. I was the one who had turned around and walked away from my Lord to follow the woman. Without a backward glance, I had continued to wander farther and farther away from my Lord.

And even there, and even then, my precious Savior had come to me in the evening hours, drawing me back.

How I love him!

Dave laid his leather journal and pen on the desk. Falling to his knees, he cried, "Lord, can you forgive me for leaving you? Please help me never to leave you again. And Lord? Thank you! Thank you for giving me discernment and understanding. Thank you for putting me back in the race!

The love of God gently enclosed him until he felt nearly overwhelmed by his Lord's embrace. Never had he felt love like this. No earthly love could compare.

Dave laughed aloud as renewed vigor surged through him.

He would begin his run again. He would once more raise his torch to the heavens. His sweet Savior would forever more be his first Love.

He lay on his bed later that night, alternately thinking and praying. He wondered if he would marry some day. He thought about runners whose lives were enriched by a faithful running partner. He remembered the fiery founder of the mighty *Salvation Army*, William Booth. William's motto was *"Go for souls and go for the worst!"*

Catherine, his partner, was a dedicated torchbearer who helped him fulfil that mission.

Catherine vowed: "While women weep, as they do now, I'll fight; while little children go hungry, I'll fight; while men go to prison, in and out, in and out, as they do now, I'll fight; while there is a drunkard left, while there is a poor lost girl upon the streets, while there remains one dark soul without the light of God - I'll fight! I'll fight to the very end!"

And war she did - hand in hand with her beloved William. They formed an army to wage war against the hosts of hell. Their troops suffered casualties of viscious and brutal murders, beatings, stonings. They marched through the streets singing, playing and preaching. Together they met the needs of a decaying humanity, crushed by sin. Their brass instruments were often battered beyond repair by those who tried vainly to stop their music, but they sang their way home dripping with a combination of blood, mud and egg yolks.

They kept singing while storming the very gates of hell into territory long held by demon forces. They marched through barrooms, prisons, dark allies. They stormed their way into danger filled ghettos and homes filled with violence.

William traveled over five million miles to preach sixty-thousand sermons. Catherine ran with him, preaching, writing, warring, studying, organizing and training a workforce of women to bring relief to hurting people.

Dave

In the couple's spare time, they reared their eight children and adopted a ninth. Seven of them became world-known preachers, leaders and song writers.

They ran, hand in hand, for thirty-five years . . . a team, one in purpose, each enriched by the other . . .

Dave recalled the wise counsel of Martin Luther:

Whoever intends to enter married life should do so in faith and in God's name. I should pray God that it may prosper according to his will and that marriage may not be treated as a matter of fun and folly. It is a hazardous matter and as serious as anything on earth can be. Therefore we should not rush into it as the world does, in keeping with its frivolousness and wantonness and in pursuit of its pleasure. Before taking this step, we should consult God, so that we may lead our married life to his glory.

"Thank you again, my Lord, for sparing me a life of heartache," Dave prayed.

He thought about John Wesley, a champion runner whose marriage was a miserable failure. His wife was not a blessing, but a hindrance. She didn't run with him but chose instead to war against him.

"In spite of her rage, Lord, he just kept running for you," Dave commented.

Dave thought of Max, a faithful runner who smiled through his tears, daily bearing the load of a divided marriage. His wife had grown bitter with hatred against the race. Now she hated him.

"I will remind Max of John Wesley the next time I see him," Dave decided.

Just before drifting off to sleep, Dave murmured, half to himself and half to the Lord, "I'm *so glad* I didn't marry her. . . "

Chapter 65

Dave

The drunkard and the glutton shall come to poverty:
and drowsiness shall clothe a man with rags.
Proverbs 23:21

The sounds and sights of the night filled the city.

A siren wailed, then began to fade from view and hearing.

As the sound grew fainter, Dave heard the soft strains of a song.

Amazing Grace, how sweet the sound!

Dave turned toward the music, foreign in this city of profanity, screams, revelry and weeping. He followed it to a small mission, sandwiched between the barred windows of a pawn shop and a theater.

Dave slipped in and sat in the back. The hollow sound of an old upright piano accompanied an elderly man's quavering words:

We've no less days to sing God's praise
Than when we first begun.

Dave looked at the men scattered in the room. The dismal, unadvertised side of drugs and liquor sat in these seats. They had no interest in the music or the message. They were here simply to secure their free meal and cot for the night. Dave was surprised that so many young were among the old.

The speaker's words caught his attention.

"Will you do it, Sir?"

He was looking straight at him.

Dave hadn't been listening. Was the man speaking to him?

He looked questionly at the speaker, and he kindly repeated his question.

Dave

"I am glad you have joined us. Do you have a message for these men?"

Dave was about to shake his head, when he realized that he did have something to say.

He walked slowly to the front of the cheerless room and faced the hopeless faces before him.

Sighing his prayer, he said simply, "I was drawn into this building by the song that has been sung throughout the world in many languages . . . *Amazing Grace.*"

His eyes rested on each man before continuing.

"I looked for hope in your eyes, but it's no longer there.

"Somewhere along the road of life, you have lost it. I don't know what disappointments, troubles and heartaches have brought you here.

"But I do know that there is not one man in this place who was more miserable or more destitute than a man named John . . .

Chapter 66

John Newton
(1725 to 1807)

He brought me up also out of an horrible pit, out of the miry clay, and set my feet upon a rock, and established my goings. And he hath put a new song in my mouth.
Psalm 40:2-3

John made his way early one morning to his favorite spot on the hillside. He sat down on a log and began to talk to God. He looked at the sea in the distance and remembered - Oh, God, it was so painful to remember - his days at sea . . .

His life at sea had begun with his first voyage in 1742, at just eleven years of age. What a wicked sailor he had been! His godly mother had faithfully taught him the Scriptures, but just before his seventh birthday, she had died. And John, no longer under her influence, had rejected God, religion, and the Bible.

He had not been content with merely ignoring God, but had delighted in mocking Him. Blasphemy and profanity literally poured from his mouth, ridiculing all that even hinted of religion. It wasn't long before his heart seemed as stone. He became cruel. Murderous thoughts filled his mind. He had no fear of God, no regard for man, no conscience. He lived a totally depraved and abandoned life. And he lived it to the fullest. He was never satisfied with just being vile himself, but his greatest pleasure in life was seducing others away from God and into sin.

He sailed to Africa to purchase slaves. He enjoyed shackling them with chains, bolting them together, dragging them onto the ship, throwing them into the hold and then selling those who survived for a big profit.

He had begun to be infatuated with the occult practices of Africa. He turned to charms, black magic, sorcery, and divinations.

In all his travels with ungodly sailors, he had never met a more daring blasphemer than himself. He daily invented new oaths to mock God. Even the sailors shunned and despised his company.

"God," he cried from the hillside. "I was like one infected with a pestilence, spreading the disease of sin wherever I went!"

John thanked God for bringing him out of such depths of sin. His heart overflowed with love, and tears streamed down his face as he remembered how blind he had been to the love and mercy of God!

"God," he prayed. "Thank you for your grace - Your amazing grace."

Opening his diary, he began to write:

Amazing grace! (how sweet the sound!)
That saved a wretch like me;
I once was lost, but now am found;
Was blind, but now I see.

He stopped for a moment then, remembering the night his heart had first begun to turn toward God for mercy.

It was during the voyage he would never forget, back in 1748. He was seventeen then. The ship he was on had been at sea for 7,000 miles, and was unfit for sailing in stormy weather. He was sleeping when the force of a violent wave broke upon the ship. He awoke with a start as his cabin quickly filled with water.

He heard a frantic shout from the deck, "The ship is going down!" He ran to the ladder where he met his Captain.

"Go back to your cabin and get your knife," the Captain yelled. A sailor took his place on the ladder as he returned to his cabin. The sailor who had taken his place had been instantly washed overboard when he reached the deck.

John joined the sailors who were plugging their clothes and bedding into the leaks, nailing pieces of boards over the holes, and frantically manning the pumps.

John laughed as he pumped, remarking, "In a few days, we will be drinking and laughing about this!" A sailor looked at him, his eyes wide with fear, tears streaming down his face.

"No, it is too late now," he replied in a trembling voice.

Fear had struck his heart as he realized that he was on a sinking ship. He ran to speak with the Captain and then returned frantically to the pumps. Without thinking he screamed, "If this does not work, the Lord have mercy on us!"

As he continued to pump, almost every passing wave broke over his head. He was roped to the deck to keep from washing away. Every time the ship descended into the sea, he expected it to rise no more.

The words he had just uttered, "The Lord have mercy on us!" echoed unceasingly in his troubled mind.

"The Lord have mercy on us! Why did I say that? For what mercy can there be for me?" he asked himself.

Even the mercy of God would not be enough for him, for he was the greatest and most wretched of all sinners. The God he had so proudly blasphemed could never forgive him. He had made the life, and even the death of Jesus Christ the subject of profane ridicule.

Now he knew God had just one message for him. It came from the dark recesses of his mind and now repeated itself over and over as he pumped water from the doomed ship.

Because I have called, and you refused; I have stretched out my hand, and no man regarded;

But you have set at nought all my counsel, and would none of my reproof:

I also will laugh at your calamity; I will mock when your fear comes;

When your fear comes as desolation, and your destruction comes as a whirlwind; when distress and anguish come upon you.

Then shall they call upon me, but I will not answer; they shall seek me early, but they shall not find me:

For that they hated knowledge, and did not choose the fear of the Lord:

They would none of my counsels: they despised all my reproof.

Therefore shall they eat of the fruit of their own way, and be filled with their own devices.

Proverbs 1:24-31

He was surrounded with black, unfathomable despair.

The ship was finally freed from water. The wind died. Would the damaged ship be able to reach port? The sails were reduced to a few tattered rags. And what would the sailors eat? All the livestock had been washed overboard. All that remained were a few fish and some food that had been set aside for the hogs.

At his first break from the pumps, John picked up the Bible he had scorned and read from Luke 11:13:

"If you then, being evil, know how to give good gifts unto your children, how much more shall your heavenly Father give the Holy Spirit to them that ask him?"

He read the verse over and over. "If this book I am trying to read was written by this Holy Spirit, then I need to ask for the Spirit to help me to understand it. And if this book is true, then this verse is true. So I will ask and see what happens."

He expected to die at any moment. The crew was dressed inadequately for the frigid cold, and there was only half of a salted cod each day for twelve sailors. Pumping continued endlessly, and between incessant labor and little food, the sailors were wasting away. One died.

Fear was John's constant companion. He knew he would either starve to death or resort to cannibalism.

The Captain continuously eyed John. John knew why. The Captain had often remarked that he looked upon John as a modern day Jonah. "A curse is present on every ship you board," he had once told him. John began to fear that the captain, in desperation, would throw him overboard in order to save the ship.

Finally, after four weeks of keeping the damaged ship afloat, they sailed into port, the last of their food boiling in the pot. All who looked upon the battered ship knew it would not have lasted even one more night at sea.

The rest of the sailors forgot God and their prayers when the danger was past - but John didn't. He continued to read the Bible. He read I Timothy 1:12-13 over and over again, a little ray of hope growing each time he read it. It was the testimony of Paul, the apostle who had himself suffered shipwreck.

And I thank Christ Jesus our Lord, who hath enabled me, for that he counted me faithful, putting me into the ministry; who was before a blasphemer, and a persecutor, and injurious: but I obtained mercy, because I did it ignorantly in unbelief.

So Paul had been a blasphemer. He had persecuted Christians and had hurt the gospel of Jesus Christ. But he had obtained mercy. Perhaps there was hope for him too.

That tiny ray of hope had grown into a prayer, the prayer into a cry for forgiveness, and slowly, slowly, his heart of stone began to melt, and the light of Christ began to penetrate his dark soul.

John marvelled at the grace of God, as he again bent to write in his diary.

"Twas grace that taught my heart to fear,
And grace my fears relieved;
How precious did that grace appear
The hour I first believed!

He could have so easily died before finding Christ. There were so many times that God had miraculously spared him from death . . .

He was thrown from a horse at twelve years old, landing just a few inches from a wood pile.

There was the Sunday he planned to go sailing with his friends. He had arrived just a few minutes too late for the venture, but just on time in God's Providence. The boat was overturned and his friend and several others drowned.

He had been deathly sick and unable to sail on one voyage. His Captain had left him on a small, sandy island in the care of a black woman, the captain's mistress. She had despised him and fed him only the leftovers from her plate. He remembered crawling during the night hours through the plantation, pulling up roots and eating them raw to keep from starving to death. When he was too sick to crawl, he was kept alive by slaves who shared with him their own small amount of food.

After many weeks of delirious fever, he recovered enough to attempt walking. The woman called her slaves to look at him as he staggered and fell, and urged them to mimic his clumsy movements. They tottered along with him, clapping their hands, sneering, throwing limes and stones at him.

When he was finally well enough to sail away, he was falsely accused by another trader of stealing from his Captain.

The Captain was furious.

"Lock Newton in chains on deck every time I leave the ship!" he ordered.

He was given a pint of rice and left in the cold and rain until the captain returned from his trips to shore. He lost his fierceness during those times. He became depressed, but still his cold heart seethed with hatred against God.

There was the time he had gone shooting with friends. He had climbed a steep bank, pulling his shotgun after him. It went off so near his face that it burned away the corner of his hat.

He remembered his many treks through the jungles. Many of his companions had been poisoned by the natives. He had miraculously escaped.

There were the countless times he had been dragged to land half dead after being pitched overboard in canoes going to shore.

He remembered the night he sat in a small boat on his way to shore to perform his duties there. He was ready to let go of the ropes when he heard the shout of his Captain:

"Newton! Get back in the ship."

Another sailor was sent in his place. The boat had sunk and the man who had replaced him had drowned. The Captain, when later questioned, had no explanation for his change of plans.

He remembered the night on ship that he had instigated a drinking contest. He drank until his brain was on fire. He danced about the deck like a madman, and his hat had fallen overboard. He threw himself over the rail, his only thought to recover his hat. A sailor caught hold of his clothes when he was halfway overboard. He was barely able to pull him back inside the ship. In his drunken state, John had forgotten he couldn't swim.

"God," he cried now, "How close I came that night to perishing in that dreadful condition and sinking into eternity under the weight of my own curse."

With a heart full of love and gratitude, he wrote:

Through many dangers, toils, and snares,
I have already come;
'Tis grace has brought me safe thus far,
And grace will lead me home.

He had scorned God, mocked Him, blasphemed Him, ridiculed Him, turned others against Him. And God returned all his evil with good.

"Thank you, Lord, thank you," John whispered as he continued to write.

The Lord has promised good to me,
His Word my hope secures;
He will my Shield and Portion be,
As long as life endures.

Yes, when this flesh and heart shall fail,
And mortal life shall cease,
I shall possess, within the vail,
A life of joy and peace.

He, who had been shunned by the most vile of humanity, was now walking with God, who promised to never leave nor forsake him.

The earth shall soon dissolve like snow;
The sun forbear to shine;
But God, who call'd me here below,
Will be for ever mine.

These past years he had preached the gospel that he had tried to destroy. He proclaimed the love of God that he had shunned. He invited all to partake of the mercy he had mocked. He crusaded against the cruelties of slavery that he had profited from. And now, his life nearly over, he looked up to the sky above him.

"I'll be coming home soon, my Father," he breathed.

Who would have believed that the amazing grace of God would reach down into a ship and place a torch in the hand of the most vile of all sailors? But was there anyone who needed light more desperately? Had a blacker one than he ever lived?

What a God! What amazing grace! He would spend an eternity praising Him, but it would never be enough.

He leaned back against a tree, thinking about the glories of heaven that would soon be his, and he bent once again to write.

**When we've been there ten thousand years,
Bright shining as the sun,
We've no less days to sing God's praise
Than when we first begun.**

John crossed his finish line at the age of eighty-two. As he preached one of his final messages just before his death, he declared, "My memory is nearly gone, but I remember two things."

His congregation looked at him expectantly, and his eyes filled with tears.

"They are," he stated, "that I am a great sinner, and that Christ is a great Savior."

Chapter 67

Dave

*But after that the kindness and love of God our
Saviour toward man appeared.*
Titus 3:4

Dave returned to his seat.

The director nodded at the pianist and stepped to the front of the humble room.

He didn't even bother to brush away his tears as he stood with his eyes closed, his hands upraised, and began again to sing.

Amazing Grace, how sweet the sound . . .

An old man joined him this time. Dave turned to see the man but was disappointed to see that his eyes were leering. He heard the drunken slur of his words now.

I once was lost, but now am found . . .

And now a young man began to sing along softly.

Was blind, but now I see.

Dave wept when he signalled out this man. For tears streamed down his face and Dave knew that he was seeing the Savior who had stepped into the life of John Newton.

The song ended, and the men shuffled toward the dining room - all but one.

Dave went and sat by the man whose head was buried in his hands and whose body heaved with sobs.

"My God," he heard him pray. "Can you save *me?*"

The room had emptied when he lifted his head and saw Dave seated beside him.

"Are you sure he'll have me?" he asked.

Dave nodded.

"He came for you, my Friend. Did you know that he said, "All that comes to me, I will in no wise cast out?"

"Then I will come to him."

I'll come.

Such simple words.

But how low must man descend before he finally speaks them?

The man knelt by the old chair.

Dave thought, "He is so young - and yet already nearly destroyed by sin.

He could almost hear the heart cry of God for his tormented creation.

O that there were such an heart in them, that they would fear me, and keep all my commandments always, that it might be well with them, and with their children for ever!

The mission director came in. He knelt and put his arm around the frayed and filthy clothing of the sin-ravaged body.

Dave slipped out of the building. The city seemed even blacker in contrast to the dim light of the mission. The garish neon lights inviting fallen humanity to partake of sin and death did nothing to dispel the city's darkness.

Dave had a new bounce to his steps as he ran along the street.

"Thank you, my Christ," he whispered. "Thank you for your grace that never fails to be amazing."

Chapter 68

Dave

And he said, Who art thou? And she answered, I am
Ruth thine handmaid.
Ruth 3:9

He had seen her so many times . . . in so many
places.

The first time he was coming out of the prison while
she was going in, her Bible in one hand, her torch in the
other.

He had noticed her next coming from a Sunday School
class into the sanctuary. A group of eleven or twelve year
old girls gathered around her, jostling for her attention.

He had seen her on a cold day sitting on a bench
visiting with a destitute, shivering woman while gently
tucking a blanket around her.

Once he had spotted her in the mission serving soup,
her hair damp with sweat from the sweltering kitchen.

He had spotted her in a convalescent home reading
the Bible to three or four women in the dining room.

Her torch surrounded her with a soft glow wherever
she was, separating her from others who lived and walked
in darkness.

He had never been in the children's home. He noticed
the sign as he ran past. Slowly he stopped, turned
around and went in. Perhaps there was a troubled teen
he could help.

She was there. A smile lit her face, attracting a group
of love-starved children who swarmed around her.

Her relief was apparent when Dave walked in the
room. She handed him a sticky baby and picked up a
toddler who clamored for her attention. Dave wasn't sure
what to do with the child. The little guy wasn't thrilled
with the situation either. He let out a piercing wail.

Dave wondered how so much noise could come from
such a small person. He didn't know whether to tighten
his grip or just let go. He looked at the girl helplessly.

She laughed and seemed to take her time coming to his rescue.

"Here," she said, exchanging the baby for the toddler she was holding. "Maybe this one will like you." He was even stickier.

Dave would never have set foot in this home if he'd known just babies and toddlers were here. Small children baffled him. He wasn't sure how to hold them, didn't know what to do when they wanted his attention, and certainly had no idea how to handle one who cried.

He struggled to hold on to the squirming child without hurting him. He looked at the woman. How did she manage five or six babies and toddlers all at once and keep smiling - and stay beautiful?

Dave looked again.

She was beautiful. Light surrounded her. A radiance shone from her eyes. Her hands were gentle and loving, patting one child while wiping tears from the eyes of another.

She seemed totally unaware that the baby was tugging her golden hair out of place.

Dave remembered all the times and places he had seen her. She was never without her torch.

He sat down on a low stool near the group. He planned to stay until she left. He had to get acquainted with her. Obviously he would have to somehow figure out how to help her with these kids. He was still trying to think of a way, when a couple two or three year old boys dove at him, nearly knocking him backwards. Gingerly, he placed one on each knee. Now what? He took off his watch, thinking maybe they would take turns listening to it tick. One grabbed it and started eating it. He finally wrested it away from him and stood up. This simply wasn't going to work.

He was starting to leave when a tired looking woman entered the room and gathered the children together. She placed one in a swing, another in a high chair, had one propped on each hip, and the others surrounding her. Dave watched her with respect. There must be a trick to handling children. If there was, no one had ever taught it to him.

"Thank you so much, Ruth," the woman said. "The time you spend here is such a help."

She hugged her and added, "I sometimes don't know how we'd make it without you."

So her name was Ruth. Dave waited for her to pick up her sweater and purse and held the door open for her.

She laughed. "Thanks so much for your invaluable help with the babies," she said.

"I think it's probably my first and last time," Dave answered with a grin. "I doubt that you noticed, but I'm really not too comfortable with babies or little kids."

"I noticed," she answered, shaking her head.

They walked down the street talking.

They were still talking over coffee in a restaurant two or three hours later. Dave found it easy to talk to her. They shared their experiences, their frustrations, their hurts, their good times, their call to the race, their love for the Lord.

"I have seen you many times and in many places," Dave said.

"Can we ever do enough for Jesus?" she answered softly. "When I tire, I think of a torchbearer named Elizabeth and I keep going. Dave, there are so many needs . . . so many hurting people . . . so many sick people . . . so many neglected children and unwanted elderly . . . so many lonely people . . . so many, many people without Christ. And there are so few runners in this race. We desperately need more women like the one who has given me inspiration."

She paused and asked, "Are there torchbearers in the past who have given you inspiration, Dave?"

He smiled. They had so many things in common.

"Tell me about this runner who has inspired you," he answered.

She seemed to forget he was even there as she replied reflectively, "Her name was *Elizabeth* . . . "

Chapter 69

Elizabeth Fry
(1780 to 1845)

They are all of them snared in holes, and they are hid
in prison houses.
Isaiah 42:22

Obscenity, curses and shouts were deafening. Three-hundred nearly naked women and nearly as many fighting and screaming children pushed and shoved, cooked and ate, and lived and slept in these four tiny rooms in the infamous *Newgate Prison* of London. There were no beds, no sheets, no blankets, a few filthy rags that served as clothing, and mere scraps of food for meals. One male attendant and his young son tried, but miserably failed, to keep any kind of order.

Women pushed and shoved viciously for a place at the window gratings, where they begged those that hurried to pass them for shillings to buy liquor. For liquor was their only hope for a few hours of drunken relief.

Into this pot of boiling, foul humanity, walked a tall, dignified Quaker woman. Elizabeth Fry hid her shocked horror as she looked calmly at the women and children. She felt as if she had been thrown into a den of wild beasts. A few stared back at her, sneering at her Quaker costume of plain brown dress with its full skirt, tight waist and sparkling white cape.

Well, she had asked for this. She had read the words of Jesus, "I was in prison, and you visited me not," and they had pierced her soul and stayed there, giving her no peace until she finally appeared before the governor of the prison.

"Sir," she had said quietly, "If thee kindly allows me to pray with the women, I will go inside."

The governor smirked as he pictured this stately woman among his clawing, screaming prisoners! Laughing, he granted her permission.

And now here she was. The Lord couldn't tell her at her judgment that she hadn't at least come. The first thing she must do here was to look upon this appalling scene with eyes of mercy, not judgment. She reminded herself she had not come to condemn, but to comfort and relieve.

She removed her bonnet, wiped off a low ledge, sat down and opened her Bible.

As she began to read, the women began to grow quiet. Even the children were silent, listening to a sound they had never heard in this vile place - a sweet voice reading the words of the living God.

> All we like sheep have gone astray: we have turned everyone to his own way; and the Lord hath laid on him the iniquity of us all.
> He was oppressed, and he was afflicted, yet he opened not his mouth . . .

> Who shall ascend into the hill of the Lord? or who shall stand in his holy place?
> He that hath clean hands, and a pure heart, who hath not lifted up his soul unto vanity, nor sworn deceitfully.

> Hear, O Lord, when I cry with my voice: have mercy also upon me, and answer me.
> When thou saidst, Seek ye my face; my heart said unto thee, Thy face, Lord, will I seek.
> When my father and my mother forsake me, then the Lord will take me up.

Wide eyes in filthy faces stared as Elizabeth turned quietly to Psalm 69 and continued reading words never before spoken in this room.

> Deliver me out of the mire, and let me not sink!
> Hear me, O Lord; for thy lovingkindness is good: turn unto me according to the multitude of thy tender mercies.

For I am poor and sorrowful: let thy salvation,
O God, set me up on high.
For the Lord heareth the poor, and despiseth
not his prisoners.

Opening to the New Testament, Elizabeth read the
words of Jesus.

Blessed are they that mourn, for they shall be
comforted.
Love your enemies, bless them that curse
you, do good to them that hate you, and pray for
them which despitefully use you, and persecute
you; that ye may be the children of your Father
which is in heaven.

Elizabeth closed her Bible and looked up. The fierce
snarling and blasphemy again filled the room. Had she
accomplished nothing?
She slowly made her way home to fix dinner for her
husband and eight children. Surely God would call
someone else to minister in the prison - someone who did
not have a large family to care for.
But she was drawn back again and again. She took
clothes with her. Brutal fighting broke out, for there were
never enough garments for everyone.
Back at home, looking at her own children, she could
not help but see the wild eyes of the children being raised
in the prison.
"All right, Lord," she said. "I will teach them."
Gathering together materials, she made her way back
to the prison.
"I will teach your children to read," she told the young
mothers.
What a nightmare her first class had been! The
mothers begged to be taught too. Describing the scene
later, Elizabeth wrote, "The railing was crowded with half-
naked women, struggling together for front places with
violence and begging in loud voices for money."
But Elizabeth did not quit. Along with teaching, she
brought the women cloth, needles and thread. She
patiently taught them handwork.

And always she read the words of God from her Bible. At home, Elizabeth knelt and prayed:

O Lord, may I be directed what to do and what to leave undone; and then may I humbly trust that a blessing will be with me in my various engagements.

Enable me, O Lord, to feel tenderly and charitably toward all my beloved fellow mortals. Help me to have no soreness or improper feelings toward any. Let me think no evil, bear all things, hope all things, endure all things. Let me walk in all humility and Godly fear before all men, and in Thy sight. Amen.

One thing that would have to be left undone was her constant entertaining. She often fed from thirty to sixty at mealtime, as Quakers gathered in her home. She must give that up if she was to continue her work in the prison.

But how could she quit visiting the poor around her? Was not that another of her Lord's commands? And she simply must take time to keep the shelves in her home stocked with an abundant supply of garments and medicines for the sick. Elizabeth sighed as she gathered together an armful. Making her way through children, pigs and chickens, she walked through alleys and up broken staircases, searching out the sick, the poor, the lonely who needed her help.

The prison governor did not laugh long at this amazing woman. When Elizabeth invited him to her home to persuade him to hire a matron to supervise the women prisoners, he readily consented.

Day after day, week after week, month after month, year after year, Elizabeth continued her work. Her family grew to eleven children, but the transformation in the prison cells kept her going back and forth between the prison and her house. A drunken, scantily-clothed, cursing woman was a rare sight now. The women's prison had slowly but steadily been transformed into a place that functioned like a well regulated family.

Elizabeth had been at her work in the prison for six years when John Randolph, the renowned Virginian congressman, visited London. He wrote to his friend about his visit: "I saw the greatest curiosity in London! I have seen Elizabeth Fry in Newgate, and I have witnessed there miraculous effects of true Christianity upon the most depraved of human beings - bad women, Sir, who are worse, if possible, than the Devil himself. And yet the wretched outcasts have been tamed and subdued by the Christian eloquence of Mrs. Fry. Nothing but religion can effect this miracle!"

Elizabeth, having faithfully brought Christ to lost souls, could still not rest from her constant and often exhausting labors. For as long as there was a need, Elizabeth had to do everything in her power to fill it. She learned that many women were loaded onto convict ships and sent to the penal settlement in Australia. She determined that not one ship would leave the Thames River without her praying with the women first. She took materials to them so they could work during their long voyage, and would have something to sell when they landed.

She formed a prison committee and appointed one of its members to visit Australia and investigate the conditions the prisoners found upon their arrival there.

"There is *no* provision for the women!" she was told. "There is neither food nor lodging! In order to survive, the women must turn to crime or prostitution!"

Elizabeth hurried to the England authorities. "You must build barracks for the women! Delay is impossible!"

The officials stared at this woman who refused to take no for an answer. She insisted that they build homes immediately - so they did!

Her enemies were vocal and powerful. There were many who opposed her work and felt that prisoners deserved their deplorable living conditions.

Elizabeth turned to the Lord for strength. "I feel the rock always underneath me," she often told her friends.

She was informed of vile conditions in other countries and personally investigated prisons in the British Isles, in Scotland and throughout England. She corresponded with people in Italy, Denmark and Russia who wanted to improve prisons in their countries.

She travelled to mental institutions and hospitals in Ireland and obtained an official permit to visit any prison at any time in France. Her Lord's command to visit the prisoners took Elizabeth to Belgium, Holland, Prussia, Switzerland and Germany. Joseph, her husband who loved his wife and shared her concern for the needy, often accompanied her.

In the midst of her work among prisoners, she heard that a man had frozen to death in the streets of London.

"O Lord," she cried. "How can I rest in my warm home, knowing that there are people shivering with cold in the streets?"

She and her committee prepared shelters and stocked them with warm bedding, soup and bread. They hunted for jobs for the unemployed and organized classes to teach destitute children. She set up libraries for coast guardsmen in more than five hundred stations around Britain.

She looked around her. There were so many needs and so few laborers - so she opened an institution to train nurses.

The overwhelming needs of people kept her daily in her quiet place of prayer, finding refuge and strength from her Lord.

"My Lord, be pleased to help and strengthen me in all this. In all my perplexities, make a way where I see no way."

Kings and princes asked her for recommendations for prison reform.

She advised the king of France, "When thee builds a prison, thee had better build with the thought ever in mind that thee and thy children may occupy the cells."

King Frederick William IV of Prussia asked to visit Newgate Prison with Elizabeth Fry while he was a guest in England.

The women prisoners may have been subdued by having a king in their cell, but Elizabeth calmly sat on her ledge and opened her worn Bible to the twelfth chapter of Romans.

The women laid their work aside as she read.

So we, being many, are one body in Christ, and every one members one of another.

Abhor that which is evil; cleave to that which is good.

Be kindly affectioned one to another with brotherly love; in honour preferring one another.

Bless them which persecute you: bless, and curse not.

Rejoice with them that do rejoice, and weep with them that weep.

Be of the same mind one toward another. Mind not high things, but condescend to men of low estate. Be not wise in your own conceits.

Recompense to no man evil for evil. Provide things honest, in the sight of all men.

Be not overcome of evil, but overcome evil with good.

Closing her Bible, Elizabeth knelt to pray. King Frederick watched as the prisoners got on their knees, and then he too knelt.

"We, being many, are one body in Christ . . ."

The Quaker woman, the King of Prussia and common prisoners all knelt together before their one Creator, as Elizabeth lifted her voice to God in prayer.

She served her Lord faithfully until just a few months before her death at age sixty-five. Her last words before saying good-bye to her family were, *"I can say one thing. Since my heart was touched at seventeen years old, I believe I never have awakened from sleep, in sickness or in health, by day or by night, without my first waking thought being how best I might serve my Lord."*

Chapter 70

Dave

*Who can find a virtuous woman? for her price is far
above rubies.*
Proverbs 31:10

"**I** have tried to follow Elizabeth's example," Ruth
said softly. "I begin every day asking God to use me to
help at least one person."

She smiled. "Elizabeth was a beautiful person."

"You are the most beautiful person I have met," Dave
said without thinking. "You not only have outward
beauty, you have inner beauty."

Ruth blushed.

"We've just met, Dave."

"I feel like I have known you for years, Ruth. You're so
easy to talk to. I can't believe how much we have in
common."

It was late when Dave got home.

"Lord?" he prayed. "She's the one, isn't she?"

A deep peace filled him.

"I was ready to run alone," he added, then smiled.

"You have sent me one beautiful running partner!"

He sobered immediately. She may not want to run
with him. She seemed to enjoy his company, but she
appeared to enjoy everyone's company. She'd even been
nice to those miserable babies. He certainly couldn't
have made much of an impression with his incompetence
in the children's home.

"I think I need your help, Lord," he said. "Please tell
her I'm not so bad and please, *please* talk her into
running with me!"

Ruth was kneeling at her bed.

"Lord, could you be sending me a running partner? I
have seen Dave in different places, always at work for you
. . . always so nice to everyone. He even tried to be sweet
to those babies tonight, but he didn't quite know how. I

never thought . . . oh, Lord, if you want me to keep running alone, I will.

"But I want you to know it was so nice being with him this evening. If it is in your perfect will, please put us together - soon!"

Chapter 71

Dave

*Wherefore is light given to him that is in misery, and
life unto the bitter in soul.*
Job 3:20

Dave ran through the dark subdivision and found
the small, white house. He had received an urgent message from a concerned mother. She wanted a torchbearer to talk to her daughter.

A tired looking woman answered his knock.

He noticed the wisps of grey hair, the exhausted sag of
her shoulders, her agitated expression.

"Thank you for coming," she said. "My daughter was
in an accident. We just brought her home from the
hospital three weeks ago. She is confined to a wheelchair
and has no desire to live. As far as she is concerned, her
life is over at just seventeen. Can you help her?"

Dave breathed a prayer as he followed her to the family
room. The girl in the wheel chair glanced at him.
Dismissing him as unworthy of her attention, she stared
back at the game show on television. The listless eyes of
one so young dismayed Dave. He pulled a chair up to
hers.

"I'm Dave," he began, and could tell immediately that
neither his name nor his presence made any difference to
her.

"What is your name?" he asked softly.

Rather than answering, she tilted her head toward her
mother.

"Her name is Charlotte," her mother answered tiredly.

Charlotte!

Dave knew now what he would tell her.

He smiled.

"Charlotte, let me tell you about another Charlotte."

As Dave began to talk, the mother slipped over to the
TV and turned it off. Charlotte seemed not to even notice.

Chapter 72

Charlotte Elliott
(1789-1871)

*And the Spirit and the bride say, Come. And let him
that heareth say, Come. And let him that is athirst come.
And whosoever will, let him take the water of life freely.*
Revelation 22:17

She had spent the last three years in her bed. The
days all seemed to run together, as loneliness and
depression nearly overwhelmed her.

She recalled her carefree and joyful life before her
health had failed. How she had enjoyed her many
friends! Her mother had often said, "Charlotte! Will you
never settle down and marry and have children?"

Charlotte had just laughed away her concern. She
was having too much fun to settle into the drudgery of
caring for a home and family. She was the life of the
party, writing humorous poetry to hear her friends
laugh. They often gathered around her, as she drew or
painted their portraits, surrounded by happy friends.

But now . . . now she could no longer lift her arm to
paint pictures of her friends. Now she no longer saw
anything humorous in life to write about. For at just
thirty years of age, she had been confined to her bed, a
helpless invalid, bitter, seldom visited by her friends who
now found her company depressing.

Hours now seemed as days, days as years, and her life
stretched hopelessly before her. She knew her parents
were concerned about her mental state, but she had
fallen into black despair, and she saw no way to lift
herself out. There was nothing left to live for.

Charlotte heard her mother come into her room.

"Charlotte," she said softly, "You have company."

She turned over and faced the wall.

"No, Mother! No! Please - I do not wish to see
anyone!"

"Charlotte, Dr. Caesar Malan is here in your room to visit you."

Charlotte nearly groaned out loud but somehow stifled it. She had heard of Dr. Malan, the famous evangelist from Switzerland. Someone had probably sent him to her to see if he could lift her spirits. She had no desire to hear what he had to say, but she might as well get this visit over with.

Turning over painfully, she gazed at him. And she stared. There was a glow in his eyes that seemed to envelop her with love and surround her with light.

He began talking to her compassionately about his best Friend, Jesus Christ.

He spoke of the joy that could be hers - joy she had never known when she was well. She longed for his message to be true, but how could it be for her? No one knew the blackness of her heart and thoughts, the rebellion and even hatred she held in her heart. And there was nothing she could do to change herself. She had tried for the sake of her exhausted parents. But she was too sunk in despair to make herself worthy to approach God.

Then Dr. Malan spoke the words that would change her life.

"Charlotte, you must come as a sinner to the Lamb of God that takes away the sin of the world . . . just as you are."

Come just as you are . . .

"Will Christ receive me?" Charlotte questioned, her eyes wide. *"Just as I am?"*

"Jesus shed his blood so He could receive you, Charlotte," Dr. Malan assured her.

Charlotte, her eyes brimming with tears, looked up to Jesus. She saw a blinding Light, his hand outstretched, his eyes literally radiating love and compassion.

"Oh, Jesus!" she cried. "Please be my Savior, my Lord. Don't ever leave my side! Bring light to my dark heart!"

She felt her heart of stone melt when he filled her being.

And her days - oh, how her days had changed from that wondrous moment!

Charlotte Elliott

Yes, there had been suffering as before - pain, overpowering weakness, exhaustion - but since that day, Charlotte had never again sunk into depression. Joy such as she had never known filled her to overflowing.

"His grace surrounds me," she declared to all who visited her, "and His voice continually bids me to be happy and holy in His service - *just where I am.*"

Dave's voice grew still as he prayed silently, "God, use Charlotte's life to reach this Charlotte who needs You so desperately today."

He sat quietly looking at her, and finally, slowly, she lifted her head and looked at him. Tears were rolling down her face.

"I want Jesus too," she said simply.

Dave and Charlotte's mother knelt beside the wheel chair as Charlotte prayed quietly, "God. You know that I am another Charlotte who needs You to change me. Only you and I know how much I need you to forgive me of my sins and come into my heart and make me a new person."

Her mother was too broken to pray aloud, so Dave prayed for Charlotte. When he again sat in a chair by her side, she said to him, "Jesus did what I asked Him to do. I feel so much lighter. I feel as if a dark presence has left me, and I'm free. But . . . I didn't understand something you said when you prayed for me. You asked God to use me and make me a runner for Him. How can I run? I can't even walk!"

Dave smiled. "My story about the other Charlotte is not finished. Let me tell you about the rest of her life."

Charlotte woke in the night, her eyes wide, staring.

"My Lord," she breathed.

She heard His tender, yet commanding voice in her heart.

"Charlotte, follow me."

"Lord, I cannot follow you," she answered. "Do you not see me? Do you want an invalid in your race? I cannot run - or even walk! I have been confined to this bed for seventeen years! Find a whole person to carry your torch. I am worthless to you . . . and to everybody."

Charlotte looked upon her Savior's face. He remained at her bedside, his eyes looking deeply into her soul. Finally she lifted her trembling hand as far as her strength would allow. He gently placed the torch in her hand, and her fingers closed around it.

She no longer saw him, but she felt his presence still with her. The soft glow of the torch now lit her room.

How could she be expected to run, she wondered. She did not even have enough strength to lift the torch. But she would hold it faithfully in this room, in this bed.

She knew there would be no sleep for her tonight. Excitement surged through her. Who would have thought the Lord would call her to the race? Would he now lift her from her bed as he had with so many in the days he walked the earth with his disciples? For how else could she run?

She looked at her hand clutching the torch. She would learn later that its glow fell on all who entered her room.

Now she could only wonder. How could an invalid run for her Lord?

And then it had happened. In the early morning hours, Charlotte reached for her paper and pen. Perhaps if she wrote of her salvation, her words would reach out and help someone. She began to write . . .

Just as I am, without one plea
But that Thy blood was shed for me,
And that Thou bidd'st me come to Thee,
O Lamb of God, I come! I come!

She thought about her pride, her bitterness and her rebellion. She remembered how she had cried out to God for cleansing.

Just as I am, and waiting not
To rid my soul of one dark blot
To Thee whose blood can cleanse each spot,
O Lamb of God, I come! I come!

She recalled the restlessness of her heart, the fears, the rebellion. And she remembered coming to Christ - just as she was.

Just as I am, tho tossed about
With many a conflict, many a doubt,
Fightings and fears within, without,
O Lamb of God, I come! I Come!

Charlotte thought of the joy that had replaced her depression; the peace that had replaced her restlessness, the faith that had replaced her fear, and the contentment that had replaced her bitterness. Christ had received her - *just as she was!*

Just as I am, Thou wilt receive,
Wilt welcome, pardon, cleanse, relieve;
Because Thy promise I believe,
O Lamb of God, I come! I come!

Her hand was weak from writing, but her heart rejoiced.

"Lord," she breathed, "Use me, *just as I am,* to bring light to this dark world."

Singers began to sing the prayer penned by Charlotte.

Just As I Am echoed throughout the world, calling the weary, the oppressed, the brokenhearted to Christ.

Thousands of letters from many nations poured into the home where Charlotte lay. They were written by people who had come to Christ through her invitation.

And although Charlotte lived fifty-two years of her life in her bed, embers from her torch would continue to call the heavy-laden to the Savior all over the world for over one-hundred fifty years.

Chapter 73

Dave

The darkness is past, and the true light now shineth.
I John 2:8

As Dave left the home, he ran with a smile lighting his face. Just before he turned the corner, he stopped and looked back at the house. He knew it would never again be the same for Jesus was now inside, lighting it with his glorious presence.

"I will bring Ruth to meet Charlotte," he thought.

Thoughts of Ruth were never far from his mind . . . her gentle ways, her kind words, the love that shone through her soft, brown eyes.

He picked up the telephone and called to tell her all about Charlotte.

They talked for over an hour before he remembered why he had called.

Chapter 74

Dave

O God, thou art my God; early will I seek thee: my soul thirsteth for thee: my flesh longeth for thee in a dry and thirsty land, where no water is; To see thy power and thy glory, so as I have seen thee in the sanctuary.
Psalm 63:1-2

Dave ran into a nearly empty church on a Sunday evening. It was almost as dark inside as it was outside. The singing was spiritless. The pastor asked for testimonies. Two or three people related an experience that had happened several years earlier. By the looks of the rolled eyes and bored expressions, Dave guessed the listeners had heard the same words time and time again. Teens snickered during the service and passed notes. Dave tried to glean something from the sermon but found it difficult. The pastor seemed as bored with his subject as his listeners.

Dave's thoughts wandered, then he picked up a couple words.

". . . and we're still waiting."

Dave had missed the first part of the sentence. This church was waiting for something, but he wasn't sure what.

He listened closely for a few minutes and realized the church was waiting for a revival. They had been waiting for several years. Dave guessed unless their attitudes changed, they would be waiting for several more.

Revival was surely desperately needed.

Dave had a feeling if Charles was here speaking, he might just tell these people about the starving farmer who watched the seasons come and go from the rocking chair on his porch while wondering why there was no crop to harvest.

His thoughts drifted to the impassioned runner, set aflame by God. What Christian didn't long for a revival such as the one that followed in Charles Finney's wake?

301

Oh, he had his share of critics. Some still accused him of merely stirring up emotional fervor wherever he went.

"His results were not lasting," they objected piously.

Dave smiled and thought, "Tell that to the people in Rochester, New York."

Dave had just read that in two separate studies, one in 1940 and one finished in 1992, Rochester was designated the kindest city in America. The citizens had a simple explanation. In 1830, a striking torchbearer had run into their city. He preached daily for six months to Rochester's doctors, lawyers, businessmen, judges, bankers, workers. Then he sent them running with their torches to the destitute, the sick, the hungry, the captive. The entire city blazed with light. And over one-hundred sixty years later, Rochester is still considered *the kindest city in America.*

He wondered how this church would react if Charles were to run into this service. Dave could almost see his glowing eyes boring into hardened hearts and his long finger pointing straight at his horrified listeners . . .

Chapter 75

Charles Finney
(1792 to 1875)

*Who maketh his angels spirits, and his ministers a
flame of fire.*
Hebrews 1:7

And, behold, a certain lawyer stood up, and tempted
Jesus, saying, Master, what shall I do to inherit eternal
life? (Luke 10:25).

It was another time - the early 1800's. And another
place - Adams, New York. And this time, the "certain"
lawyer was young Charles Finney. But the age-old
tormenting question was the same.

"Master," he cried, "what shall I do to inherit eternal
life?"

The question drove him into the woods near his home,
and as he made his way into the forest, he vowed, "I will
give my heart to God, or I never will come out of here."
Charles fell to his knees. Making a log his altar, he
prayed fervently, wrestling with God. The minutes
stretched into hours. But this young lawyer, who made
his profession with convincing words, could not reach the
throne of heaven. He was distracted by the sounds of the
forest. Each time he heard a rustle of leaves, he jumped
up guiltily, fearing that someone walking near him would
see him on his knees praying.

He grew increasingly frustrated with himself and this
whole business of praying - and with God! He was
making an attempt to pray - why did God seem so far
away?

He heard another fluttering of leaves, and he quickly
looked toward the sound. He finally realized his problem
was pride. Why, he was so proud, he was afraid that
someone would catch him on his knees - before the
Creator of the universe! Why shouldn't he, a mere man,
be kneeling before his God?

He began to weep and confessed his pride. Hours later, he left the woods. For the first time in his life, he had peace of mind and heart.

He was alone in his office later that same day when he felt the presence of Jesus Christ enter the room. The room lit up as Christ stood before him. Charles Finney was immediately reduced from a brilliant young lawyer to a sinner in need of a Savior, a child in need of a Father. He fell on his face before his Lord, literally bathing Christ's feet with his tears.

"Waves of liquid love flowed through my body," he later wrote of his awe-inspiring experience, "cleansing me, baptizing me, filling me!"

Charles ran from his office, gripping his torch that would light his world. The world stared at this new runner. His brows were shaggy, his nose beak-like, his mouth expressive - but it was his eyes that kept men from dropping their gaze. They seemed to literally glow and penetrate hearts with their radiant light.

The next morning began as other mornings. Charles was at work in the law office when a client came in to inquire about his case.

Charles looked at the man and saw, not a client that would bring him gain, but a soul who needed a Savior. He realized he would never again be content practicing law.

"Go to another lawyer," was the strange advice this lawyer had for his client. "I will no longer be pursuing a career in law. I am going to become a preacher of the gospel." Closing his books, Charles Finney walked out of his former life.

He knew what his decision would cost. He was leaving behind his pursuit of all the world had to offer him. He fully understood that by running with Christ, he would acquire his enemies. Yet he knew the message that was already burning in him would never be quenched in a law office.

Preparation for running this race differed from preparing for a career in law. His life's work would now be to present the case for Jesus Christ. His congregation would be the jury, and he would bring them to the point of decision. He prepared for the work by fasting and praying, seeking strength from God. Then he began to run.

He ran into churches and into meeting halls. His message was strange, offensive and unpopular - especially among preachers. They watched in mounting horror as their congregations, along with the unchurched masses, thronged to hear his message. Their voices of opposition grew louder as his crowds grew larger.

"There is too much human emotion in your meetings," they accused.

Charles shook his head in amazement at the popular belief that no one should be emotional concerning the state of his soul.

He was resting in his home one evening, the open fire warming his tired body. A visitor knocked at his door, and Charles wearily let him in.

"How can you say I can repent and turn to God?" the man asked. "I have no feeling or emotion whatsoever regarding the condition of my soul."

Charles walked over to the fire and picked up a red hot poker. Turning toward his visitor, he threatened to strike him with it.

His visitor recoiled in terror.

Charles returned the poker to the fire and turned toward his cowering visitor, his eyes penetrating to his very heart.

"Sir, you are demonstrating feeling and emotion when you are threatened with a mere poker from my fire. You should demonstrate some feeling about the salvation of your eternal soul that is destined for the raging fires of hell."

His accusers raved on.

"He permits women to pray in mixed public meetings!"

Charles continued to allow women to join his prayer meetings and mingle their voices with the men's in prayer. He welcomed the prayers of women and encouraged them to obtain a good education so they could teach their children.

Then Charles incurred further wrath from his enemies by moving a bench to the front of the churches and halls where he preached.

"These are our *anxious benches*," he explained. "I will call those who want to seek salvation through Christ forward to these benches."

"Anxious benches! What will Finney think of next?" the preachers grumbled.

Charles ignored their complaints. And night after night, the benches were filled with people repenting of their sins and receiving Jesus Christ as their Savior.

Church meetings were never held on any days but Sundays . . . until Charles Finney came to town.

"We will hold services Monday, Tuesday, Wednesday, Thursday, Friday, Saturday - and Sunday," he announced.

The religious leaders who objected to change met together to complain about this strange runner.

"He is holding meetings every day of the week! We all know that church services should be held only on Sundays!"

When these same leaders heard him address God in prayer, they were amazed.

"Have you heard Finney pray? He talks to God in everyday language! He isn't showing reverence, talking to God in such a manner!"

There were always a few in every church who were horrified when some of the city's poor and lowly people came and heard Charles preach that the invitation to receive Christ included them. They were even more dismayed when he insisted they be allowed to not only enter the church, but get saved, join the church, and then sit wherever they chose to sit!

"What about our pew rent? He thunders against our churches charging rent to sit in the pews! He is against our charging high rates to sit in the best pews! Why, we could have the poor sitting in the front of our churches! And without our income from pew rent, how will our church expenses be met? He insists on free seating for anyone who wants to enter the church!"

Charles rebuked them for their conceit and ran on, preaching the message of the gospel to all who would listen.

Men came to his meetings, vowing to kill him. For light from his torch was beginning to shine into homes and into churches where men preferred darkness.

Skeptics went to his meetings to sneer. Many of them were converted. Others left in disgust, desperate to stop him but not knowing quite how.

Charles ran through villages, towns and cities. Stores closed so people from all walks of life could attend the controversial meetings.

Professors in the theological seminary in Auburn, New York wrote to ministers in areas before Charles could arrive, warning them to oppose his wretched ministry.

Spies were sent out to find something in his life that could be reported to damage his influence among the people. Charles knew why they had come, but his weapon against them was unwavering love. They cowered as the light from his torch exposed their motives. Many found themselves eagerly sitting on the anxious benches that they had criticized. They returned to those who had sent them with a glowing report of their salvation.

The lawyer, who was training Charles before he entered the race, scoffed at both the race and the runner. It was incomprehensible to him that this brilliant young man had abandoned a law career to enter this despicable race. He continuously met friends and acquaintances who had heard Charles preach and were now witnessing to him of their conversion. The prominent lawyer finally decided to make peace with God himself.

"But I will not find God in the woods where Finney found Him!" he declared vehemently. "I will get my torch lit properly, in a church or in my own parlor!"

God would teach him that he did not light men's torches on men's terms. It was not until he walked to those same woods that he was gloriously saved.

Charles announced prayer meetings beginning at daybreak. When attendance at these prayer meetings began to dwindle, he ran to the houses of Christians.

"Wake up! Wake up! Don't you know it's time to pray?" he called loudly, beating on their doors and windows. People jumped guiltily from their beds to make their way sleepily to church to join Finney in prayer.

Charles Finney

He ran into a cotton factory at New York Mills. When he got within eight or ten feet of a young woman trying to mend a broken thread, she sank to the floor, bursting into tears. Work stopped in the room, as other workers stared at her. Then they too began to weep, until nearly all in the large room were in tears, confessing their sins before God. Conviction of sin spread throughout the mill. The factory owner called his superintendent over to him.

"Stop the mill," he instructed. "Let the people attend to religion; for it is more important that our souls should be saved than that this factory run!"

The workers were called to the mule room, where Charles spoke to them. When he left the cotton mill, the entire factory was ablaze with light.

Charles ran into Rome, New York, and preached on Sunday in a church there. Many people gathered on Monday in a home to listen to him again. Charles began to speak, but there was so much conviction of sins that he simply prayed quietly to his heavenly Father. As he conversed with God, people felt the presence of God fill the room. They began to sob and to sigh. Charles dismissed the service, and they left, weeping, to return to their homes.

Early Tuesday morning, he was called to visit homes all over Rome. The pastor joined him as he went from home to home, leaving them ablaze for God. In the afternoon, families came from every direction of town to gather in a large room. The meeting lasted until night as people crowded in to hear the Gospel.

A prayer meeting was held each morning. In the afternoon, he met with people who wanted to be saved. Every evening he preached. And after just twenty days, more than five-hundred people had found Christ.

Charles ran to Philadelphia, preaching to the lumbermen who had brought their logs down the Delaware River to sell. Many were converted. As they passed by the shanties of other lumbermen on their way back home, they stopped to tell them of their salvation. Soon over five-thousand people in an eighty-mile radius, who had attended no church, no revival meeting, and had heard no preacher, found Christ after simply hearing the joyful witness from these faithful lumbermen.

Charles Finney

Charles ran on to Reading, Pennsylvania, passing a merchant whose main business was making whiskey. He had just built a large distillery with all the latest improvements, and it was one of the most modern distilleries of the day. Then he met Jesus Christ, and when Charles left Reading, the merchant was tearing down his distillery, explaining to all who passed, "I will neither work it, nor sell it to be worked!"

Every morning, Charles was up long before daylight, praying. He fasted frequently. He literally warred against the powers of darkness in prayer. And he saw over 100,000 sinners converted in 1830 alone.

He ran into sin-blackened cities, and when he left, the city would be blazing with light, its ballrooms and theaters and bars turned into revival centers. The area where Charles ran became known for years afterward as the "Burned-over District".

He ran to London in 1849, where 1,500 to 2,000 men, women, and children were saved each evening he was there.

Now there were torches lit all over America and England. The runners, like Charles, were praying and fasting. In 1858-59, over one million Americans were saved as a direct result of these united prayer meetings.

Only once did Charles' hand falter during his race. Lydia, the girl who had prayed for his conversion, the companion who had become his running partner for twenty-three years, the mother of his three daughters and two sons, his beloved, crossed her finish line triumphantly. Sorrow nearly overwhelmed Charles, leaving him powerless to run, his mind reeling with his loss. He fell on his face before God, and God gently touched his fallen runner. He filled him with love and comfort and renewed him with strength and vigor. Lifting him to his feet, God placed the torch back in his hand.

Charles ran his race well, leaving a glow of light in his wake. At eighty-three years of age, he still stood erect as a young man, his mind alert, his torch held high and steady.

Two weeks before completing his eighty-third year, he crossed his finish line victoriously.

Charles left behind him not only millions of converts, but also principles that future runners who desire revival in their ministry can follow.

Those looking at his life believed that the revival that accompanied his meetings was a miracle sent from God. But Charles emphatically stated, "A revival is not a miracle! A miracle is an event that does not happen through the established order of the natural world. A miracle is a divine intervention of nature by God.

"When a farmer sows his seed and a crop springs up, we do not consider this a divine miracle," Charles went on. "The growth of the crop is in the natural order of the world that God created.

"A farmer must labor in order to reap a harvest! It is up to him to plow the field, plant the seed, and even bring in the harvest! God will not do the work the farmer must do! A crop cannot be produced without the blessing of God upon it. But God has not chosen to produce a crop in an empty field while the farmer sits idly on his porch!

"Can you imagine the farmers in our land being told that God will give them a crop only when it pleases Him, and that for them to plow and plant and labor as if they expected to raise a crop is very wrong?

"The world is our field. Our seed is the Word of God. Preaching is the sowing of the seed. The results are the springing up and growth of the crop.

"Yes, we need God's blessing, just as the farmer needs plenty of sunshine and rain! That is God's part! But no farmer will reap a harvest without laboring!"

His eyes then bored into the hearts of his accusers, exposing their jealousy of the harvest he was reaping.

"You tell me that I am taking the work of revival out of the hands of God and that I am interfering with his sovereignty, and going on in my own strength to produce a revival! And now, suppose the farmers should believe such a doctrine. Why, they would starve this world to death!

"The same lack of results will follow from the church's being persuaded that promoting revival and presenting the gospel to the lost is not the responsibility of Christians.

"Because of these teachings, generation after generation of souls have gone down to hell, while the church has been dreaming, waiting for God to save sinners without us doing our part of plowing, and planting and reaping!

"This lie has been the devil's most successful means of destroying souls."

His accusers turned away, unable to ensnare or to stop this runner with their arguments against his work.

Charles turned to those who were willing to learn from him and run with the torch in future generations.

"There are principles you must follow to promote a revival," he instructed them.

(It would do us well to listen in.)

1. **You must preach messages against sin!** It is sin that must be confessed and forsaken!

2. **You must teach Christians to obey God!** Just as in the case of a converted sinner, the first step for the backslidden Christian is a deep repentance, a breaking down of the heart, a getting down into the dust before God, with deep humility. After one truly repents, his life will be one of daily obedience to God.

3. **The church must see the lost state of sinners and their eternal fate.** The hearts of many Christians are as hard as marble. The love of God must soften their hearts, so they will begin to labor zealously to bring others to Him. They must be grieved that others do not love God, and must want everyone to love Him as they do. And they must determine to witness to their neighbors, friends, and family. They must be filled with a tender and burning love for lost souls. They must have a longing desire for the salvation of the whole world. They must be in agony for individuals whom they want to see saved - their friends, relations, enemies. They must not only urge them to give their hearts to God, but they must intercede for their salvation in prayer.

4. **The power and lust for the world must be broken in the lives of the Christians.** You must teach them to set their affection on heaven, and not on the charm of this world.

5. **When Christians get themselves right with God,
sinners will be saved.** Harlots, drunkards, infidels, and
all sorts of abandoned characters will be converted. The
church must welcome them and love them.

Charles paused and looked around at his listeners,
shaking his head.

"It is no good to preach to people whose hearts are
hard and waste and in a fallow state. The farmer might
just as well sow his grain on the rock! Seed sowed on
rocks will bring forth no fruit!

"You, as well as your listeners, must begin a self-
examination of your heart, your life, your actions, your
true character. Write down your sins. They were
committed one by one - repent of them one by one! Go
over them as carefully as a merchant goes over his books.
Do not be in a hurry!"

He then gave them a list of headings to write their sins
under.

Ingratitude

How often have you received blessings from God, and
never thanked Him for them?

Lack of Love toward God

God is a jealous God! He wants your unwavering
affection and love! How often have you offended Him?

Unbelief

How many times have you charged God with lying by
your unbelief of His express promises?

Neglect of the Bible

Neglect of Prayer

Lack of Love for the Souls of Man

Do you have compassion? Do you care that their
souls are destined for hell? Are you praying for their
salvation?

Neglect of Family Duties
How have you lived before your family? Do they see you praying fervently? Are you a spiritual example for them?
Neglect of Watchfulness Over Your Own Life
Have you neglected to watch your conduct and have sinned before the world, the church and God?

Neglect to Watch Over Your Brethren
Do you bear their burdens? Are you even acquainted with them? Are you meeting their physical and spiritual needs, or just pretending to love them?

Neglect of Self-denial
Are you willing to deny yourself of comfort and convenience for the Lord? Do you willingly suffer reproach for Christ? Do you deny yourself luxuries to save a world from hell? Do you give out of your abundance - or do you deny yourself and sacrifice willingly for Christ?
Worldly-mindedness
Do you look at all your possessions as God's - not yours? Do you seek wealth out of lust or ambition?

Pride
Are you more concerned with decorating yourself for church than about preparing your mind for the worship of God? Are you more concerned with how you appear outwardly before men than how your soul appears in the sight of God? Do you seek to divide the worship of the church - to draw attention to yourself and your appearance, rather than to God?

Envy
Are you pained to hear some people praised? Is it more agreeable to you to dwell upon their faults than upon their virtues; their failures than upon their successes?

Censoriousness
Do you have a bitter spirit, speaking of Christians without love?

Slander

Do you speak behind people's backs of their faults? Slander can be telling lies or the truth with the design to injure another.

Levity

Have you been reverent in the presence of God?

Lying

Lying is designed deception - making an impression contrary to the truth, by your words, looks, or actions.

Cheating

Have you dealt with others in the same way you would have them deal with you?

Hypocrisy

Have you confessed sins you had no intention of forsaking?

Robbing God

Have you misspent your time, squandering the hours God gave you to serve Him? Have you squandered money on your lusts?

Bad Temper

Hindering Others from Being Useful

Have you weakened the influence of others by insinuations against them? Do you hinder the labor of others, by destroying people's confidence in them?

Write down each heading, listing your sins beneath each one. Go over this list four times! Drive the plow through! God does not break up the fallow ground! He told us to!"

"Make restitution to those you have wronged! Then, and only then, the soil will bear fruit an hundredfold!"

And so Charles finished his race, leaving behind him not only people, homes, churches, and even taverns and ballrooms ablaze with light, but also a path for other runners to follow that would bring the light of revival to a complacent people, a backslidden church, a proud society, a sin-laden nation, a world staggering in darkness.

Chapter 76

DAVE

We are orphans and fatherless.
Lamentations 5:3

Dave knelt before the wide-eyed girl.

"What is your name?" he asked gently.

The small girl shrank back from him, her terror filled eyes darting quickly to those of the older girl by her side.

"Her name is Jenny."

Dave looked up at the speaker. It was hard to tell how old she was, but he guessed she was no more than ten. Her eyes were already weary of life, and there was a hopelessness about her that wrenched Dave's heart.

He had glanced their way when he was passing them. And then, the words spoken by his Master nearly two-thousand years earlier were repeated in his heart.

I was hungry, and you gave me no meat.
I was thirsty, and you gave me no drink.
I was a stranger, and you took me not in.
I was naked, and you clothed me not.

He had retraced his steps and now stood looking at the older of the two children.

"And your name?" he asked softly.

She looked away, as if ashamed to identify herself.

Dave barely heard her mumble, "Beth."

"Well, Beth and little Jenny, will you two wait right here for a few minutes? I don't like to eat alone! I'll just run back to the store down the street and get some food, and we'll have a picnic together."

Jenny's face lit with eager anticipation, but Beth just shrugged.

"I'll be right back," Dave said, as he turned toward the store.

"My Lord," he prayed, brushing the tears from his face. "These children are hungry and dirty and have lost all hope. Where are your people?"

315

He stopped, staring at the huge church he was passing. He looked up at the cross atop its spire, its brilliant stained glass windows, its massive structure.

Then he turned and looked again at the two children sitting alone on the bench. They were less than a block from this church that claimed Jesus as its Lord. Seeing Jenny watching him eagerly, he continued toward the store.

He shopped more carefully than usual, choosing foods that would provide nutrition for several days. Then he hurried back to the girls.

Opening the plastic tablecloth, he spread it on the ground beside the bench. Jenny jumped down to help him, her eyes on the sacks anchoring it to the ground. He noticed out of the corner of his eye that Beth was watching him, but when he smiled at her, her eyes darted quickly away.

He opened three bottles of fruit juice, peeled back the flap on the small milk cartons and polished the apples with a napkin before setting one at each place setting.

He removed the wrapping from the paper plates with jolly clown faces staring up at him. *Happy Birthday* was written across the top. He doubted if either of the girls had a birthday today, but the plates were on sale, and he knew Jenny at least would like them.

Jenny, however, didn't give them more than a quick glance. Her eyes stayed on the bag of food.

Dave felt tears filling his eyes. Why would a child care about a clown when her stomach churned painfully for food?

Quickly he removed bread, cheese and meat.

"Jenny. Beth. Before we eat, I am going to thank my Father for you and for this food. Sometimes when I talk to him, I close my eyes. You may join me if you would like to."

Four eyes stared at him intently as he shut his.

"Father," Dave prayed simply. "Thanks so much for my two new friends. I didn't want to eat all alone today. And we all thank you for this food we're going to eat together. Most of all, we thank you for Jesus, your wonderful Son. Amen."

Dave

The girls were already eating when he opened his eyes. He nibbled on his apple, studying them openly for the first time. Their attention was solely on their meal, and he knew that both had forgotten he was even there. They didn't even notice that he ate only part of an apple. He had just eaten his dinner moments before finding them.

It was hard to keep his eyes off little Jenny. What would this child look like if she was fed and bathed and dressed properly? Her eyes looked hollow in her thin face. Ill-fitting, dirty clothes hung on her body. He wondered how the ugly bruises on her arms had come to be there. Her hair was dull, lifeless, dirty and uncombed.

Then his eyes strayed to the cross on the church spire rising in the air just down the street.

He waited until their frantic eating slowed. Then he said quietly to Beth, "Beth, where is your home?"

For the first time her frightened eyes looked straight into his. Then she answered so quietly that he strained to hear her mumbled words.

"We don't have a home now."

"And where is your mother?"

She looked down then and he leaned forward to hear her answer.

"She's looking for work."

Dave hesitated and decided against asking about a Dad.

"Where are you staying at night?"

Fear covered the child's face. Jenny filled the silence.

"Wherever we can, Mister. Last night our mother didn't come for us, so we slept right there," she said, pointing to the ground under a tree.

"Do you stay here until your mother comes?" Dave asked Beth.

Again it was Jenny who answered.

"If people don't tell us we have to leave, we stay where we are. But if they make us leave, we come right back when they go away, so our mother will know where to find us."

He kept working as he asked, "How long have you been waiting here for your mother?"

Jenny looked up at Beth, who mumbled, "Three days."

Dave wrapped the food that remained on his plate in napkins and placed it in a sack. Then he stood up. He could feel the watching eyes of both girls.

"I have to go now, Beth and Jenny. You have made my dinner a happy one. Now I want you to take these sacks of food. I am a runner and can't be carrying bags of groceries with me."

As he spoke, he set the sack of leftovers and the sack he hadn't opened on the bench. As he turned to leave, he looked into the eyes of Jenny and then Beth.

"Jenny and Beth, I just want to tell you one thing before I leave. There is someone who loves you both very, very much. His name is Jesus. He is the one who told me that it would be good to stop and have dinner with you. I'm so glad he did, because this is one of the most enjoyable dinners I have had in a long time."

Dave ran out of words. How could these two sisters, huddled on a bench, sleeping alone on the ground, their thin bodies craving food, their eyes straining for the sight of their mother, comprehend the love of Jesus?

"My Lord," Dave cried silently as he turned away. "Where are your people that will show these children your love?"

His steps did not pause as he turned to walk up the granite steps of the church. He did not hesitate as he walked into the ornate, silent cathedral and followed the signs to the office.

A young man greeted him.

"Please, Sir," Dave said. "I must see the rector of this church."

"What is this concerning?" the young man asked.

Dave's eyes softened.

"Two beautiful children who live near this church. Their names are Beth and Jenny."

"Wait here," the man answered and disappeared.

Dave stood waiting, wondering what kind of man he would be meeting. Just seconds later, he grinned. Standing before him was a large, middle-aged man with warm eyes and a ready smile. Dave knew instantly that this was a man he could open his heart to.

Dave was still grinning when he emerged from a side door, the big man at his side. Together they walked down the block toward the bench. But his grin faded quickly when Dave saw the bench was empty. He hurried toward the spot. Then he motioned to the man to follow him. The plastic tablecloth was spread under the tree, a bed for the two children who lay asleep, their arms entwined around the sacks that were placed between them.

The big man stood silently, tears flowing unheeded down his cheeks.

He motioned Dave to the bench, and they sat quietly for a few moments.

Then the man broke the silence.

"I will send someone to get them tonight."

Dave shook his head.

"I doubt that either of them will leave willingly. They stay here waiting for their mother."

"Then I will send someone to stay with them."

He sighed heavily.

"Dave, what can we do? I don't want to be like the men you told me about earlier. I don't want to be the priest that passes by or the Levite that crosses the street. I want to be like the Samaritan that Jesus commended. There are so many needs in this city. Where do we start?"

Dave smiled.

"Sir, you could start with Jenny and Beth."

Both men turned toward the two children.

"How long will you be here, Dave?"

"I was leaving when I saw the children."

"Will you stay and speak to as many board members as I can gather together this evening?"

"I will."

Dave looked at the men gathered before him. He didn't want to prejudge, but they certainly did not look like men who would concern themselves with the plight of two ragged children.

With a prayer for wisdom, he told them about Jenny and Beth.

During a slight pause, one man spoke.

"I believe you plan to ask us to involve ourselves with these two children and probably other children in similar circumstances as well. Do you not realize there are multitudes of these homeless people? Are there not shelters for them? Do you know anything about their mother? Statistics say she is undoubtedly a drug addict, a drunkard, and probably selling her body to support her habit. I believe you should know before you continue, that my personal opinion is that these children should be referred to the appropriate government agencies . . ."

"Marvin," the booming voice of the pastor interrupted. "Please allow Dave to finish, and then we will discuss our views in this matter."

Dave noticed the flush that heated Marvin's face. He recovered his poise quickly, but not before Marvin saw the look of hostility in his glance toward the pastor. Dave knew then that Marvin would be against whatever the pastor wanted to do.

"Sirs," he said, looking directly at Marvin. "We are all aware that homeless people line many of our nations' streets. If the government agencies were successful at caring for them, I would not have brought this matter to your attention. And Jenny and Beth would not be sleeping less than a block from this church on a plastic tablecloth."

Then he addressed Marvin.

"You, Sir, asked what we could do. We could be obedient to our Lord's command to simply feed the hungry, give shelter to the stranger and clothe the naked."

"It all sounds great, Young Man," Marvin replied, barely controlling the anger in his voice.

"But regardless of appearances, we are not a wealthy church!"

A smile lit Dave's face as he looked at the men seated before him.

"My Friends, God does not need a wealthy church to meet the needs of the poor.

"For you see, he is a wealthy God!

"Please give me just a few minutes of your time. I want to tell you about one man who, by faith, tapped into our God's vast storehouse of endless supplies."

Chapter 77

George Mueller
(1805 to 1898)

And the stranger and the fatherless which are within thy gates, shall come, and shall eat and be satisfied; that the Lord thy God may bless thee in all the work of thine hand which thou doest.
Deuteronomy 14:29

The girl was small for her age. Her ragged dress hung loosely on her emaciated little body. It had been days since she had eaten more than a few scraps of food at a time. And she had fought off dogs and other children even to get those! She could no longer even remember what it felt like to be without gnawing hunger pains.

Food had often been scarce when her mother was alive. But there had always been something to partially fill her. Since her death, there had been nothing except what she found that had been thrown away by others. How long had she made her home wherever she happened to wander? Sometimes she had slept under a bench, once or twice in an abandoned building.

She clutched the crumpled paper in her hand as she walked down the strange street, staring at the numbers on the houses.

Smoothing the paper, she stared again at the words. The message was strange - and probably too good to be true.

It offered a home to girls between the ages of seven and twelve. It said there would be no charge. And it said only orphans would be welcome.

She wasn't sure of her age. Was it eight - or had she turned nine? Her mother would have remembered.

Brushing the tears quickly from her eyes, she knew she at least was certain about one fact. She was an orphan! There was no one in the world who cared whether she lived or died.

She stared at the house she had nearly passed. The numbers matched. But it was huge! She looked up . . . one, two, three stories high! And . . . the house was beautiful! Dare she knock? What would she find inside - kindness - or terror?

She went slowly to its massive door, and standing on her tiptoes, pulled back the knocker. She gripped it tightly for a moment, and then fearfully let it fall.

George jumped to his feet. Someone was knocking! Could it be his first orphan? He had just asked God last evening to send him some orphans!

He chuckled as he nearly ran to the door.

Wasn't that just like God?

Six-thousand orphans were living in degradation, vice and poverty in Bristol's prisons and streets.

Somehow their needs had become his. Their hunger had prevented him from enjoying a good meal. Knowing they had no bed hindered him from getting a good night's sleep. Finally in desperation, he had prayed for a house for thirty children. He had decided to bring in girls between the ages of seven and twelve.

The place had been ready for its orphans for a few days now. He had given fliers advertising his home all over Bristol - but where were the orphans?

Then he had heard the voice of his God speak to his heart. "George. You forgot to pray for the orphans!"

He laughed. He had prayed in the funds to rent this house for a year. He had prayed in good Christian helpers. He had prayed in food. He had prayed in clothing for the girls! Now God expected him to pray in the orphans!

So . . . last night he had prayed that God would send him the orphans!

He opened the door and looked down at the little ragged girl standing before him, naked fear in her eyes.

A brilliant smile lit his face.

He was so glad she was in rags! She would love the beautiful clothes he had waiting for her upstairs!

And how she needed to eat! Wait until she saw the feast he had prepared for his first guest!

She hesitantly and fearfully handed the smiling man the paper. Could it really mean what it said? Would this beautiful house become her home? Would this kind looking gentleman become her father?

George stepped back, motioning her to enter with a wide sweep of his hand. At the same time he called out behind him, "Come quickly, everyone! Our first little girl is here!"

The girl gazed wide-eyed as the foyer filled with smiling people. They looked at her with love shining through their eyes. They all seemed to be talking at once. She simply stared.

She was the first. The home was soon filled to capacity with thirty chattering, happy girls. George, thirty years old, happily married and the father of one daughter, was now the busy Dad to thirty more girls!

He rose early each morning to pray for their daily needs.

He prayed in spoons, dresses, blankets, cups, calico, helpers, pillow cases, plates, coal, milk, rent money, shoes, bonnets, petticoats, apples, bacon, sugar, wool, combs - and whatever else was needed at the moment. Always the answers came.

There was the gift of money from one poor woman. George knew she herself was nearly destitute, and taking her gift in his hand, he went to her home to return it.

"I know you yourself have needs and debts," he began.

"But I received a small inheritance from my father!" she interrupted. "And it was enough to pay all my debts and give some to my mother. The rest I gave to you for your orphans!"

"What will you live on?" George asked.

"My heavenly Father will care for me," was her firm answer. "The Lord Jesus has given His last drop of blood for me, and should I not give *all* the money I have?"

Many days George found money outside his door, placed anonymously in a pan or in a sack.

But his joy in seeing the answers to his daily prayers was clouded by a burden.

For the word had spread. Almost daily now, orphans of every description found their way to his home - little boys, little girls, some bringing with them their tiny little brothers and sisters. George had to turn them away, for his home was filled to capacity.

He went again to his knees. "Father, I need another home for more children," he prayed simply.

In less than a year, thirty-one year old George Mueller became the Dad to sixty orphans.

Still the orphans arrived. And what should he do with the children who had no place to go when they turned thirteen years of age?

Another home was purchased. This one would house forty boys, ages seven and older.

George was thirty-two now. He spent much time on his knees, praying in food, clothing and shelter for eighty-one children and nine full-time staff members.

In his spare time, he taught three-hundred fifty children in day school and three-hundred twenty children in Sunday School and pastored a church!

Some days the responsibility of it all nearly over-whelmed him. These children were looking to him for all their needs! He had no money! Would God continue to provide?

Then one day he read Psalm 68:5 and found the promise that planted unshakeable faith in his heart.

A Father of the fatherless . . is God in his holy habitation. God - the Father of the fatherless!

If God described Himself as a Father of the fatherless, why, he would never have to worry or be concerned about his orphans again!

For these were not *his* orphans! They were God's!

And *he* was not their father! God was!

And fathers, George realized, a smile lighting his face, were obligated to care for their children!

Grabbing a pen and paper, George wrote:

"This shall be my argument before him in the orphans' hour of need. He is their Father, and therefore has pledged Himself to provide for them and to care for them. I have only to remind Him of the need of these poor children, in order to have it supplied. This word, 'a Father of the fatherless' contains enough encouragement to cast thousands of Orphans, with all their needs, upon the loving heart of God!"

He continued in prayer for the daily needs of his children, but he never again worried that God would not bring the needed supplies.

A friend once asked him, "George, what would you do if there was no food for the children at mealtime?"

George didn't even hesitate. He had learned the answer to that question long ago!

He replied confidently, "Such a thing is impossible, as long as the Lord gives us grace to trust in Him, for 'whosoever believeth on Him shall not be ashamed!' But if we ever forsake the Lord and trust in an arm of flesh or regard iniquity in our heart - then we may pray and utter many words before Him, but He will not hear us!"

When small items were brought in - George took time to thank his heavenly Father for sending them. He thanked his God for *every* gift - whatever its size or value.

During one six month period, money and supplies arrived with only minutes to spare before the children sat down to eat.

The cook shook her head wearily, but George, perfectly calm, remarked, "It is worth being poor and greatly tried in faith. For we have every day precious proofs of the loving interest which our kind Father takes in everything that concerns us!"

He now was feeding over one-hundred children a day, supporting two Sunday Schools, giving away Bibles and several hundred tracts and books.

And he couldn't neglect the adults! They had needs too! Four evenings a week, he taught three-hundred fifty illiterate adults how to read and write. He prayed in the money for their books and writing materials, so all could freely attend his two adult schools with no charge. At the end of each class, George read the Bible to his students.

George also supported six day schools.

And could he forget the missionaries who had forsaken their countries and homes for Christ? He supported missionaries in Jamaica, Australia, Canada, the East Indies and China!

And still the orphans came.

George Mueller

At age forty-one, George purchased seven acres and built a home for three-hundred children and thirty staff and teachers.

At age fifty, George built another house for four-hundred girls. When he was fifty-four, he purchased eleven and a half acres and built yet another home to house four-hundred fifty more children!

God, truly the Father to the fatherless, sent in daily supplies for one-thousand, one-hundred fifty orphans and their huge staff.

George Mueller, realizing he had tapped into the treasure house of heaven itself, could not stop praying and providing as long as there was one child in Bristol, England, who had no parents, no home, no food, no bed.

He built two more large homes for eight-hundred fifty more children and prayed in the money to purchase eighteen more acres.

He now was responsible for the daily needs of two-thousand children and two-hundred staff members.

He would never forget the morning they all gathered for breakfast - at an empty table. There was no food in the homes. There was no money to purchase food. George had vowed never to ask man for help. His needs would be made known to God and God alone.

As over two-thousand people sat down to eat, George was not prostrate in his prayer closet, weeping before God for food.

Instead, he stood confidently to give thanks to his faithful Father for His daily provision.

"Dear Father," he prayed simply, "we thank Thee for what Thou art going to give us to eat."

A knock was heard. The village baker, laying awake with thoughts of George's orphans, had finally dressed and hurried to his bakery at 2:00 A.M. and was now delivering fresh bread for the breakfast of over two-thousand two-hundred people.

And another knock! This time the milkman stood at the door, explaining that his cart had broken down right outside the Orphanage. Could he be allowed to empty his cart of milk inside, so he could repair his wagon?

At ninety-one years of age, George Mueller said to a visiting pastor, Charles R. Parsons:

"For nearly 70 years, every need in connection with this work has been supplied. The orphans from the first until now have numbered 9,500, but they have never wanted a meal. Hundreds of times we have begun the day without a penny, but our Heavenly Father has sent supplies the moment they were actually required. There never was a time when we had no wholesome meal.

"During all these years, I have trusted in the living God alone.

"In answer to prayer, $7,500,000 have been sent to me. We have needed as much as $200,000 in one year, and it has all come when needed. No man can ever say I asked him for a penny.

"We have no committees, no collectors, no endowment. All has come in answer to believing prayer.

"God has many ways of moving the hearts of men all over the world to help us.

"There is no limit to what God is able to do! Praise him for everything! I have praised Him many times when He sent me ten cents, and I have praised Him when He has sent me $60,000!"

Pastor Parsons asked him, "Did you ever have a reserve fund?"

George looked at his visitor with amazement.

"To do so would be an act of the greatest folly!" he replied emphatically. "How could I pray if I had reserves? God would say, 'Bring out those reserves, George!'

"Oh no, I never thought of such a thing! Our reserve fund is in heaven! I have trusted God for $1. I have trusted him for thousands and never trusted in vain. Psalm 34:8 says, *Blessed is the man that trusteth in Him!*"

Pastor Parsons hardly dared to ask him the next question. But he only had one hour with this man, and he just had to know his answer.

"You have never thought of saving for yourself?"

George Mueller had been sitting calmly, leaning slightly forward.

But now he jerked erect, and, for what seemed like several moments, searched his interviewer's face, his eyes penetrating to his very soul. He was clearly roused! His eyes flashed fire!

Finally he withdrew from his pocket an old-fashioned purse with rings in the middle separating the coins.

He laid it in the hands of Pastor Parsons and answered quietly, but firmly, "All I am possessed of is in this purse - every penny! Save for myself? *Never!* When money is sent to me for my own use, I pass it on to God!

"As much as $5,000 has thus been sent at one time; but I do not regard such gifts as belonging to me! They belong to Him, whose I am and whom I serve.

"Save for myself?

"I dare not save! It would dishonor my loving, gracious, all bountiful Father!"

Pastor Parsons looked at this runner and thought about the works that resulted simply from faith in God's promises.

His faith provided a home for over nine-thousand children, supported nearly two-hundred missionaries, educated nine-thousand scholars in one-hundred schools, and prayed in and gave out four million tracts and tens of thousands of Bibles!

Between the ages of seventy and eighty-seven, this man, still pulsing with vigor and energy, had traveled over 200,000 miles to forty-two countries, preaching the gospel to over three million people!

Pastor Parsons had yet one more question.

"Do you spend much time on your knees, praying?"

George's face seemed lit from within as he answered, "Hours every day. But I *live* in the spirit of prayer. I pray as I walk, when I lie down, and when I rise. And the answers are always coming. Tens of thousands of times my prayers have been answered. When once I am persuaded a thing is right, I go on praying for it until the end comes. I never give up!

"In answer to my prayers, thousands of souls have been saved! I shall meet tens of thousands of them in heaven!"

He paused, and when Pastor Parsons was silent, George went on, almost to himself.

"The great point is to never give up until the answer comes. I have been praying every day for fifty-two years for two men, sons of a friend of my youth. They are not converted yet, but they will be! How can it be otherwise?

There is the unchanging promise of Jehovah, and on that I rest. The great fault of the children of God is that they do not continue in prayer. They do not go on praying! They do not persevere! If they desire anything for God's glory, they should pray until they get it!

"Oh, how good, kind, gracious, and condescending is the One with whom we have to do!

"He has given me, unworthy as I am, immeasurably above all I have asked or thought!

"I am only a poor, frail, sinful man, but he has heard my prayers tens of thousands of times and used me as the means of bringing tens of thousands of souls into the way of truth in this and other lands.

"These unworthy lips have proclaimed salvation to great multitudes, and very many people have believed unto eternal life."

Pastor Parsons again hesitated, and then said softly, "I cannot help noticing the way you speak of yourself."

George Mueller answered instantly.

"There is only one thing I deserve and that is Hell! I tell you, my brother, that is the only thing I deserve. By nature I am a lost man, but I am a sinner saved by the grace of God. Though by nature a sinner, I do not live in sin. I hate sin! I hate it more and more, and love holiness more and more!"

As Pastor Parsons left George Mueller, he recalled the story told of George by Charles Inglis, a well-known evangelist.

When I first came to America thirty-one years ago, I crossed the Atlantic with the captain of a steamer who was one of the most devoted men I ever knew. When we were off the banks of Newfoundland, he said to me: "Mr. Inglis, the last time I crossed here, five weeks ago, one of the most extraordinary things happened that has completely revolutionized the whole of my Christian life. Up to that time, I was one of your ordinary Christians. We had a man of God on board, George Mueller, of Bristol. I had been on that bridge for twenty-two hours and never left it. I was startled by someone tapping me on the shoulder. It was George Mueller.

"Captain," said he, "I have come to tell you that I must be in Quebec on Saturday afternoon." This was Wednesday.

"It is impossible," I replied.

"Very well, if your ship can't take me, God will find some other means of locomotion to take me. I have never broken an engagement in fifty-seven years."

"I would willingly help you, but how can I? I am helpless," I answered.

"Let us go down to the chart room and pray," he said.

"I looked at this man and I thought to myself, What lunatic asylum could the man have come from? I never heard of such a thing."

"Mr. Mueller," I said, "do you know how dense this fog is?"

"No," he replied, "my eye is not on the density of the fog, but on the living God, who controls every circumstance of my life."

He went down on his knees, and he prayed one of the most simple prayers. I thought to myself, "That would suit a children's class, where the children were not more than eight or nine years of age."

The burden of his prayer was something like this: "O Lord, if it is consistent with thy will, please remove this fog in five minutes. You know the engagement you made for me in Quebec for Saturday. I believe it is your will."

When he had finished, I was going to pray, but he put his hand on my shoulder and told me not to pray.

"First," he said, "you do not believe God will do it, and, second, I believe He already has done it. And there is no need whatever for you to pray about it."

I looked at him, and George Mueller said, "Captain, I have known my Lord for fifty-seven years, and there has never been a single day that I have failed to gain an audience with the King. Get up, Captain, and open the door, and you will find the fog is gone."

I got up, and the fog was gone.

On Saturday afternoon, George Mueller was in Quebec.

Dave paused, quietly looking at each man gathered before him. Then he went on.

George Mueller left us not only an example of living by faith, but its definition.

When he was asked what faith was, he answered, "Faith is the assurance that the thing which God has said in his Word is true, and that God will act according to what he has said in his Word. This assurance, this reliance on God's Word, this confidence is faith.

"Probabilities are not to be taken into account. Many people are willing to believe regarding those things that seem probable to them. Faith has nothing to do with probabilities. The province of faith begins where probabilities cease, and sight and sense fail.

"Impressions, probabilities, appearances are not to be taken into account. The question is - whether God has spoken it in his Word.

"Trials, obstacles, difficulties, and sometimes defeats, are the very food of faith.

"God has never failed me! Trust him for yourself and discover how true to his Word he is!"

Chapter 78

Dave

But whoso hath this world's good, and seeth his brother have need, and shutteth up his bowels of compassion from him, how dwelleth the love of God in him?

I John 3:17

Dave looked at the members of the church board. None of them returned his gaze. Two got up to refill their coffee cups. The others simply looked down.

John felt Dave's eyes upon him. Finally he looked up.

"Look, Dave. Your story is great. I'm sure it worked for George. But we're not men of great faith, as he was. We're not . . ."

"Wait a minute," Dave interrupted. "You don't understand! George Mueller did not start out any different than any of you! In fact, probably none of you spent your youth as he did! He was a thief, a liar and a drunkard!

"He wasted his time reading novels. He was always in debt - he was even imprisoned as a teenager for running up debts that he had no intention of paying!

"While in college, he faked a robbery, smashed his trunk and guitar case and claimed his room was broken into, just to get money from sympathetic friends and professors!

"His free time was spent in taverns, where he drank ten pints of beer in one afternoon!"

All eyes were back on Dave now.

One man showed interest for the first time.

"This same Mueller you were telling us about - was a drunk?" he asked.

"This same George Mueller. But when he was twenty years old, he attended a home Bible study with a friend, where he received Christ as his personal Savior and Lord.

"George was a new man! He never again drank in a tavern. His lying ceased! He became a soul winner on campus, giving gospel tracts to all he met. He visited the sick, prayed with them, held meetings in his dorm, preached in villages and towns surrounding the university, and walked fifteen miles to hear one good sermon. George met Jesus Christ, and he was a new man!

"And this Jesus, Gentlemen, whom George met, is the same Jesus you profess to serve!"

Dave looked straight at John, who seemed to be the spokesman for the rest.

"You see, Sir, it's not a wealthy church we need here. It's simply a man or a group of men who realize we serve a God of great provision! It's not a man with a huge bank account. It's simply a man who realizes there is an unlimited account in the treasure house of heaven!

"George Mueller did not begin his work by caring for nine-thousand orphans. He began with one - and his faith grew as his Lord provided for her. You see, Friends, a mustard seed of faith grows with the need.

"Couldn't you, as a church, begin a walk of faith by caring for just two small girls who desperately need your love? Couldn't you show them the meaning of the cross that they can see from their bench . . . "

"Excuse me," the pastor said, his voice, as usual, in full volume.

All eyes were upon him as he left the room.

Dave had obviously failed to move these men to action. The pastor, who he had considered his one ally, was gone. There was no use in continuing his plea. The men simply ignored him and conversed with one another.

The pastor returned after a few minutes, and John moved to adjourn the meeting until the problem of the two children could be looked into further.

The motion was quickly seconded and the meeting was brought to an abrupt end.

The men left quickly, leaving only the pastor and Dave.

For the first time since meeting the pastor, there was an awkward silence between them.

Finally the man spoke.

"Dave, you said what you came to say. I don't know if your story reached the hearts of these men or not. I'm sorry to say that I doubt that it did. I do know that I personally have made a decision today. I will care for Jenny and Beth and any other needy children who wander into my neighborhood - with or without the approval of my church, and with or without my position as pastor of this church."

A big hand reached out to clasp Dave's.

"I will no longer sit in the bleachers and view God's runners! I am going to join old George and run this race myself. Up until now, neither I nor the members of this church have involved itself enough to get our hands dirty. It's time we take a look at the real world around our fine sanctuary! Now, let's go see how those two little girls are doing."

He started out the door, but Dave stood still, his heart nearly bursting with joy.

"Well, come on, Dave," the mighty voice filled the room. "What are you waiting for?"

"Can we pray before we go?"

And kneeling in the room, Dave asked God to give the new runner love and courage and a torch that would light up his neighborhood.

The man prayed as he spoke, his voice thundering out his petitions to his God.

Then they ran to the bench together.

Just before reaching the girls, Dave stopped short. A tiny, well-dressed, perfectly groomed woman sat between the two girls, an arm pulling each one close to her immaculate clothing. A blanket covered their legs against the chill of the evening. She was quietly talking and both girls were listening with wide eyes. Jenny gripped a cookie.

The new runner looked at Dave and laughed loudly.

"No, that's not their mother. That is my beautiful little wife, Doris. I excused myself during the meeting to call her and tell her about these kids. You can continue your run now. There's no need to worry about the kids in our neighborhood. Doris would have been at this business long ago if I hadn't kept her busy with things that really don't matter much. You go on now. We'll take it from here."

The girls didn't even glance Dave's way as he left them.

But he knew there was one who did.

Looking up, he spoke to him.

"Jesus, it's okay here. You have found a beautiful couple to work through. Jenny and Beth will believe you love them now."

He realized he was talking much louder than usual and chuckled as he lowered his voice to its normal volume.

His smile faded, as he looked to the towns and cities beyond.

"Oh, God, please touch the hearts of your people. There will always be some who cross the street to avoid those who are hurting. But give us some more good Samaritans like this beautiful couple I have just met!

"Lord, I guess what I am really asking, is that you raise up a George Mueller in every neighborhood! How desperately our children need them!"

Chapter 79

Dave

For all the city of my people doth know that thou art a virtuous woman.
Ruth 3:11

They were back in the restaurant where they had first gotten acquainted. Ruth had been helping in the children's home again and Dave had been speaking to a group of young people.

"I met Charlotte," she was saying. "Dave, that girl is an inspiration to me! She has such a beautiful outlook on life. I have never seen a mother and daughter with such a beautiful relationship with one another. They begin each day with prayer and singing . . . have you ever heard them sing, Dave? Their voices blend perfectly." She sighed. "What I wouldn't give for a voice like Charlotte's!"

Dave flipped open his address book and pointed an address out to her.

"Ruth, are you sure you went to the right house?"

Ruth didn't bother to look at the address.

"Yes, I went to the right house! How many Charlottes are there in wheel chairs that you won to the Lord?"

Dave closed the book and put it back in his shirt pocket.

"I was teasing. But the two people you just described don't sound anything like the two people I met."

He smiled.

"Of course, I met them B.C."

She smiled back.

"Before Christ," she said softly. "What were they like then, Dave?"

He shook his head.

"Let's just say that you wouldn't have left their house encouraged or inspired by the music they were making together. Did you say you'd been with Tom too?"

She nodded. "We went to the park where he used to live. He showed me the bench that was his bed and the table where he met you each morning. He wanted to find some boys he knew, and your Uncle Joe didn't want him to go alone."

"Oh, no! I was hoping Tom wouldn't go back to his old friends!"

"He went back, all right. We found two of them. You should have seen their faces when they saw Tom with a Bible in one hand and a torch in the other!"

"Tom?" Dave asked. Then he grinned. "I know. I knew him B.C. How's Uncle Joe?"

Ruth shook her head. "I love your uncle, Dave. You would never know by being around them that they weren't father and son. Uncle Joe was pacing the floor when we got back but tried to act as if he wasn't worried a bit. Tom was just as anxious to get home. I think he was afraid Uncle Joe and his house would both be gone. He told me today that he has never had a room with a bed and three meals a day."

"It's seeing Christ transform people like Charlotte, Uncle Joe and Tom that makes this run so exciting," Dave remarked. "I realize we need to run and speak the Word even in the places we see no results. But I'm glad God didn't tell me what he told Jeremiah when he called him to run. No wonder they call him the weeping prophet. What a discouraging job he had. Can you imagine responding to a call like his?"

Therefore you shall speak all these words unto them; but they will not hearken to you: you shall also call unto them; but they will not answer you.

"I thank God every day for the Charlottes, Joes and Toms!"

"I do too," Ruth said thoughtfully. "I feel like Jeremiah on some days and in some places. Then I remember that we run the course God sets for us. Perhaps years down the road someone may remember our witness and turn to Christ. Others may not remember our words until the judgment day when it's too late. I try to remember at the end of a discouraging day that I have done what God asked me to do and I need to leave the results to him."

She paused and then added, "I see very few results at the mission."

She noticed Dave's anxious expression and squeezed his hand that was holding hers.

"I know you worry about me going to the mission, Dave, but I trust in my Lord's promises just like you do. You're the one who told me to memorize Psalm 91," she reminded him. "He is *my* refuge and fortress as well as yours! "

Dave frowned. "I guess it's easier for me to trust God to protect me than it is to trust him to protect you. You're a brave girl."

Ruth shook her head. "I don't feel brave at all. I read about people who are brave and they put me to shame. Think of Corrie ten Boom who hid Jews during Hitler's reign and was imprisoned in Ravensbruck. She ran fearlessly even in a terror-filled German concentration camp. She ran throughout the world when she was sixty and seventy years old. Dave, Corrie landed in foreign airports, not knowing either the language or any people. God always took care of her!"

"I still say you're a brave girl."

"Brave," she scoffed. "I don't know the first thing about being brave. Dave, let me tell you about a woman who was brave. Her run took her straight up to the coldest, highest mountain range in the entire world. Did you know that since 1950 people who enter Tibet have to first have their heart and lungs tested in Beiging? The Lord sent Annie there with a weak heart! Oh, and did I mention that her guide was a murderer? Let me tell you about someone really brave . . . "

Chapter 80

Annie Taylor
(1855 to . . . her finish!)

He giveth power to the faint; and to them that have no might he increaseth strength.
Isaiah 40:29

The doctor of Cheshire, England, stood looking sympathetically at the frail child.

"Don't bother educating her," he advised her parents. "Your daughter has valvular heart disease and will die as a child."

But the doctor could not know that God would once again choose the weak of this world to confound those who are mighty.

He didn't see ahead to a thirteen year old girl. Annie, still frail, knelt in a small church to receive Jesus as her Savior. She chose him that day for her dearest friend.

He had no vision of the day that Annie, at age sixteen, would sit listening to a missionary, absorbed as he presented the urgent need for runners in distant and strange lands.

"We need *men*," he stated. "And they must be *strong* men, willing to hazard their lives for their Lord!"

Annie leaned back in her seat, sighing with disappointment, knowing she would never qualify for this great race.

She buried her heartfelt desire and chose instead to be educated in the fields of art and medicine. She completed twelve years of intensive training in Italy, Germany, and the London Hospital.

But all through the years, she was unable to still the voice of her Lord. Finally she knelt at his feet, her weak heart racing wildly, and accepted the torch from his hand.

It was settled. Her load was lifted. She made plans to go to Tibet.

Her announcement was met with shock and dismay.

"Annie! Do you realize where you are going?"

"I do," she nodded, smiling. "I am going where God has instructed me to go."

"But Annie! Surely God wouldn't send you to Tibet! Don't you know it is the highest place in the world? Your weak heart will never stand the high altitude of Tibet!"

"I have placed my great Physician in charge of my heart," Annie replied calmly.

The word spread and more came with their dire predictions.

"Annie, the country of Tibet has the most rugged and difficult terrain in the entire world. The only ones who dare go there are hearty mountain climbers who go to climb Mount Everest."

"And me. I too will go to Tibet."

Then she laughed.

"There is no need for worry. I have no intention of climbing a 29,000 foot high mountain!"

Her eyes took on a faraway look.

"Please don't worry. My life is in my Master's hand. Remember, we have received no orders from the Lord that are impossible to carry out, and He has told us to go into *all* the world!"

On September 2, 1892, her long journey began.

She found a guide and they joined a caravan of Mongols.

She wore heavy sheepskin, the wool turned toward her body to keep out the frigid winds and bitter gales that raged in the cold mountains throughout the year. Her meals often consisted of raw goat and sheep.

Annie slept wherever shelter could be found, in a cave, tent, often in a snowdrift. She cooked her meat when she was able in her only utensil, a tin basin. More than once, Annie's hand was frozen to its side.

During the trip, she learned that her guide was a murderer. She caught him eyeing her constantly and realized he had marked her as his next victim.

But the God who had summoned her was running with her. She trusted him to be her shield, buckler, and ever-faithful companion.

She awoke some nights, gasping for breath, her heart racing. She begged God to stop the palpitation of her weakened heart, so she could continue her course.

Annie ran a route that would make the most valiant and healthy runner tremble. Annie knew she was not strong, so she held on tightly to the one who was.

Most evenings, she extracted her small diary and pencil from her bundle to write her thoughts, her hand stiff from the bitter cold. One starry evening, Annie paused before writing. Her thoughts returned to her home in England, her fine clothing, her warm house, her delicious meals, her soft bed. Then Annie looked around at her frozen white world, walls of rocks jutting above and beyond her.

She smiled as she wrote, "The ground is my bed, the stars my curtain, and the wind pretty bad about my head."

She glanced over at the sleeping form of her ruthless guide, then added, "It is quite safe here with Jesus!"

Annie could hardly contain her excitement as she reached her destination.

Her first stop was a Tibetian monastery. Her smile faded. Formidable statues towered above her, their jewels gleaming. Scores of worshipers lay prostrate before them. Some stood chanting before a repulsive idol, inserting pins into its robes to increase their mental powers.

The floor, ceiling and walls were covered with paintings and hangings of mythical Buddhist figures. An eerie glow flickered, cast by thousands of butter candles. Pagodas and thrones awaited the demonic rituals of the powerful lamas. Aged women spun their prayer wheels endlessly, tonelessly chanting, chanting, awaiting an answer that would never come from gods who did not exist.

Annie shuddered as the power of evil flowed toward her, threatening to suffocate her in its grip. This was a blackness such as she had never known The midnight hour of the caves where she had slept did not compare to the spiritual darkness of this night. She reached out frantically for her Lord, then felt his strength and power flow through her.

And Annie lifted her torch.

"Jesus has power over evil spirits," she cried! "Jesus can set you free!"

The nuns paid her no heed. As she left, she heard their futile chant, knowing it had been prayed for over twelve-hundred years. It had never and would never avail anything.

"O, the jewel in the lotus.

"O, the jewel in the lotus."

Annie backed out of the monastery, demons keeping their distance from the light she had dared to bring into their abode.

She ran throughout the forgotten land of Tibet. She met no other runners, for there were none in that strange and dark land.

But the people . . . how she loved the people. Christ had died for them and she now lived for them! They were so friendly! The sturdy little people surrounded her. They wanted to know all about her. She had never met such curious people! Wherever she walked, children fought for the privilege of holding her hands.

One quarter of all the men and boys were Buddhist monks, trusting in the ceaseless journey of reincarnations to eventually bring them purity.

She told them of Jesus and his amazing love, offering them his free salvation.

Crowds thronged her as she painted the gospel message on story cards. She passed them out to three-thousand people.

She gave out a thousand Tibetian and Chinese Bibles. Some copies made their way to the lamas.

Annie recorded joyfully in her diary, "I hear the lamas in all the monasteries are now reading the gospel!"

She introduced many to Jesus. One by one, they began to approach him, their hands outstretched to receive their own torch. Pockets of light were now scattered throughout the country.

Annie ran valiantly, this girl who was pronounced ineligible for the race by all but her Lord. She ran fearlessly, carrying God's promise in her diseased heart, "Be of good courage, and I shall strengthen your heart!"

Those back home who listened with dread for news from her or about her were sent only reports of victory.

They at last realized that a torch shines brightest in the blackest part of the earth, and that Christ's strength is seen most clearly in the weakest of his vessels.

Annie, rejected by the world as unfit for its use, ran a path that took her uphill to a forbidding land and a forsaken people. She held gospel meetings, read the Bible, invited people to prayer meetings. She played a tiny organ, singing the gospel message in her high and cheerful voice. She used her medical training to care for the injured and the sick, many times exhausted herself.

One of her favorite Bible verses was, "Ask of me and I will give thee the heathen for your inheritance, and the uttermost parts of the earth for your possession."

When Annie crossed her finish line, falling into the arms of her beloved friend, she must have heard his delighted words, as he welcomed her home:

"Well done, good and faithful servant. Well done, Annie!"

Chapter 81

Dave

A virtuous woman is a crown to her husband.
Proverbs 12:4

"**W**asn't Annie something, Dave?"

Dave nodded. "She was one courageous lady who knew her God and trusted him for protection. You've made your point, Ruth. God takes good care of his people. I'll try not to worry about you."

He laughed.

"Just as long as you don't head for Tibet!"

She didn't laugh with him.

"I don't know where God will lead me, Dave. I am willing to go wherever he leads. I don't just go where I feel like going and expect him to follow me. My heart's desire is to follow him."

Dave nodded. "It's okay if he leads you to Tibet, Ruth. I just hope that wherever he leads us, he will lead us there together."

He leaned forward, taking both her hands in his.

"Ruth, I've fallen in love with you. I thought I was in love with someone once. But I didn't even know what love was until I met you. I can't believe there's a girl like you left in this corrupt world. I never dreamed I would meet someone like you!"

Pleasure colored her face.

"I love you too, Dave. I loved you the first time I saw you."

"The *first* time! You couldn't have! I was at my very worst among all those babies!"

She smiled. "It's true. I went right home that night and asked God if it would be possible for us to run together."

"I did the same thing - the first night!"

A waitress walked by to lock the door and officially close the restaurant. One glance at the lovebirds in the corner made her decide to clean the other section first. She noticed they hadn't touched their food.

"Will you be my wife, Ruth?"

344

She answered softly, quoting the beautiful vow of a Ruth before her:

"Whither thou goest, I will go; and where thou lodgest, I will lodge: thy people shall be my people, and thy God my God: Where thou diest, will I die, and there will I be buried: the Lord do so to me, and more also, if aught but death part thee and me."

The vows in their future wedding would never mean as much to Dave as Ruth's beautiful acceptance of his proposal.

The waitresses were vacuuming the floor when Dave and Ruth finally became aware of their surroundings and hurriedly left.

Dave took her in his arms at her door and kissed her. He pulled back quickly. "Ruth! Why the tears?"

She pulled him back to her. "I'm just happy, Dave. Women cry when they're happy."

"I guess I have a few things to learn," he murmured against her hair.

He was halfway home when he started running faster. He had forgotten to tell Ruth about a couple things that had happened today. He decided to call her the minute he got home.

She laughed when she heard his voice.

"I was just wishing you would call, Dave! I thought of something I hadn't told you."

"That's why I called! I thought of things I forgot to tell you!"

"You first."

"Uh . . . let's see. Can you believe it? I can't remember! It seemed important while I was running home. I feel pretty silly. You tell me what you wanted to say."

Silence.

"Ruth?"

"You're not the only one who feels silly. I forgot what was so important too. I think I just wanted to hear your voice."

She laughed. "After all, it's been twenty minutes!"

They talked for another hour or so and Dave agreed to meet her the next evening. Dave was scheduled to speak at a church and Ruth was conducting a Bible study with a group of women in the inner city.

She looked at the women sitting in front of her. Their clothes were faded and worn, but their faces were glowing with joy. Most of them were still young, but lines were already furrowing their faces. Ruth knew that in spite of working long and hard hours, they just barely survived financially. How she loved each one of them. Studying with them was one of the high points of her week. They had asked her to be their teacher, but she always left enriched with their wisdom. They mined spiritual gems in God's Word that countless others walked right over.

Following their spirited study, discussion, testimonies, and prayer, they dismissed to chat. Ruth was preparing to leave when Betsy approached her.

"Ruth," she began in her lively voice, "God wants me to run with the torch."

Ruth glanced at the flaming torch Betsy was holding.

"Whatever are you talking about, Betsy? You've been running with the torch ever since you asked Jesus to save you!"

"I know. I guess what I meant to say is that I feel God has called me to be a missionary."

"A missionary! Are you sure?"

"Yes, I'm sure. But I have some big problems to overcome. I never was very smart in school. I had to quit and go to work when I was in tenth grade. Even if I hadn't been forced to quit, I probably would have anyway. I never read a book until I met Jesus. Now I read the Bible all the time. That's the only book I've ever read. As I said, I'm not too smart."

Ruth looked at the big girl before her. She was the no-nonsense type. She always came straight to the point in her conversation. Her witness was the same. Since she had met Jesus, she simply introduced everyone she met to her beloved Savior and Friend. Ruth could picture her being a very effective missionary. She had already made her own neighborhood her mission field and several of the women in the Bible study group were brought to Christ by Betsy.

Ruth would never forget the first time she had heard Betsy pray with a friend of hers.

"Jesus, this is Mandy. She wants to meet you like I did, and she needs you to save her like you saved me. I've told her all about you, but I would appreciate it if you would come and meet her for yourself."

Ruth had smiled the first time she heard the prayer, but she had heard it often since.

"Jesus, this is Lynn . . .Jane . . . Belinda . . . Cindy . . . Nancy . . . Sandra . . . Shelly . . . "

The list of names went on and on.

Now Ruth caught herself praying the same way.

"Come sit at the table with me, Betsy. I want to tell you about a parlor maid named Gladys. She wasn't very smart when it came to books either. But wait till you hear what God did with her . . . "

Chapter 82

Gladys Aylward
(1902 to 1970)

Consider what I say; and the Lord give thee
understanding in all things.
II Timothy 2:7

Her face paled.

"But I *must* go to China! God has told me to go!"

The spokesman for the committee was quickly losing patience.

"Gladys," he said with finality. "You have been studying with this missionary society college for three months. More study will accomplish nothing. You simply will *never* be able to learn the Chinese language. *Never.*"

He looked at the thirty year old woman standing before him. Whatever made her think God would want her in China? She was poor and practically illiterate. She needed to face reality and get back to her job as a parlormaid.

He saw the tears streaking down her face, but remained stern. Sending Gladys to China was out of the question.

Making her way home, Gladys vowed, "Then I will seek support elsewhere."

The answer was always the same, spoken sometimes rudely, sometimes gently.

All who knew her breathed a sigh of relief when she found employment as a housemaid. She kept to herself, but no one complained, for she was a faithful and hard worker.

The weeks and months passed by. Each payday, Gladys counted and recounted her savings. When she at last had enough, she purchased a one-way ticket to Tientsin, China. She left Liverpool on October 15, 1932, carrying a battered suitcase, filled with food and clothing. She was left almost penniless.

She was forced from the train before it reached China. Gladys gazed at her strange surroundings and listened to conversations she could not understand

Then she straightened her shoulders. God was expecting her in China. She trudged through blizzards, the bitter wind whipping through her thin coat. All around her, soldiers fought the Russo-Chinese War. She miraculously escaped their flying bullets.

The populace of Yancheng, China, gazed in wonder at this decrepit, smiling figure entering their city.

Love shone from her eyes. She became one with them, rapidly learning to speak, read and write Chinese fluently. They learned to love her before falling in love with her God.

She was there when the Japanese invaded China. Gathering one-hundred children around her, she led them through the mountains to safety.

All around her were littered the tragic by-product of war. Orphans . . . *so many orphans.* Her heart went out to them.

Gladys was sixty-eight when she finished her race. She left behind many converts in Yancheng, an orphanage, and . . . the bewildered missionary committee.

Chapter 83

Dave

Thou therefore endure hardness, as a good soldier of Jesus Christ.
II Timothy 2:3

"**B**etsy is so excited, Dave," Ruth told him later that evening. "She thought God only called intellectuals to the race. She didn't know what to do when God called her."

"What did she think of Gladys?"

"She decided if God could use Gladys, he could use her."

"Did you know I almost didn't run because I felt so inadequate?"

"You? What made you feel inferior?"

"I was afraid God would make me speak in front of people. The very thought terrifies me."

"You spoke tonight!"

Dave looked at her blankly.

"Tonight, Dave. You said you were going to speak at a church tonight."

Dave waved his hand. "Oh, that. I wasn't preaching or anything."

"What were you doing then?"

Dave thought a minute.

"Now that I think about it, I guess you could say I was preaching. I've never thought of myself as a preacher and probably never will. If the Lord had asked me to speak when I first started running, I would have run in the opposite direction. But now telling people about Jesus has become my life. I guess it doesn't make much difference whether I'm telling one, ten or fifty. I can't think of anything I'd rather do.

"You know, Ruth, when we start this race we have no idea what God will have us do. I don't think Bruchko ever planned to eat live grubs!"

Ruth nearly choked on her sandwich.

"Live grubs!"

"Live grubs. Haven't you heard of Bruce Olson, nicknamed Bruchko by the Motilone Indians?"

"He really ate live grubs, Dave?" Ruth asked in a low voice.

"Sure. He was served a plate full of squirming grubs."

Ruth was quiet, so Dave went on telling her about Bruce.

"God called Bruce at nineteen years of age out of Minnesota and placed him in the Andes Mountains among the Motilone Indians. No one had ever seen a Motilone Indian. They were known only by the trail of riddled bodies they left behind when anyone approached their village. They lived in a wild jungle area on the border between Venezuela and Columbia.

"Bruce couldn't get accepted by a mission board either. He was young, broke, unhealthy, and as a child couldn't even tolerate the rigors of his boy scout activities. He would sneak off whenever possible and read a good book. The mission board was convinced he was best suited to sit in a warm house in a civilized country.

"Instead, God sent him to crawl through a dense jungle in South America. His body was pierced by thorns and covered with red welts from bites of strange bugs.

"He finally slept, but woke up to the sight of naked men surrounding him. He was pierced with arrows, whipped by strangers, and shot in the thigh. He tried to stay friendly while most of his blond hair was pulled out and was bruised, battered and tortured.

"Incidentally, Ruth, Bruce didn't like the grubs any better than you would. He tried to eat them to prevent starvation, but the squirming worms didn't stay down."

Dave smiled at her. "Did I mention, Ruth, that each grub was about the size and shape of a hot dog?"

Ruth turned whiter and shuddered as she pushed her plate away.

"I hope the Lord doesn't send Betsy to the Motilones," she said weakly.

"Oh, he won't," Dave answered cheerfully. "He might send some of the Motilones here as missionaries. Did I mention that the entire village of Motilones are now

351

running with the torch throughout South America? Bruce is still there with them."

"I think Betsy could do it. But I sincerely hope the Lord never puts me to the test."

"Do what?"

"Eat grubs, Dave. The thought of it turns my stomach."

Dave sighed. He had just told her about a great torchbearer, his victorious race, and an entire village lit up as a result. And Ruth was still thinking about grubs. Women were definitely different creatures.

He had to admit though, she wasn't the only one who hoped she would never be served grubs on a platter.

Chapter 84

One Aged Woman

Without shedding of blood is no remission.
Hebrews 9:22

Dave found himself running through an unfamiliar town one Sunday morning. He joined a group entering a church. He craved fellowship with fellow runners. But he searched the church vainly for just one carrying a torch.

The congregation was listless, the singing joyless, the prayers poetic words with no expectation of an answer from the throne room of God.

The Scriptures were read, but were themselves dead, without the touch of the life-giving Spirit upon them. The sermon was without power, the church without Christ, the service without purpose, the congregation without light.

Dave's mind drifted to an earlier time, another service, another sermon . . .

Jesus reached out to light her torch.

"No, Lord! Who am I to enter your race? I am old, well beyond the age to run! I am shy - why, everyone knows how timid I am! Please, Lord, find someone else to run for you!"

The Lord gave her no answer. His hand, holding the fire meant for her torch, remained outstretched. She turned away from him to go about her daily chores. But often, throughout the day, she stopped what she was doing to plead with him to leave. She reminded him of others, far more capable than she to run in his race.

Still he stayed, his eyes seeming to bore into her very soul. She tried in vain to ignore him.

The hours passed slowly. He remained in her home, patiently waiting for her to come to him.

Finally she turned and weeping, crept to him, kneeling at his feet.

That was the day he lit her torch.

She didn't feel a whole lot different, even though her obedience had brought her a great relief. But she didn't know what he wanted her to do, where he wanted her to run.

So she continued to do just what she had always done, going where she always went. Nothing extraordinary happened.

Until that one special day.

Her church was joining others at a large religious service being held at the *Golden Gate Exposition* in San Francisco.

She, with others in the city, had anxiously waited to hear the famed speaker. But now she listened with mounting horror. He chose his words craftily, eloquently attempting to destroy all faith in the cleansing power of the blood of Jesus Christ!

She looked on the faces around her. Only a few looked disturbed! Many were listening to his words raptly, smiling and nodding as he spoke! The master of deception, Satan himself, was using this man to woo God's people away from the cross!

Her heart pounded, her hands gripped her Bible as she listened.

Then she rose to her feet, unaware of the curious glances and stares of those around her. For her eyes were fixed on a blood-stained cross and a man nailed to its beams, struggling in agony just to draw his next breath. His face was bruised and swollen. Blood poured from his wounds.

She gazed upon the mockers at his feet, ridiculing, taunting, shaking their fists at God's sacrficial lamb.

And those mockers merged into the one today who stood before this vast crowd of people, mocking her Lord's redeeming blood.

Tears streamed down her upturned face as she lifted high her torch. Without thought or plan, she began to sing softly.

There is a fountain filled with blood
Drawn from Immanuel's veins.
And sinners plunged beneath that flood
Lose all their guilty stains.

One Aged Woman

As she began the second verse, a hundred people stood to their feet, a hundred voices blended with hers:

The dying thief rejoiced to see
That fountain in his day.
And there may I, though vile as he,
Wash all my sins away.

By the time the second stanza had been sung, a thousand faces turned from the mocker who stood before them, his voice silenced by one aged woman carrying the torch. A thousand people, their eyes now upon the cross on Calvary's hill, lifted their voices, singing the third stanza triumphantly:

Thou dying Lamb, thy precious blood,
Shall never lose its pow'r.
Till all the ransomed church of God
Are saved, to sin no more!

Dave didn't know the woman's name. The story had been passed down by those who had attended the conference, and her name had been lost in its telling. He grinned as he thought how surprised she must have been when she realized that her torch had lit that entire arena with the fire of God.

He returned to the present, where the service was drawing to a close and the people around him were restlessly preparing to leave.

"Oh, God," he breathed. "Where was your torch bearer when this church was drawn away from your cross? Where were your prayer warriors? Where were your soldiers, ready to contend for the faith? Did someone here fail to respond when you chose them to enter your race?"

All that remained now was a ritual of death.

Dave slipped quietly out the door.

But even as he grieved for those who dutifully attended a darkened morgue week after week, his heart was joyously singing . . .

There is a fountain filled with blood . . .

Chapter 85

Dave

The people that walked in darkness have seen a great light: they that dwell in the land of the shadow of death, upon them hath the light shined.
Isaiah 9:2

The day didn't seem properly finished without a telephone call to Ruth. They were both enthusiastically sharing their day's events when Ruth said, "Dave! I was visiting my cousin on campus when I noticed a brilliant light. I asked who was carrying the torch and she laughed and said, "Oh, that's Ray. Ever since some guy named Dave visited him the other day, all he talks about is Jesus and the Bible."

"I went over to listen to what he was saying and, Dave, he was preaching - right outdoors! A group was gathered around listening to him. A few of them were asking their ridiculous questions and making their derogatory comments. Ray wasn't phased by anything they said. He had a quick answer for every question. He told them before he was born again he had made the same foolish remarks. He invited anyone to talk to him anytime, day or night, about his Savior and announced a meeting he was going to hold this weekend to discuss the Bible.

"He held up his Bible and said that people had been tortured and killed to make sure we had copies to read, and we had better start reading it. Most of the crowd drifted away, but two stayed to talk to him. I overheard him tell them that he hadn't had anything to live for until he met Jesus.

"Do you know him? You aren't the Dave he was referring to . . . are you?"

Dave couldn't believe the news. Could it be Ray - preaching? He couldn't imagine it.

"Ruth, does this Ray have curly black hair and blue eyes, and is he about six feet tall? Does he have sort of a sneer on his face?"

Dave

She hesitated before answering. "That may be him. He has curly black hair and I think he has blue eyes. He's probably about six feet. But there definitely was no sneer on his face. This guy was lit up, Dave. He was excited and happy and in love with Jesus. He said he is going to spend the rest of his life telling people about his Savior!"

Dave couldn't visualize Ray without his cynical sneer. Ray . . . *preaching?*

Dave could hardly sleep for excitement. He wondered how Phil reacted to Ray's salvation.

"Who knows what God will do with Ray?" Dave thought. "Perhaps he will be another James Stewart."

It was impossible to think about James without smiling. His race had begun on a football field before thousands of fans and he had literally blazed a trail of light wherever he ran. He was used to being challenged by scoffing hecklers. In fact, there were times he joined a crowd and became a heckler himself . . .

Chapter 86

James Stewart
(1910 to 1975)

Go ye therefore into the highways, and as many as ye shall find, bid to the marriage.
Matthew 22:9

James awoke with a start. He hadn't heard anything but could feel the presence of someone in his room. Then he heard a sob.

With disgust twisting his features, he clutched his football to his chest and turned away from his mother. But even with his eyes closed and his back to her, he could not shut out the picture of her kneeling by his bed, praying silently for his soul.

Why couldn't she just leave him alone and accept him the way he was? Most mothers would be proud that their son was on his way to becoming one of Scotland's greatest football players!

While the country had already begun cheering, she sobbed and looked pitiful. He had always loved his mother but a deep bitterness was swiftly replacing his love.

He patted his football tenderly. If he couldn't have football and his family both, he would choose football. He had long since decided he would live for no one or nothing else.

He was only thirteen when he was chosen as Scotland's choice of boys for the international team. Coaches and fans alike encouraged his dream of becoming the greatest center forward Europe had ever known.

Football . . . Scotland's national passion.

Hundreds of thousands stood freezing in the bitter cold all night long just to secure tickets to the big games. He would give those loyal fans something to see! His name would one day be praised not only in Scotland but throughout the world.

If his mother wanted to weep about it, then let her weep.

Yes, he was obsessed with the game. How else would he get to the top? He practiced before others woke up in the morning and was still practicing long after they lay asleep. Football magazines littered his room. He listened to every word spoken by professionals just to glean one more tip. Then he practiced hours on end to perfect it.

He was fourteen now. Already every senior football club had their eyes on him. A tremendous career lay before him and everyone knew it.

"Everyone but Mother," he mumbled bitterly.

Her sobs were getting louder.

"Jim! Jim!"

He faked sleep, but she said her piece anyway.

"Jim, I offered you to God for his service before you were born!"

He snorted. Who was she to offer his life to God? He would live his life as he chose. And he chose football, thank you.

"Jim," she continued, as though he had spoken his sneer aloud. "It was not for football that God gave you to me. There is only one thing that matters. That is being one-hundred per cent for Jesus Christ."

"That might matter to you," he wanted to shout. Instead he said to himself, "But it matters not one bit to me."

Finally she left the room.

The next night it was more of the same. Would she never leave him alone?

He got used to her presence and was able to sleep right through it until one night. The new urgency in her voice woke him up.

"It's now or never, Jim," she said firmly. "You must surrender all to the claims of Jesus Christ. *Now.*"

Jesus Christ.

There were football fanatics.

Jesus apparently had his share of fanatics too.

Why did his own mother have to be one of them?

As if one wasn't enough in his family, his brother joined the radicals. David, known as a walking sports encyclopedia, had always amused his friends by spouting out scores and statistics like a ticker tape. Who would ever think he would end up spouting Bible verses instead?

And his father. He sat in his chair every evening, without fail, between nine and ten o'clock, singing hymns out of Sankey's hymn book.

His family wasn't alone. Church services just weren't the same anymore. Staid sermons became impassioned pleas. Preachers often broke down, weeping for souls. Sinners trembled with conviction, and usually there were between fifty and eighty of them receiving Christ as their Savior . . . and Lord.

It was the *and Lord* that bothered him.

The preachers never offered salvation to a willful rebel. They gave him just two options: *all . . . or nothing*. James realized that the *all* included his football career.

He may not be part of the home scene, but he was big in the football crowd. Every boy envied him when the director of the leading football club gave him a season ticket to the director's box. Sitting in that box in a stadium that accommodated over 100,000 people was a heady experience for a fourteen year old!

Back in church, James continued to resist the call of God. His awesome Presence permeated every service. Vibrant testimonies by sinners who had surrendered to Christ were followed by joyful songs of praise. James gripped his seat and refused to be budged.

And then . . .

He expected God to be in church.

But it was a real shock to meet him while playing a championship football game. Thousands of people were there. And it was on the football field, right in the middle of the game, that God came to James. He didn't ask for his life this time. He demanded it.

It was a bitter cold night. While his teammates shivered, sweat poured from his face.

"Oh, Lord," James moaned. "Why *here?*"

His thoughts raced.

Should he walk off the field?

Should he kneel and pray . . . *here?*

"God," he prayed silently. "If you will just let me finish this game, I will surrender to you the moment the referee blows his whistle."

James played the rest of the game. The second the final whistle blew, he looked up to heaven and cried, "O God, save me now for Christ's sake. O Lord Jesus, I thank you for shedding your blood for me that I might be saved. O blessed Holy Spirit, forgive me for all the times I have stifled your convictions!"

He ran from the stadium, through the shoving crowds, and straight to his mother. Flinging open the door, he cried, "Mother! I'm saved! I'm saved!" And James burst into tears.

His mother merely glanced his way.

Quietly she said, "Yes, James, I know. God told me that you would be saved this week. I have arranged for you to give your testimony at an open air meeting in the center of the city with other Christian young people."

James' love of football was replaced with a burning love for souls. He went to work delivering groceries. His official Scottish title was *message boy.*

He carried their groceries to their homes and knocked on their doors. Then he stammered, "Friend, I am a message boy and you know my job is to come and bring provisions to your home. But I am also a message boy for God and I have come to ask you to make provision for eternity. PREPARE TO MEET THY GOD!"

He ran to Sunday Schools to speak to children who had watched him play football. He went door to door in his neighborhood giving out tracts. In those first few weeks, more than a thousand families invited him in to hear his testimony. He preached in the open air wherever he could find an audience. He walked the streets, wearing sandwich boards over his shoulders with Scripture texts written on the front and back placards. At other times he carried a leather pouch hung on a strap and tied around his shoulder. He balanced a big heavy pole in the pouch on the upper end of which were his *talk texts.* They worked like window blinds. As he preached, he pulled them up or down to illustrate his sermons.

It was at his first open air meeting that a seventeen year old youth strode to the front of the crowd of several hundred people. Standing before the men he shouted, "If God could save James Stewart, he could save the devil!"

The men grinned, waiting for the preacher boy's reaction and hoping for a fight.

"He is right," James said simply. "A mighty miracle has taken place in my life, similar to the miracle John Newton experienced. Let me quote you two verses of the beautiful testimony John put to music. You know the song. It's *Amazing Grace.*"

> In evil long I took delight,
> Unaw'd by shame or fear.
> Till a new object struck my sight
> And stopped my wild career.

> I saw one hanging on a tree
> In agony and blood,
> Who fix'd his languid eyes on me
> As near his cross I stood.

James rejoiced as God touched and saved drunkards, men without hope, young people, adults, children, potential suicides.

He teamed up with Sergeant Wheeler, a famous detective who became a powerful open-air evangelist. Wheeler regarded the teeming masses of all Britain as his congregation. He was a strong man with a booming voice. He was insulted when invited to preach indoors.

"Preaching indoors is child's play, James," he would thunder. "We'll leave that for the softies!"

One of their favorite places to preach was the race track. During the twenty minute interval while bets were being placed for the next race, James and Sergeant Wheeler simply set up church before a stand of ten to twenty thousand people.

One would open the service by shouting, "Well, friends, we are glad you have come! We are sorry to be late, but we will start our service now. We will begin our service this afternoon by singing *What a Friend We Have in Jesus.*

"What, you haven't got your hymnbooks with you? That is a pity. We will excuse you this time, but don't forget to bring hymnbooks with you tomorrow. We will sing a hymn everyone knows. We will begin with *Jesus Lover of My Soul.*

"What? Nobody singing? What's the matter with you all? Are you a bunch of backsliders? Well, we will have to sing a duet for you."

And they did.

The racing fraternity regarded them as one of their own. No matter what city the race was being held in, James and the Sergeant would be there first, waiting for the crowds to come hear them preach. They knew of no better way to preach to so many thousands of people without spending money to rent halls and advertise.

James picked up the racing lingo and adapted it to his use. A tipster would move through the crowds shouting, "A dead cert! A dead cert!" Then he would sell bets for the horse certain to win.

James would go walking right behind him shouting, "A living reality! A living reality! It's a dead cert and a living reality that you are going to die! You had better get right with God here!"

Another time he would follow the tipster whose cry was, "Two to one, bar one; two to one, bar one; two to one, bar one." James came right behind him yelling, "Bar none! Bar none! Whosoever will may come! If you are barred out of heaven, you bar yourself!"

When the race began with the roar, *"They're off,"* James and the sergeant hurriedly pulled down the gospel banners and knelt and prayed quietly until the race was finished.

They endured punches in the stomach, being knocked to the ground, the juice of overripe tomatoes oozing down and staining their faces, and mocking sneers. None of the ridicule phased either of them.

One bookmaker screamed at the sight of them, "Are you here again? Get out of my sight! The very sight of you makes me sick! Why don't you stay where you belong?"

James replied firmly, "You are going by your racing book and we are going by our Book. We have got our marching orders. Our Lord Jesus said *'Go ye into all the world and preach the gospel.'* Isn't this part of the world? Now you just keep quiet while we preach!"

When the races were over, their gospel wagon would be found lumbering to a market square in the heart of whatever city the races were held. They parked it carefully in their reserved spot. Then they opened up the side of their wagon and preached to one or two thousand shoppers. They did this every evening.

One evening news reached them that the bookmaker who had pleaded with them to leave the racetrack had been gloriously saved and was now a Methodist preacher in Northern England!

Many Sunday evenings three to four thousand people gathered in the public park to listen to Sergeant Wheeler and James. The most renowned evangelists of the British Empire counted it a great privilege to stand on the wagon platform with the sergeant.

Crowds of hardened men brushed tears from their eyes as he spoke. At the close of the service, hundreds would kneel on the ground and receive Christ as their Savior.

James ran to Hyde Park of London where forty people often stood on forty soap boxes speaking on forty different themes. Hecklers were always part of the crowd.

"Scottie, do you believe that the whale swallowed Jonah?"

"Sure I do!"

The heckler would turn triumphantly toward the crowd. "Ha! Did you hear him? He believes the whale swallowed Jonah." Turning back to James he laughed, "We sure don't believe it!"

James was never without a quick answer. "If you don't believe it, that's not my fault. But I'll tell you what I will do. When I get to heaven, I'll ask Jonah!"

"Ha! Suppose he's not there, Scottie Boy?"

"Then you can ask him!"

The heckler would be stopped only for a moment.

"The fool hath said in his heart, *There is no God*!" James would shout. "Do any of you who don't believe in God have more questions? Now not everyone at once! Just one fool at a time. One fool at a time, please."

Finally one would shout from the crowd.

"Where did Cain get his wife?"

"Ah! Now I know what's wrong with you. You are interested in somebody else's wife! If you are not careful, you will get into trouble! Is Cain's wife really your trouble?"

"Yes."

"She is the reason you can't come to Christ?"

"Yes."

"If I tell you who Cain's wife was, will you get converted? Will you accept Christ as your Savior? Will you step out from this crowd and ask God to save your soul?"

"Yes."

"Well then, I will tell you who Cain's wife was. She was Mrs. Cain, of course!"

The crowd kept coming, the hecklers kept heckling and souls continued getting saved. James was sometimes still there after midnight, persuading lonely people to cast their cares and sins upon a loving Savior.

The leader of an atheistic society in London stood on the stone wall at Tower Hill quoting famous atheists and mocking the Bible.

If the atheist reached Tower Hill before James, he would set up in James' usual place. The policeman who controlled the mobs would not let James set up. On those days, James simply switched from preaching to heckling.

"How do you know there is no God?" he would call out to the atheist. "How do you know the Bible is not true? Prove to us that death ends it all!"

One such day James turned to the crowd and shouted, "Do you see that man there?" He pointed at the atheist.

"One day by the power of God, he is going to stand in that very same place preaching the gospel of the Lord Jesus Christ!"

Only a short while later, the atheist lay dying. He was terrified. Finally he begged God for mercy and God healed both his soul and body. He returned to his spot and climbed up on his soap box.

"Jesus saves!" he cried. The crowd stared in shock. Wasn't this new preacher the former atheist? What was he doing carrying a torch? Many turned to Christ.

When most people were home sleeping, James was carrying food and doughnuts to the derelicts who slept on the Thames Embankment or the homeless who sought shelter for the night under the railway arches. He visited one after another, offering doughnuts, friendship, and the love of his Savior.

James turned then to Eastern Europe.

The first signs of war rumbled throughout the nations. While people were fleeing their countries, James Stewart ran cheerfully from one to another. He paid no attention to uniforms or borders. He ignored laws that prohibited the preaching of the gospel.

The first stages of war were now being fought. Undaunted, James ran into Prague and rented the largest music hall in the city. People filled the auditorium, and about four-hundred received Christ every evening.

He ran on to Budapest.

Families were homeless and daily battling hunger. People lined the roads, searching through the littered bodies for their lost loved ones.

It was dangerous to leave one's home. Many were murdered for the clothes on their backs.

In the midst of this devastation, James ran into a church. It had been partially demolished. Over two-thousand Christians were gathered inside. Thousands more stood outside in the sub-zero temperatures. Often James preached to groups of twenty-thousand at a time.

Snow fell on the shivering congregation. Yet they stayed, pouring their hearts out to the Lord.

James learned the meaning of fervent prayers while with those people. He felt as if he was in the midst of a mighty sob, ascending to the heart of God. The people would pray for two or three hours. They began in unison to praise God for his goodness and glory.

"Don't ask the people to sing, James," he was advised by one preacher. "Our people are too weak from hunger. The exertion of singing will be too much. Many are in the beginning stages of starvation. It takes all their strength just to sit."

James ached with compassion as he looked over the congregation. There was no heat in the building. Actually, the building itself was a mass of solid ice.

People were covered with blankets and bundled in coats and hats. The organ was frozen. The organist's hands were so stiff with cold that she could no longer play.

Ushers brought James hot bricks to stand on so he could continue to preach without freezing his feet.

But, oh, what joy!

Such hunger for the Word of God!

Crowds followed him home after every service. They stood in the freezing cold at one o'clock in the morning, begging to hear more preaching.

James' interpreter talked to them until day break.

The following morning, the building would fill with men for their special service.

James had only one worry.

"Oh, God!" he cried. "Am I doing something wrong? Why are things going so well? I am not being attacked by Satan!"

The attack came. He was arrested and accused of being a spy. The Soviets were undecided whether he was a British or Nazi spy. They knew he was one or the other. Why else would he be the most traveled foreigner in Europe?

James cheerfully turned their accusation times into gospel meetings.

Moscow was unsure what to do with him.

America and Britain demanded his release.

"Do not leave! Above all, do not preach!" he was sternly commanded.

Finally he was released. He hated to leave, but he knew he was leaving behind him a trail of torchbearers. Even in the midst of Europe's terrible tragedy, the light would not go out.

His race that began on a football field never slowed.

To his dying day, James faithfully lived his heartfelt prayer:

Let me burn out for Thee, dear Lord,
Burn and wear out for Thee;
Don't let me rust, or my life be
A failure, my God, to Thee.

Use me and all I have, dear Lord,
And get me so close to Thee
That I feel the THROB
Of the great heart of God;
Until I burn out for Thee.

Chapter 87

Dave and Ruth
(Tomorrow)

The night is far spent, the day is at hand: let us therefore cast off the works of darkness, and let us put on the armour of light.
The path of the just is as the shining light, that shineth more and more unto the perfect day.
The sun shall be no more thy light by day; neither for brightness shall the moon give light unto thee: but the Lord shall be unto thee an everlasting light.
Romans 13:12
Proverbs 4:18
Isaiah 60:19

"It's getting darker, Dave."

Dave squeezed her hand.

"I know, Love."

"Some runners have quit the race."

"Yes. Paul told us Demas quit too. He loved the present world more than our Lord."

"How could anyone forsake the living Lord for a dying world? Dave, God has been so good to us."

"We serve a faithful and loving God, Ruth. He's been with us every step of the way."

The warmth of his smile lightened her step.

"And he has given me a faithful and loving wife. How long have we been running together now?"

"Four years."

"Four years of shared memories."

"Dave, what do you think our future holds?"

"We can't be sure what the next hour holds, Hon. But I do know there seems to be growing antagonism against the race. The world is growing blacker and desperately needs more light."

He looked around him as he spoke.

369

Dave and Ruth

"There are so many totally dark places . . . some neighborhoods, factories, homes, schools, stores . . . even some churches."

He slipped his arm around her.

"Ruth, we know there is only one hope for the world's future. LIGHT will return and darkness will flee his glorious presence. Our **Champion Runner** has promised to come back again!"

"Oh, Dave, how I long for his coming. We run here and there, trying desperately to bring light. But there is too much darkness and too few lights. Sometimes our task seems overwhelming."

Dave pulled her closer.

"Don't ever get discouraged, Ruth. Our race will soon be finished. Jesus is coming back in all his splendor and beauty. Ah, what a day! The sun will have no need to shine in the presence of his brilliance."

He looked up to the heavens.

"Oh, Lord! I can't wait," he cried. "Come quickly, Lord Jesus!"

Renewed vigor surged through them as they ran in silence, contemplating the triumphant celebration of victory to come.

Their Lord *would* return!

The race *would* be forever won!

Dave spoke quietly in the stillness of the moment.

"Until that glorious day, Ruth, I have one more hope for our future."

"What is it, Dave?"

"I pray daily for more torchbearers."

The Call of the Lord

The harvest truly is plenteous, but the labourers are few; Pray ye therefore the Lord of the harvest, that he will send forth labourers into his harvest.

Behold, I say unto you, Lift up your eyes, and look on the fields; for they are white already to harvest.

I must work the works of him that sent me, while it is day: the night cometh, when no man can work.

Watchman, what of the night?
Watchman, what of the night?

A Torchbearer's Answer

Then said I, Here am I; send me.

Matthew 9:37-38
John 4:35
John 9:4
Isaiah 21:11
Isaiah 6:8

Appendix

Notes

Chapter 4
1. Henry Van Dyke, *Out-Of-Doors In the Holy Land.*

Chapter 13: Polycarp
1. John Fox, *Fox's Book of Martyrs.*
2. *Christian History*, Issue 27, Vol. IX, No. 3.
3. Henry C. Sheldon, *History of the Christian Church.*
4. Bruce L. Shelly, *Church History In Plain Language.*
5. Ruth A. Tucker, *From Jerusalem to Irian Jaya.*

Chapter 14
1. Jeff Rennicke, *The Fleeting, Eternal Snowflake,* Reader's Digest,

Chapter 15: Lawrence
1. John Fox, *Fox's Book of Martyrs.*

Chapter 18: Martin of Tours
1. *The New Encyclopaedia Britannica*, 15th Edition.
2. Justo L. Gonzalez, *The Story of Christianity.*
3. Henry C. Sheldon, *History of the Christian Church.*
4. Ruth A. Tucker, *From Jerusalem to Irian Jaya.*

Chapter 21: Augustine
1. *The New Encyclopaedia Britannica*, 15th Edition.
2. *Christian History*, Issue 15, Volume VI, No.3.
3. Henry C. Sheldon, *History of the Christian Church.*
4. Augustine, *The Confessions of Saint Augustine.*

Chapter 23: Patrick
1. *The New Encyclopaedia Britannica*, 15th Edition.
2. Henry C. Sheldon, *History of the Christian Church.*
3. Ruth A. Tucker, *From Jerusalem to Irian Jaya.*

Chapter 25: Columba
1. *The New Encyclopaedia Britannica*, 15th Edition.

Notes

2. Ruth A. Tucker, *From Jerusalem to Irian Jaya*.

Chapter 28: Gregory the Great
1. *The New Encyclopaedia Britannica*, 15th Edition.
2. Bruce L. Shelly, *Church History In Plain Language*.

Chapter 30: Boniface
1. *The New Encyclopaedia Britannica*, 15th Edition.
2. John Fox, *Fox's Book of Martyrs*.
3. Ruth A. Tucker, *From Jerusalem to Irian Jaya*.

Chapter 32 : Anskar
1. *The New Encyclopaedia Britannica*, 15th Edition.
2. Ruth A. Tucker, *From Jerusalem to Irian Jaya*.

Chapter 33
1. Paul Lee Tan, ThD: *Encyclopedia of 7,700 Illustrations: Signs of the Times*.
2. *Vocatio*, Volume 6, No. 1.

Chapter 34: Adalbert
1. *The New Encyclopaedia Britannica*, 15th Edition.
2. John Fox, *Fox's Book of Martyrs*.

Chapter 35
1. *Christian History*, Issue 27 (Vol. IX, No. 3).

Chapter 36: Alphage
1. John Fox, *Fox's Book of Martyrs*.
2. *The New Encyclopaedia Britannica*, 15th Edition.

Chapter 37: Gerard
1. John Fox, *Fox's Book of Martyrs*.
2. *The New Encyclopaedia Britannica*, 15th Edition.

Chapter 38: Stanislaus
1. John Fox, *Fox's Book of Martyrs*.

Chapter 41: Waldo
1. *Christian History*, Volume VIII, Number 2, Issue 22.
2. Bruce L. Shelly, *Church History In Plain Language*.
3. *The New Encyclopaedia Britannica*, 15th Edition.

Notes

Chapter 42
1. *The Annals of America*

Chapter 43: John Wyclif
1. *Christian History*, Volume II, No 2, Issue 3.
2. John Fox, *Fox's Book of Martyrs*.
3. *The New Encyclopaedia Britannica*, 15th Edition.
4. Henry C. Sheldon, *History of the Christian Church*.
5. Bruce L. Shelly, *Church History In Plain Language*.

Chapter 45: John Hus
1. *The New Encyclopaedia Britannica*, 15th Edition.
2. Bruce L. Shelly, *Church History In Plain Language*.
3. Henry C. Sheldon, *History of the Christian Church*.
4. John Fox, *Fox's Book of Martyrs*.

Chapter 47: Girolamo Savonarola
1. *The New Encyclopaedia Britannica*, 15th Edition.
2. Justo L. Gonzalez, *The Story of Christianity*.
3. Henry C. Sheldon, *History of the Christian Church*.

Chapter 48
1. *The Annals of America*.

Chapter 49: William Tyndale
1. *Christian History*, Volume VI, No. 4, Issue 16.
2. *The New Encyclopaedia Britannica*, 15th Edition.
3. John Fox, *Fox's Book of Martyrs*.
4. Bruce L. Shelly, *Church History in Plain Language*.
5. Henry C. Sheldon, *History of the Christian Church*.

Chapter 50
1. *The Annals of America*.

Chapter 51: Martin Luther
1. *Christian History, Issue 39* (Vol. XII, No. 3).
2. *Christian History*, Issue 28 (Vol. IX, No. 4).
3. Henry C. Sheldon, *History of the Christian Church*.
4. *The New Encyclopaedia Britannica*, 15th Edition.
5. Merle Severy, *The World of Luther*, National Geographic, Vol. 164, No. 4.

Notes

6. C. Douglas Weaver, *A Cloud of Witnesses*.

Chapter 53: Auguste Hermann Francke
1. *Christian History*, Volume V, No. 2.
2. Ruth A. Tucker, *From Jerusalem to Irian Jaya*.

Chapter 56: Count Zinzendorf
1. *The New Encyclopaedia Britannica*, 15th Edition.
2. *Christian History*, Volume I, No. 1.
3. Ruth A. Tucker, *From Jerusalem to Irian Jaya*.
4. Kenneth W. Osbeck, *101 Hymn Stories*.

Chapter 59: David Brainerd
1. *The Life of David Brainerd (Chiefly Extracted from his Diary)*, (Baker Book House, 1978).
2. Winifred M. Pearce, *David Brainerd*.
3. *The Annals of America*.
4. *The New Encyclopaedia Britannica*, 15th Edition.

Chapter 62: Susanna and John Wesley
1. *Christian History*, Volume II, No. 1.
2. Wesley L. Duewel, *Ablaze for God*.
3. *Christian History*, Issue 28 (Vol. IX, No. 4).
4. *The New Encyclopaedia Britannica*, 15th Edition.
5. Howard A. Snyder, *The Radical Wesley*.
6. Edith Deen, *Great Women of the Christian Faith*.

Chapter 66: John Newton
1. John Newton: *Letters of a Slave Trader Freed by God's Grace*, Paraphrased by Dick Bohrer.
2. John Newton, *Out Of The Depths*.
3. Ernest K. Emurian, *Hymn Festivals*.
4. Kenneth W. Osbeck, *101 More Hymn Stories*.
5. Kenneth W. Osbeck, *101 Hymn Stories*.

Chapter 69: Elizabeth Fry
1. Edith Deen, *Great Women of the Christian Faith*.

Chapter 72: Charlotte Elliott
1. Edith Deen, *Great Women of the Christian Faith*.
2. Ernest K. Emurian, *Hymn Festivals*.
3. Kenneth W. Osbeck, *101 Hymn Stories*.

Notes

Chapter 74
1. John S. Tompkins, *Our Kindest City*, Reader's Digest, July 1994,

Chapter 75: Charles Finney
1. Charles G. Finney, *An Autobiography* .
2. *Christian History*, Volume VII, Number 4, Issue 20.
3. *The New Encyclopaedia Britannica*, 15th Edition.
4. Paul Lee Tan, ThD: *Encyclopedia of 7,700 Illustrations: Signs of the Times.*
5. The Annals of America, *Lectures on Revivals of Religion*, New York, 1838.

Chapter 77: George Mueller
1. Arthur T. Pierson, *George Muller of Bristol.*
2. Roger Steer, *George Muller: delighted in God!.*
3. A. Sims, *George Mueller Man of Faith.*

Chapter 80: Annie Taylor (and Tibet)
1. Lois Hoadley Dick, *Live*, Radiant Life, Volume 65, Number 4, Part 8.
2. Fred Ward, *In Long-Forbidden Tibet*, National Geographic, Volume 157, No. 2.
3. *The New Encyclopaedia Britannica*, 15th Edition.

Chapter 82, Gladys Aylward
1. Edith Deen, *Great Women of the Christian Faith.*

Chapter 83: Bruchko
1. Bruce E. Olson, *Bruchko.*

Chapter 84: One Aged Woman
1. Paul Lee Tan, ThD: *Encyclopedia of 7,700 Illustrations: Signs of the Times.*

Chapter 86: James Stewart
1. James A. Stewart, *Heaven's Throne Gift.*
2. James A. Stewart, *Revival Behind the Iron Curtain.*

We've Come This Far By Faith
by Carolyn Wilde

Paul and Carolyn were deeply in debt when an automobile accident led Paul to make a life-changing commitment to put God first in his life, and their extraordinary, living-by-faith adventure began.

We've Come This Far By Faith is a heart-warming book, not just about a family who learned to trust their God for their needs, but about a living, faithful, loving God who cares for His children.

We've Come This Far By Faith will challenge and inspire you to trust God to guide and take care of you as you put His principles into action in your life. The comment most often heard from readers of **We've Come This Far By Faith** is, *"I stayed up all night reading this book! I just couldn't put it down!"*

We've Come This Far By Faith will give you that extra faith you need to step out on the sea of life with your eyes and faith firmly fixed on Jesus Christ! He will not let His followers sink, no matter how the storms around us rage!

**Available at fine Christian
book sellers everywhere and through**

Solid Rock Books, Inc.
979 Young Street, Suite E
Woodburn, Oregon 97071
(503) 981-0705

Seven Biblical Principles for Financial Peace of Mind

by Paul and Carolyn Wilde

How many people do you know who have financial peace of mind? Do you have it?

The number one cause of divorce today is fighting about money! **MONEY!**

Worrying about it causes ulcers, migraines, divorces, murders, thefts, prostitution, suicides . . . the list could go on and on, but God's Word sums it all up by saying our love for it is the root of all evil.

Did you know there are seven principles we must follow if we want the blessing of God upon our lives?

You may follow two or three of them – but do you know and follow all seven?

We, as Christians, especially in the coming days of financial turmoil and economic collapse of the monetary system as we know it, need to know and put into practice every single one of these principles. Then, and only then, will you have financial peace of mind.

This book will show you what these seven principles are and how to practice them!

Other products from Solid Rock Books, Inc. include:

☑ **Books**

☑ **Audio Tapes**

☑ **Video Tapes**

For a *FREE* catalog, please write to:

Solid Rock Books, Inc.
979 Young Street, Suite E
Woodburn, Oregon 97071
(503) 981-0705